IN QUEST OF IDENTITY

IN QUEST
OF IDENTITY

Patterns in the Spanish American Essay
of Ideas, 1890-1960

MARTIN S. STABB

THE UNIVERSITY OF NORTH CAROLINA PRESS
CHAPEL HILL, 1967

199
S 77 i

ACKNOWLEDGMENTS

SUPPORT FOR THIS STUDY CAME FROM TWO SOURCES. IN 1962 the American Philosophical Society provided funds for the early stages of the work, especially for travel to libraries. At the same time the Research Council of the University of Missouri granted me a semester's leave in which to carry out the basic research. This same body has periodically given me additional support in the form of smaller grants to cover costs of typing, materials, travel, and miscellaneous expenses. This project could not have been successfully carried out without this aid and therefore I am deeply indebted to both the American Philosophical Society and the University of Missouri Research Council.

My debt to individuals is also great, though somewhat more difficult to determine. Professors John A. Crow and the late Manuel Olguín, both of the University of California at Los Angeles, were my first mentors in the study of the Spanish American essay, and any contribution which I may have made to the field stems from their early encouragement. My debt to my own students is substantial, since a good portion of the material contained in this book was originally conceived during the give-and-take of a seminar in the Spanish American essay which I regularly teach. Among my colleagues at the University of Missouri who have helped me I am especially indebted to a good friend and severe critic, Professor R. E. McGrew of the Department of History, who read the entire text and made many valuable suggestions.

Columbia, Missouri   Martin S. Stabb
February, 1967

CONTENTS

IN QUEST OF IDENTITY

I / INTRODUCTION

AS THIS STUDY NEARS COMPLETION, SPANISH AMERICA
continues in the midst of a profound revolution: a revolution whose
ideological dimension is no less important than its economic, social,
or political dimensions. In assessing this revolution those who are
unfamiliar with the Hispanic world—especially North Americans—
are quite likely to underestimate the intellectual forces at work just
as they are likely to place too much importance on socio-economic
factors. The degree to which the intellectuals shape the destiny of
different nations or regions varies greatly. If we examined the
totality of a culture, different weights must be assigned to the component parts; and in Spanish America the intellectual component—
the influence generated by teachers, philosophers, and men of letters
—weighs much more heavily than it does in the United States.

The point may be demonstrated in several ways. Take, for
example, the universities and other institutions of higher learning.
Hispanic America has relatively few such institutions and a relatively
small percentage of highly educated men, yet the course of her
history has been closely tied to the academic world. The existence
of the "National University," an institution virtually alien to the
North American mind, is extremely significant in this regard. The
fact that in Spanish America university teaching has, until very
recently, been considered a part-time occupation has made the
relatively sharp North American distinction between the academic
man and the man-of-affairs much less clear. Bank officials teach
economics, practicing lawyers teach political science, and oddly
enough postal administrators may teach literature or even philosophy. The impact of student groups must also be taken into
account in assessing the role of the universities in Spanish American
life. In the first place these groups—with all their vigor, non-

conformity, and political activism—seem to be more generally accepted by the society as a whole than are their recent counterparts in the United States. In the second place Spanish American student groups transcend the narrowly defined university environment in that their members frequently continue to participate in the group's activities long after completing their formal education. Given the nature of these organizations it is not surprising that their political activism has often been translated into political power: witness the development of the important APRA (Alianza Popular Revolucionaria Americana) party growing out of Peru's student-led university reform movement of 1919, or the recent and dramatic events in Cuba which had their beginnings in what the casual observer in the late forties must have considered just another typical *movimiento estudiantil* at the University of Havana.

The weight of the intellectual sector within the totality of Spanish American culture is impressively demonstrated by noting the considerable number of thinkers and literary men who have gained high office in these nations. The contrast with the United States is striking. This nation did not elect or propose Horace Mann as president, yet Argentina did make the essayist and educational theorist, Domingo Faustino Sarmiento, its chief executive. Would anyone in the United States have thought seriously of proposing a writer of regional novels and social protest such as Steinbeck as a presidential candidate? Unlikely, yet it was just such a man—the celebrated novelist Rómulo Gallegos—who was elected president of Venezuela in 1946. North American readers may be surprised to learn that Victor Raúl Haya de la Torre, one of the leading candidates in the Peruvian presidential election of 1962, is an essayist of hemispheric repute who has published serious papers on such esoteric themes as the relationship of Einsteinian relativity to the philosophy of history. They might also be surprised to learn that Juan Bosch, former president of the Dominican Republic and of late the center of political controversy in the Caribbean, was a short story writer of considerable stature long before his name graced the Associated Press wire services. Of course not all Spanish American presidents or other governmental leaders have been writers and intellectuals: by the same token North America has had an occasional Jefferson or Wilson in public life. Nonetheless I believe that in addition to the greater relative number of intellectuals in Spanish American public life, as compared with North America, there is in the lands to the South a different popular attitude toward the man of letters who would seek public office. The fact that Woodrow Wilson was a professor of political science and president of a great university before his election is usually treated as a curiosity in the context of American politics. In Spanish America, by contrast, the academic titles of doctor or licenciate, or the fact that a man has written a good novel, are unquestionable assets for the political aspirant. Understandably this situation has a negative side: given the limited diffusion of general education in many countries, it is all too easy to take advantage of the blind respect paid the academician or littérateur. But whether the well-educated man uses his privileged position for good or evil is beside the point. The fact remains that his activities as a writer, philosopher, professor, or poet do not disqualify him for an active part in determining his nation's destiny; rather, they enhance his chances of playing such a role.

To return to my original point, this study deals with the intellectual expression of what may rightfully be considered a genuine revolution. I shall attempt to trace this movement as it manifests itself in a Spanish American literary genre particularly sensitive to ideological battles, the essay. The time span to be covered will be roughly seventy years—from the last decade of the nineteenth century through the first six decades of the twentieth. But before we begin, the revolution itself and the milieu which produced it must be examined briefly.

Stated in very general terms, this ideological revolt was directed against that view of human affairs which holds that the totality of man's existence may be empirically analyzed and understood. Under attack too was the corollary idea that the individual and the society may be technologically manipulated. The revolutionaries, by contrast, affirmed that human affairs are highly problematical, that they are suffused with contingency and the unpredictable, that the rational-scientific approach to the world of nature has only limited value in explaining the human condition. They found—and are continuing to find—that man cannot readily be defined, that his being cannot be made to "stand out" from a clearly discernible background: in short, that man has great difficulties in viewing himself as simply another object in nature. In their rejection of the scientific-rationalist approach to the human condition, Spanish American intellectuals reacted sharply against certain of its specific manifestations: positivism, bourgeois liberalism, and the belief in progress, understood as the unending increase in man's well-being through technology.

To this point I have been describing what the revolutionaries were trying to destroy. But with what could they fill the ideological vacuum that they had helped to create? Hopefully this question will be answered in the main body of this study. A tentative reply may, nonetheless, be helpful here. The writers whom we shall soon meet were searching for a radically different approach to the problem of man—some new way of looking at him which would, on the one hand, grant him autonomy from both the determinism of science and the constrictions of theology and, on the other, would exalt and liberate the uniquely human aspects of his nature: his creativity and his emotive life. In this search they have not been alone. Indeed the Spanish American expression of this movement is only one manifestation of a general ideological revolution which is still in progress throughout the Western world. Granted the wide diffusion of this revolution and admitting its European roots, what is the rationale for its study within the Hispanic American context? Aside from its obvious value in helping us understand contemporary Spanish America, there are, I feel, other good reasons. One of these lies in the fact that the region occupies a uniquely "intermediate" position in today's world: Spanish America's traditions and her historic trajectory are not as fixed as those of western Europe, while her sense of identity is not as ill defined as that of the very new "emergent" nations. A number of Spanish American writers have sensed the import of this situation and have suggested that the continent's unique destiny is to serve as a bridge between the highly developed sector of the world and the "new" countries of Asia and Africa. They feel, moreover, that Spanish America's ethnic complexity and her experience in dealing with Europe and North America have served to qualify her especially well for this role. In short they suggest that in the process of solving her own problems Spanish America may provide new solutions to the problems facing all twentieth-century men regardless of race or nation.

Our view of Spanish America opens upon the fading years of the nineteenth century. What strikes the eye first is the vigor and prosperity of the major cities. The situation was most dramatic in the South: Buenos Aires—called *La gran aldea* (the overgrown hamlet) —only a few years earlier had bypassed the 300,000 mark and was rapidly becoming a true metropolis. Italian, English, Yiddish, and German spiced and corrupted the Spanish of her founders. Financed to a great extent by British capital, the railroad network each year penetrated deeper into the rich heartland of the country. Two weeks' work in the New World would pay the way for an immigrant's third class passage to the Río de la Plata. For a time the Argentine government itself paid the new immigrants' passage. In Mexico City, the northern focus of Spanish American activity, a similar spirit was in evidence. If fewer Europeans were immigrating, then Mexicans would create their own Europe high on their lovely plateau. And so, under the leadership of the sometimes-benevolent dictator Porfirio Díaz, Mexico City was rebuilt along decidedly Parisian lines: the tree-lined, monumental Paseo de la Reforma would be the Mexican Champs Elysées, and the Chapultepec park would be known as the *bosque* of Chapultepec, echoing the French Bois de Boulogne. And if Paris was the *cité lumière*, then Mexico would be the first fully electrified city of Spanish America. In addition to the impressive campaign for beautification and electrification, the last decades of the century saw great progress in railroad construction (financed mostly by foreign capital), in the draining of the swampy Valley of Mexico, and in the beginnings of the petroleum industry. The value of exports increased steadily and agricultural production soared. Foreign investors came to consider Mexico, with her glittering land, mining, and plantation ventures, as the new realm of El Dorado. A small but influential class of newly rich occupied the very comfortable homes lining the Paseo and other fashionable *bulevares*. Many members of this new class held important official and semi-official positions among Díaz' inner circle of advisers—the celebrated *científicos*: hard-headed "men of science" who professed the tenets of French positivism; or stated more accurately, the Mexicanized version of Comtian thought, generously augmented by the social organicism of Herbert Spencer and the latter-day Darwinists.

Like Buenos Aires and Mexico City, other urban areas reflected in varying degrees the period's material well-being and passion for cosmopolitanism. The sober white-collar worker of Valparaiso or Santiago might, for example, affect the briar pipe and tweeds of the many Britishers who ran Chile's important coal and shipping industries; while the more volatile, more "typically Latin" young man of Caracas or Lima fell naturally into the stereotype of the Parisian *boulevardier* of the *belle époque*. The over-all pattern was, however, essentially the same in all of the continent's major cities. Despite an occasional set-back—such as the Argentine depression of 1890—in every large urban center the bywords of the time were progress, prosperity, optimism, and Europeanization.

The contrast provided by the smaller towns and the country was striking. The traditional Hispanic pattern of land tenure, maintained by the custom of primogeniture and fortified by nineteenth-century laissez-faire economic politics, served to exaggerate the endemic problem of the inequitable distribution of wealth. Mexico's case is one of the more dramatic: during the Díaz era (1877-1910) the value of exports skyrocketed and basic commodity prices trebled, while the *jornal*—the basic wage of the agricultural worker or day laborer—remained virtually unchanged. The Indian and near-Indian masses of the Andean countries (Peru, Bolivia, and Ecuador) fared no better. In the Río Plate countries there were perhaps more crumbs falling from the banquet table of progress and prosperity, yet not many miles away from the bustle of Buenos Aires or Rosario, the "new Gauchos"—Italians, Basques, even eastern European Jews—lived in primitive huts and eked out a precarious existence as sharecroppers or marginal cattlemen on the fringe of the great *estancias* of the wealthy. And in the far Northwest of Argentina Indians still worked the overlord's sugar plantations within a socio-economic system more reminiscent of Spanish colonial days than of the dawning twentieth century.

Even more striking than the economic gulf which separated the rising metropolis from the backlands was the radically different way of life, the radically different attitudes and tastes of city dweller compared with country dweller. Perhaps nowhere in that portion of the world where European languages were spoken was this contrast greater than in late nineteenth-century Spanish America. In the country—and here we must include many of the smaller provincial cities as well as the strictly rural areas—illiteracy was the rule rather than the exception; the church's educational and psychological hold on the people remained unchallenged; the language retained its purity and *casticidad* (indeed it often reflected archaisms of the Conqueror's day); and except for periodic check-ups on his foreman, or for an occasional fling with a naive country girl, the well-to-do landholder made certain that the greater part of his life would be spent with his cronies in the national capital—or better, in Paris, London, or Rome. Intellectuals and creative men fled the hinterland at the first opportunity; and in those countries where the dust of the provinces stifled even the atmosphere of the national capital, they crossed borders and succumbed to the magnetic attraction of the great metropolises. Thus Mexico City became an intellectual center not only for Mexicans, but for Guatemalans, Nicaraguans, and

Dominicans as well. Similarly the Río Plate drained an intellectual watershed of even greater size than its hydrographic area: for many Bolivian, Paraguayan, and Uruguayan writers, success in Buenos Aires became the diploma of literary achievement.

The literary activity of the larger cities contrasted with that of the country as the elegant English Brougham contrasted with rural oxcarts or burros. While the backlanders read catechism, the pretentious but dull *diario de provincia*, or the tired lyrics of Spanish romanticism, the urban literati might sample Baudelaire, Leconte de Lisle, Zola, and the Goncourts. The more sophisticated could dabble in Oscar Wilde or perhaps the Russian novelists. Instead of religious orthodoxy they might expose themselves to Comte, Spencer, James, or Nietzsche. They could journey to France by boat or by book, and upon returning they could gather in clubs and cafes to establish their own literary movement: *modernismo*. Amidst the glitter of cosmopolitan society, surrounded by an ever-increasing array of mechanical marvels, and surfeited with the century's material abundance, they could forget the crumbling streets of the provincial towns, the smell of the cane fields at dusk, the tired resignation in the eyes of the *negrita* or *chola*, heavy with the child of the *señorito*. But could they? The vogue of cosmopolitan *modernismo* was of short duration; and only barely hidden amidst the well-chiseled lines of its most famous exponents there was, I think, a strong current of dissatisfaction. There is a thinly veiled mood of desperation in their escape to a world of Parnassian statuary, of formal gardens, and of decadent aristocrats. At times this underlying desperation came to the surface. Rubén Darío, often considered the initiator of *modernismo*, could be as embittered a critic of the bourgeois order as any ardent radical. Witness his short prose piece of 1888, "El rey burgués" ("The Bourgeois King"), in which the gross, insensitive monarch forces the poet to prostitute his art by becoming a mechanical organ grinder. A general tone of alienation, of being out of joint with the times, is evident in the work of virtually all the *modernistas*. In their escapism they seem to have sensed, albeit dimly, that their literary efforts were in some way inauthentic, that they were failing to face the enigma of their own identity, and that in severing the umbilical cord which joined them to the land and the common folk, they had cut themselves off from what might well be their richest source of creative nourishment. In much of the *modernista* poetry there is a kind of tiredness, a pose perhaps of world-weary ennui. The poets seem to be saying that the progress and prosperity of the times really did not impress them greatly. They appear to be imprisoned in a golden cage of their own making, waiting to be transformed into a more ethereal substance and so, to escape. Thus Darío will have his *princesa* dream of flying off on the winged horse of her mythical Prince Charming, while Darío's contemporary, the essayist José Enrique Rodó, will choose Ariel, Shakespeare's "aeyrie spirit," as his ideological mentor.

This undercurrent of intellectual restlessness was further strengthened by specific political events. Foremost among these was the emergence of the United States as a strong and aggressive power whose vigorous culture and whose political ambitions threatened Spanish America's very existence. The defeat of Spain in 1898 underscored this insecurity and fear: given the obvious decadence of the mother country, what chance for success might her childeren expect? These doubts were further aggravated by the peculiar state of Spanish America's economic order. As we have seen, the wealth and well-being of the large cities was accompanied by misery and backwardness in vast areas of the interior. Spanish American intellectuals were becoming increasingly aware of the specious nature of the continent's prosperity and of the need for radical programs of economic amelioration. Yet they could not look toward the United States for a model of material betterment, since they quite understandably viewed *yanqui* culture as alien and threatening. Though the Hispanic intellectual saw the need for a better economic order in his continent, he distrusted the North American's pursuit of success, his worship of progress, and his insensitivity to the world of the aesthetic. Stated somewhat differently, many Spanish American intellectuals found themselves in an ambivalent position: although they wished that their region might enjoy the material bounty of the dawning twentieth century, they distrusted the world of technology and progress—particularly as embodied in the culture of North America, the *coloso del Norte*, as it came to be called. Most of all, they feared that in attempting to emulate the "advanced" countries, they would lose their own identity, their own unique—if yet not fully developed—manner of being.

To sum up, at the turn of the century Spanish America found herself confronted by complex choices of ideological orientation as well as by pressing problems of self-discovery and self-definition. These concerns crept into all manifestations of her literary life, but it was the essayists who expressed them most directly. The essay, faithful to its creator, Montaigne, characteristically reveals a thread of doubt, a degree of skepticism, and a tendency on the part of the author to consider more than one side of a given question. Given the nature of the issues confronting Spanish America at this period, it is no wonder that her writers should turn to the genre par excellence of tentatives and alternatives.

The present book should be thought of as a series of interrelated studies, each of which centers on one general theme characteristic of a given group, decade, or generation of writers. It is not intended to be a comprehensive survey of the contemporary Spanish American essay as a literary genre. My basic criterion for one essayist's inclusion and another's exclusion is the degree to which each man's ideas are germane to the theme under consideration. As is frequently the case when dealing with writers whom Spanish Americans dub *pensadores*, a number of the figures studied are essayists in only the broadest sense of the term. Some are amateur social scientists, others historians, while a few are, in their own fashion, philosophers. Likewise, a number of major literary figures who have cultivated the essay have been entirely omitted or only briefly noted. Those who have a professional interest in Spanish American literature may be surprised to find relatively little material dealing with questions of style or literary structure. Moreover, I have not sought to place the writers' studies within the usual framework of chronologically ordered literary periods. In short, though I am concerned with the essay as a vehicle of expression, the focus of this study lies more in the area of ideas—of intellectual history set against the backdrop of the total culture—than it does in the area of literature per se.

II / THE SICK CONTINENT

AND ITS DIAGNOSTICIANS

IT IS DIFFICULT TO APPRECIATE THE EXTENT TO WHICH science set the course of Spanish American intellectual life during the closing decades of the past century. The philosophic embodiment of the scientific attitude, positivism, not only dominated the thought of the period, but enjoyed a position of semi-official privilege as well. Highly influential educational institutions, such as Mexico's National Preparatory School and Argentina's Paraná Normal School, were founded by devotees of the Comtian system. Generations of young intellectuals left these and similar institutions revering the "Law of the Three Stages" and distrusting anything which was even vaguely tainted by metaphysics. One of the most striking examples of positivism's acceptance may be found in Mexico, where the dictator Porfirio Díaz was surrounded by a group of advisers who, by virtue of their positivistic orientation, were known as the *científicos*.

An important expression of positivism's scientific approach to man and his society was a strong interest in race and racial theories. The biological thought of the nineteenth century—diffused through such popularizing movements as Darwinism, social organicism, and the relatively new discipline of physical anthropology—provided abundant material upon which the racial theorizer could draw. Moreover, the fact that Spanish America had a population of great ethnic complexity naturally led her thinkers to consider race in assessing the continent's problems. The effect of the Spanish-American War must also be taken into account in this connection. Although it was Spain rather than Spanish America who had suffered defeat, the weakness of the mother country at the hands of the vigorous and ambitious Anglo-Saxon certainly disturbed the Hispanic world. The popular mind undoubtedly saw in the defeat of a swarthy southern "race" by a blue-eyed northern "race" a good example of the triumph of a "more fit" people over an "inferior" group. Thus it is understandable that during the decade immediately following the conflict many Spanish American writers should analyze political and social problems by means of the intellectual apparatus which social organicism and such race-centered theories as linguistic paleontology or anthroposociology might provide.[1] From the latter movements they acquired notions of Nordic or "Aryan" superiority along with the inevitable idea of the natural inferiority of "southern" peoples—Latins, Negroes, and non-Europeans in general. From the social organicists they adopted the concept of society as a living, growing organism, and thus subject to disease which might inhibit normal development. If something was wrong with the society, then the vocabulary of the times demanded that it be called a "sickness." A glance at the titles of a number of essays of the period bears this point out. In 1899 the Argentinian Agustín Álvarez published his *Manual de patología política*; in the same year a pamphlet titled *El continente enfermo* was published in New York by the Venezuelan, César Zumeta; several years later in 1905, another Argentinian, Manuel Ugarte, wrote his *Enfermedades sociales*; while the Bolivian Alcides Arguedas, produced his famous *Pueblo enfermo* in 1909. Regardless of the fact that the fundamental tenets of these writers may differ widely,[2] the similarity of what one critic has dubbed the "surgical" approach to the continent's problem, is striking. This attitude is not confined to the above essayists. In the work of the

1. Anthroposociology, a movement which began in the 1880's and continued through the first decade of the twentieth century, concerned itself principally with relating the social and cultural development of peoples to their biological "race." The anthroposociologists apparently took for granted that a definite correlation existed between physical groupings and cultures. Modern students of racial theory find their methodology poor, their assumptions unfounded, and much of their thinking to be heavily laden with gross racism. The myth of Aryanism (derived from the half-truths of linguistic paleontology), and *ad hoc* notions of "superior" versus "inferior" races often appear in the writing of the movement's leaders: Vacher de Lapouge in France, Otto Ammon and E. Gumplowicz in Germany, and C. C. Closson in the United States. Although these men have virtually been forgotten, their ideas influenced a number of better known sociological thinkers, particularly in France. For more information on anthroposociology and its influence see Jacques Barzun, *Race: A Study in Modern Superstition* (New York, 1937), pp. 218-22; and Louis L. Snyder, *Race, A History of Modern Ethnic Theories* (New York, 1934), pp. 164-68.
2. Ugarte, by way of example, was a devoted Socialist, whereas Arguedas, a member of a wealthy landholding family, supported decidedly conservative positions in ideology and practical politics. Furthermore, the fact that all of these writers use "surgical" terminology does not make their views of race—the focus of the present chapter— necessarily identical.

Argentinian C. O. Bunge, *Nuestra América* (1903), the "clinical" approach is very evident, as it is in much of the thought of Peru's Francisco García Calderón. More often than not, in the thinking of these writers, the unhealthy virus producing the illness was to be found in the racial make-up of the population. What is not under consideration here—and the point must be emphasized—are questions of racial relations and racial prejudices among Spanish America's masses. That the common people remained generally uncontaminated by the racism of these writers is, I think, clear; but a discussion of this point lies outside the scope of our study.

In addition to the generalized influence of social evolutionism and anthroposociology, certain specific European sources may be detected in the work of this group of essayists. Of the popular European "raciologists" of the period, the French social psychologist, Gustave Le Bon appears to have exerted a particularly strong influence. A few passages from his then popular work, the *Lois psychologiques de l'évolution des peuples* (1894), will serve to establish the intellectual atmosphere in which Bunge, Arguedas, and García Calderón wrote.

The key concept in Le Bon's raciology is his notion of the "national soul":

> Each race possesses a psychic constitution as fixed as its anatomical constitution. . . .
> . . . close examination reveals that the majority of individuals of a given race have a number of common psychological traits which are as stable as the anatomical traits that permit us to classify species. Like these traits, psychological characteristics are regularly and faithfully reproduced through heredity.
> This aggregate . . . constitutes what may justifiably be called the national character.[3]

The relationship between the national soul and social organicism is also basic: "A race may be compared to the mass of cells that constitute a living being. These billions of cells have a very short existence, whereas the existence of the being formed by their union is relatively long."[4] Most important, Le Bon firmly believed that the "racial character," the "national soul," or simply the "nature" of a given race was immutable. He repeatidly asserts that the milieu—whether it be thought of in terms of the physical environment, political institutions, or any other *circonstance extérieure*—is

3. Gustave Le Bon, *Lois psychologiques de l'évolution des peuples* (9ᵉ éd.; Paris 1909), pp. 9-10.
4. *Ibid.*, p. 12.

powerless to alter fundamental group traits.[5] As one might expect he divides mankind into a neat hierarchy of superior and inferior races, with the European naturally on top. Moreover, this superiority is physical, intellectual, emotional, and even moral.[6] Consistent with his basic views, he maintains that education can never transform a member of an "inferior" race into the equal of the white man: the Negro who is, for example, given all the advantages of a European education will only acquire the superficial veneer of the superior race: "this negro may accumulate all the diplomas in the world without ever reaching the level of an average European."[7] On the crucial question of miscegenation, an almost verbatim echoing of Le Bon is evident in many Spanish American essayists. The core of the French thinker's position is that the product of racial mixing will always be inferior to the parent stocks. He claims that miscegenated groups suffer a "disassociation" of character and morality, that they are incapable of creating or maintaining a culture, and that what society they do have is "degenerate" or "anarchic."[8] In his discussion of *les métis* Le Bon was chiefly concerned with the mixture of whites and Negroes: significantly, when he sought concrete illustrations for his theories he turned to the Caribbean: "All of these republics, without a single exception, are perpetually prey to the most bloody anarchy, and, despite the impressive wealth of their soil, one after another they flounder amidst all kinds of corruption, insolvency, and despotism."[9]

One of the most complete raciological analyses of Hispanic America to appear in this century was *Nuestra América* (1903) by the Argentinian, Carlos Octavio Bunge (1875-1918). Bunge's methodology—his fundamental scientism, his manipulation of Le Bonian ideas, and his frequent reliance on social organicism—provides a valuable point of departure for our investigation of the sick continent and its diagnosticians. The route which Bunge's thinking will follow is indicated early in his book: "What I would call the practical objective in this work is to describe, with all its vices and in all its forms, the politics of Spanish America. In order to understand this, I must first investigate the collective psychology which produces it.

5. *Ibid.*, pp. 174-75.
6. *Ibid.*, pp. 24-33.
7. *Ibid.*, p. 33.
8. *Ibid.*, p. 45.
9. *Ibid.*, pp. 114-115.

And, to know this psychology I shall first analyze the races which make up the native Spanish American."[10]

The first of the races to be analyzed is the Spanish. He finds that the "dominant quality" of this group is arrogance, the origin of which "is lost in the darkness of prehistory, because it is found more in geography than in race."[11] Although geography seems to be given priority over race, Bunge notes that this arrogance is evident even today in the American of Spanish descent, as well as in the *peninsulares*.[12] His thinking is typically racist here: an acquired trait persists "in the blood" although the historical and geographical agents which originally produced it no longer prevail. Bunge next analyzes the distinct regional groups of Spain. Finding the Castilians to be the dominant force in shaping the "national soul," he asks: "Why is it that the Castilian has formed a particular breed and has imposed his own standard of purity [*casticidad*]? This gives rise to a most difficult historical problem: that of the origin of one group's dominance, that of innate preponderance, of original supremacy...."[13] He resolves this problem in terms of a rather simplistic social Darwinism: among contending "sub-races" the fittest survive and their domination "is the mark of their superiority ... imposed upon the weak groups, the dominated ones."[14] In addition to Castilian arrogance and "innate superiority," Bunge discusses several other traits which the Spanish American has inherited from the mother country. Most important among these is a sense of Christian piety and morality, which he finds existing in present day Spanish Americans of pure European stock as "innate" characteristics.[15]

When Bunge turns his attention to the nonwhite elements in Spanish America's racial composition, his deeply engrained racism is very apparent. The Indian, he feels, is characterized by "passivity" and "oriental fatalism," and these traits account for the Spaniards' easy conquest of the Indian empires of Peru and Mexico.[16] The Negro receives similar treatment. After a brief moment's consideration of the validity of the concept of superior versus inferior races, he proceeds to analyze the "positive facts" regarding the Negro's attainments. These he finds to be entirely lacking: the

10. Carlos Octavio Bunge, *Nuestra América: Ensayo de psicología social* (6ª ed.; Buenos Aires, 1918), p. 49.
11. *Ibid.*, p. 59.
12. *Ibid.*, p. 61.
13. *Ibid.*, p. 101.
14. *Ibid.*, p. 53.
15. *Ibid.*, p. 189.
16. *Ibid.*, p. 123.

Negro has not invented anything, he is not capable of intellectual leadership or of artistic creativity. His typical traits are "servility and vanity."[17] That Bunge believes the Negro to be inferior, or at best undesirable, is clearly shown in a number of other instances: on one occasion he states that the sexual temperament of the African renders him less "virtuous" than the European;[18] at another point in *Nuestra América* he expresses approval of the "logic" of the North American attitude toward this race;[19] and in discussing the early years of Spanish American independence, he is apparently shocked that the equalitarian-minded revolutionaries went to such extremes as erecting statues of Negroes in public squares.[20] Similarly, his characterization of the mulatto plainly reveals his utter disdain for this group: "Impulsive, perfidious, petulant, the mulatto is a complex amalgam of the Spanish and African spirit . . . . He is as touchy and as fickle as a woman, and, like a woman, like a degenerate, like a devil himself, he apsires to be strong, but is necessarily weak . . . . He lacks personal valor. In dangerous situations he has difficulty in overcoming his fear; but by means of tricks and fraud, he can escape his enemy with reptilian undulations."[21] The mestizo hardly fares better. He is accused of "rapacity," of intensifying and aggravating the Spaniard's arrogance, and of having a love for brutality inherited from his Indian ancestors. In short, both the mestizo and mulatto reflect the worst of their parent stocks: "Both impure, both atavistically anti-Christian, they are like the two heads of a mythical Hydra which encircles, constricts, and strangles in its gigantic coils, a beautiful and pale virgin: Hispanic America!"[22]

Bunge's views on atavism—attributed, incidentally, to what he calls the "Darwinian theory of hybridization"—lead him to the conclusion that "the mestizo tends to reproduce a kind of primitive man, or, at least an ancient and pre-Christian man. And all this, naturally, in a very general way, with, as we shall see, many mitigating circumstances and logical exceptions . . . ."[23] In describing the atavism and degeneration of the hybrid Bunge pinpoints several unfortunate traits: "psychic inharmony," sterility, and lack of a moral sense.[24] A basic assumption underlying this very unfavorable

17. *Ibid.*, p. 136.
18. *Ibid.*, pp. 146-47.
19. *Ibid.*, p. 136.
20. *Ibid.*, p. 133.
21. *Ibid.*, p. 148.
22. *Ibid.*, p. 149.
23. *Ibid.*, p. 139.
24. *Ibid.*, p. 141.

view of the hybrid is "psychophysical correlation." Like Paul
Broca and the anthroposociologists of the nineteenth century, Bunge
accepts this correlation at face value when he writes "every one who
is physically a mestizo . . . is morally a mestizo."[25]

Having established these fundamental concepts regarding the
non-European, Bunge analyzes the effects of Negro and Indian blood
upon the political and social structure of the continent. He apparently feels that the *sine qua non* of modern society is "a sense of
morality . . . the fruit of Christianity."[26] This sense, which Bunge
maintains exists in the European as innate and inherited, is lacking
in the colored races; hence the great mass of nonwhite Spanish
Americans are simply incapable of distinguishing good from evil.[27]
In addition to this general lack of morality in Spanish American life
and politics, a number of other social and political defects are credited
to "bad blood." Bunge feels, for example, that the servility and
fatalism of the Indian and Negro account for the fact that many
countries are particularly susceptible to *caciquismo* (political bossism).
Anticipating objections to this notion, Bunge finds it necessary to
explain away the fact that "European" Argentina had herself been
dominated for two decades by one of Spanish America's most in-
famous *caciques*, Juan Manuel Rosas: "The susceptibility to domination by a *cacique* of Spanish American nations is in inverse proportion to European blood. Thus the tyranny of Rosas in Buenos
Aires—the most European part of Spanish America—was also the
bloodiest in her history."[28]

If one accepts this hastily contrived explanation of Argentine
history and agrees with Bunge regarding the *cacicabilidad* of pop-
ulations dominated by mixed blood, it follows that the republican
form of government is, as Bunge states, "suitable only for the purest
of European races."[29] Thus, for most of Spanish America, faith in
democracy is held to be an unfortunate carryover from the equalitarianism of the French Revolution. Against this "cursed disease

25. *Ibid.*, p. 140. Paul Broca was a prominent French anthropologist and a contemporary of Darwin. Coincidentally, Broca founded the Anthropological Society of
Paris in 1859, the same year that the *Origin of the Species* appeared. Broca's group
devoted itself chiefly to anthropometrics—the precise measurement of the human
anatomy, particularly the skull. In general, the Paris Society remained aloof from
the theories of evolutionism. For further discussion of Broca and his group see Barzun,
Race, pp. 159-61.
26. Bunge, *Nuestra América*, p. 146.
27. *Ibid.*
28. *Ibid.*, pp. 247-48.
29. *Ibid.*, p. 246.

which still leads us . . . toward pernicious Utopias,"[30] Bunge suggests
the remedy of "the POSITIVE STUDY of history, politics, economics,
and sociology."[31] As a good example of the proper manner of
achieving progress in a nation dominated by non-European peoples,
he applauds the "scientific" positivism of the Díaz regime in Mexico.[32]

A book such as *Nuestra América* would have little appeal to present-day Spanish Americans. The author's racism is only the outward
manifestation of attitudes which run counter to contemporary
thought and sensibility. The most striking feature of Bunge's view
of the New World (at least the Hispanic portion of it) is that it
cannot measure up to what he considers the only culture worthy of
emulation, the European. Equally unacceptable to modern thinkers
is his pretentious "scientific" manipulation of human masses and his
disinclination to deal with the individual. The complete falseness
of his "objective" positivistic pose is frequently revealed by violent,
impassioned outbursts against specific groups, particularly the
mulatto and mestizo. In short, the scientism of Carlos Octavio
Bunge is in sharp opposition to the ever-increasing humanism
characteristic of contemporary Spanish American writers.

It is not surprising that Bolivia, a country almost totally peopled
by Indians and mestizos, has produced much literature on the
nativist theme. Alcides Arguedas (1879-1946), who shows this
interest in his novels *Wautu-Wauru* (1904) and in his better known
Raza de bronce (1919), has written several essays dealing with the
Andean region and its inhabitants. The best known of these works
is the essay *Pueblo enfermo* (1909) in which Arguedas discusses the
Indian, the mestizo, and questions of race at considerable length.
Of interest too is his *Danza de las sombras* (1934), a rambling collection of travel notes and personal memoirs, most of which were
written well before the book's date of publication.

Like Bunge, Arguedas undertakes the investigation of his region's
problems with a desire for a realistic, "surgical," hardhead approach.
In keeping with this spirit, he urges his compatriots to face the facts
of national backwardness and political chaos directly: "we must
agree, frankly, vigorously, and directly, that we are *sick*; or rather,
that we have been born sick and that our total collapse may be
certain."[33] The causes of this sickness are then sketched out in

30. *Ibid.*, p. 264.
31. *Ibid.*
32. *Ibid.*, p. 308.
33. Alcides Arguedas, *Pueblo enfermo* (3era ed.; Santiago de Chile, 1937), p. 176.

broad terms: "Heredity, lack of culture, laziness, and poverty; here you have in summation the real underlying causes of the sickness of our countries. . . ."[34] Arguedas traces the ills of the Andean countries (the phrase "our countries" here and throughout the book indicates that his attention is not directed solely to Bolivia) to both "inheritance" *and* environmental forces: lack of culture, poverty, etc. A basic problem in analyzing the thought of Arguedas—and of others like him—revolves about the sense in which "heredity" is used in reference to group traits. A writer who ascribes qualities or defects of a people to "the Spanish heritage" or "the Indian heritage" may mean either that such traits have been culturally transmitted— passed on by custom and tradition—or that they are actually inherited biologically—"in the blood," as it were. An examination of this question in Arguedas' essays is the first step toward understanding his view of Spanish American reality.

Arguedas' characterization of the Indian occupies an important place in this analysis. The native American, he asserts, "carries in his blood" a marked lack of foresight; he possesses an "atrophied" aesthetic sense; and the Indians' willingness to die in battle "comes to the poor unfortunates by heredity."[35] Although these traits are apparently considered innate in the American native, a few other characteristics are ascribed to environmental conditioning. In an early chapter of the *Pueblo enfermo*, for example, Arguedas maintains that the hypocrisy and deceit of the Indian was developed as a defense mechanism against the brutality of the conqueror.[36] In a similar manner, the Indian of today finds that feigned stupidity affords him an escape from distasteful work.[37]

Arguedas discusses the Bolivian mestizo, or *cholo* at great length. Significantly, this group fares considerably worse in his view than does the pure Indian. Speaking of alcoholism and laziness, he asserts that while there is some justification in the Indian's being a sluggard and drinker, these vices are found in the *cholo* simply "by inclination."[38] Arguedas' over-all characterization of the *cholo* stresses his "atavistic" traits, though the Bolivian writer does concede him a degree of intelligence and an "enviable" ability to adapt to his environment. Moreover, "he is generous, intelligent, and considerate. . . ." Having taken brief note of the few good *cholo* characteristics, Arguedas goes

34. *Ibid.*, p. 180.
35. Alcides Arguedas, *La danza de las sombras* (Barcelona, 1934), II, 271.
36. Arguedas, *Pueblo enfermo*, p. 51.
37. Arguedas, *La danza*, II, 350.
38. *Ibid.*, p. 345.

on to present the catalogue of his faults. These include a lack of sense of duty, a lack of discipline, bellicosity, egocentrism, vanity, hypocrisy, servility, and lack of loyalty.[39]

Given this view of mestizo character, it is not difficult to predict how Arguedas will "explain" his region's social and political shortcomings. In language reminiscent of Bunge he states that "mestizo blood" has molded society to the point that "we are burdened with impudence, cheating, falseness, and other evils which unavoidably turn man aside from the pursuit of moral perfection, the highest goal of life."[40] It is to miscegenation that Bolivia owes its slow development of democratic institutions;[41] it is because of a "certain uniqueness in the Indo-Hispanic character" that the people lean too heavily upon the state for all their needs; and, had Indian blood not predominated in his country's racial composition, Bolivia would have adopted "all kinds of moral and material advances, and would be today at the same level as many of the more favored nations."[42] Again Bunge may be recalled when Arguedas states that "with mestizos and *cholos* one cannot utilize institutions made for pure-blooded and thoroughly educated peoples."[43] We note here that democratic institutions are practicable among peoples of "pure" blood *and* who have been prepared by a long period of education for such institutions. Once again, the environment as well as the purely biological inheritance are given as two causes producing one situation, and the relative importance of one against the other is difficult to determine.

On occasion Arguedas will consider geography and climate from a rigidly environmental point of view. A host of regional characteristics are explained in this manner. Owing to the "harshness and aridity of the wilderness" the highlander of the Andes is "tough, spiteful, egoistical, cruel, vindictive, and jealously hateful."[44] Furthermore, as a result of the bleakness of the inter-Andean plateaus, the Aymará Indian is cheerless, unimaginative, and unpoetic.[45] In the tropical regions, by contrast, one may find "a race made more gentle by the climate . . . (whose) members lead a tranquil, affable, pleasant life" and who appear "helpful and obliging toward stran-

39. Arguedas, *Pueblo enfermo*, pp. 57, 62-63.
40. *Ibid.*, p. 218.
41. *Ibid.*, p. 90.
42. *Ibid.*, p. 32.
43. Arguedas, *La danza*, II, 83.
44. Arguedas, *Pueblo enfermo*, p. 36.
45. *Ibid.*, pp. 34-35.

gers."[46] Despite these desirable qualities, a truly tropical climate has a fundamentally bad effect on a group; for in such an environment life is too easy and man is not forced to provide for future periods of scarcity. One might suppose that since Arguedas accepts this kind of analysis, the Indian or *cholo* of the high, barren, relatively cold Andean plateaus would, by contrast, be considered a model of industry and activity. However, Arguedas refrains from carrying his reasoning to this kind of conclusion; in keeping with the pessimistic tone of much of his thinking he prefers to point out only the undesirable interpretation of a given situation.

To what extent can the cultural environment—education, in particular—counteract undesirable traits produced by physical environment and "innate" racial characteristics? In short, can the *pueblo enfermo* be cured of its ills? At least in his later writings, Arguedas expresses confidence in the ability of education to erase, or at least to modify, these negative qualities. He notes that it is fruitless to blame Bolivia's geography for her backwardness, and that the troubles of the region are not simply a result of the "mental insufficiency" of the race. He thus concludes that "the great national problem is primarily . . . pedagogical."[47] This view represents Arguedas' thinking in the year 1934; earlier, in the first edition of *Pueblo enfermo*, while asserting that the Indian is capable of being educated, he holds that such training must be limited to the native's immutable temperament; that while he may make an excellent soldier or farmer, he will always be "incapable of anything requiring initiative." And as late as 1937, in the third edition of this same work, Arguedas agrees with Juan Bautista Alberdi's conservative, mid-nineteenth-century view of popular education: "make the *roto*, the *Gaucho*, the *cholo* . . . go through all the processes of the finest educational system, and in a hundred years you will not make of him an English worker who labors, consumes, and lives in dignity and comfort."[48] In essence Arguedas holds that the Indian or the mestizo can and should be educated to a degree, but that it would be vain to hope that they could reach the highly civilized level of the white European. His remedy for Bolivia's *enfermedad* reveals

46. *Ibid.*, p. 76.
47. Arguedas, *La danza*, II, 337.
48. Alcides Arguedas, *Pueblo enfermo. Contribución a la psicología de los pueblos hispano-americanos.* Carta-prólogo de Ramiro de Maeztu (Barcelona, 1909), p. 237. Note that all other references to this work are from the third edition (1937). In general there is little substantive difference between these two editions, although the exact phraseology varies somewhat. Important, too, is Arguedas' addition of several chapters—including one in which he supports Hitlerian racism—in the later edition.

the typical attitude of the landholder: the national welfare will best be served by educating the Indian and *cholo* to a point at which his maximum potential as an agricultural worker or soldier is reached. That Arguedas sincerely believed that the non-European was incapable of going beyond this point is implicit throughout his thinking, regardless of his occasional expressions of faith in education.

The theory that miscegenation produces degeneracy and the complementary notion that racial purity leads to a superior culture occupies a central place in Arguedas' thought. Here again a parallelism with Bunge may be observed; as in the case of the Argentine writer, terms such as "atavism" and "degeneration" are frequently found in Arguedas' discussion of the mestizo. Significantly, Arguedas' position on these questions remained essentially unmodified throughout his career as a writer. As we shall see, much of the theorizing which found in miscegenation the *causa causarum* of the continent's ills was of relatively short duration; few writers of recent decades have held to racistic interpretations of Spanish American reality. However, as late as 1937, in the third edition of the *Pueblo enfermo*, Arguedas is unequivocal in his view that racial mixing is *the* explanation of Bolivia's backwardness: "in short, I repeat that miscegenation is the most obvious and the most enslaving phenomenon in Bolivia, and it is the only thing that explains reasonably and satisfactorily our present backwardness."[49] As in the 1909 edition, he seeks support for his position in the literature of European raciology. By the thirties, however, such support could no longer be found within the ranks of the scientific anthropologists and social psychologists. As the critic Zum Felde notes, Arguedas' thesis was never corrected in the light of modern race concepts: his racism in fact became so entrenched that he could only find substantiation for his views in the writings of that distinguished raciological "expert" of recent history, Adolf Hitler. Thus the pages of the 1937 edition of *Pueblo enfermo* are filled with citations from the Spanish translation of *Mein Kampf* and with approval of Hitlerian notions of Aryanism, the superiority of pure races, etc.[50]

To sum up, Arguedas traces the national *enfermedad* to the maleficent heritage derived from both Indian and Spaniard, and to the "degenerative" effects of the intermixture of these two groups. His views on the mestizo clearly imply that miscegenation itself produces a group which not only incorporates the undesirable

49. Arguedas, *Pueblo enfermo*, p. 264.
50. *Ibid.*, pp. 264-65.

characteristics of the two parent stocks, but in fact, exaggerates and intensifies these defects. "Heredity" is used in two senses; that of immutable, blood-carried traits and that of environmentally produced characteristics. The role of the principal cultural force, education, is important but limited. The non-European can only be educated to a certain level; the Hitlerian view that cultural forces are impotent when confronted by the determinism of the blood is endorsed. It follows that there are immutably inferior and superior races. Occasional slips, too, reveal his beliefs: speaking of the Indian's reaction to extreme exploitation, he notes that "then the Indian will become aroused, and will forget his *obvious* inferiority. . . ."[51] (italics mine). Since he feels that there will always be a large group of only partially educated "inferior" Indians and mestizos, he holds little confidence in the success of democratic institutions. In a few relatively rare instances, Arguedas expresses the opposing view that nations of the Andean region can follow the example of the true democracies (the United States is held up as the worthiest model of these) and by doing so "attenuate certain racial peculiarities and modify material conditions; that is, change the form of those great molds in which the soul of a people is cast. . . ."[52] Despite these occasional rays of hope, despite his unconvincing assertion that he is not "a fanatic on the subject of race,"[53] and despite his recognition of the fact that science has been unable to discover what physical criteria actually determine races,[54] Arguedas remained essentially a racist. His closed view of racial development, his certainty that cultural forces could not materially change the undesirable, "inferior" traits inherent in non-European "blood," and finally his acceptance of Hitlerian raciology lead inevitably to this conclusion.

The work of Arguedas is an extreme example of the general intellectual orientation of the diagnosticians of the sick continent. Science—understood always as "European science"—explains the individual as well as the group, and what science cannot account for is either ignored or else crops up as an unresolved inconsistency. As we shall note as our study develops, scientism of this kind was, by the first few decades of the present century, already under attack by many Spanish American writers. In this context, the Peruvian essayist Francisco García Calderón (1883-1953) occupies an ambiv-

51. *Ibid.*, p. 47.
52. *La danza*, II, 384.
53. *Ibid.*, p. 154.
54. *Pueblo enfermo*, p. 31.

alent position: as a follower of José Enrique Rodó (whose impact will be discussed later) he shows at least a superficial reaction against this restrictive scientism. Nevertheless his work remains permeated with racistic notions derived from the social organicists and particularly from Gustave Le Bon. That a French source should figure prominently in his writing is understandable since García Calderón was—even by Spanish American standards—an extreme Francophile. The bulk of his work, including his widely read survey of the Latin America of his day, *Les démocraties latines de l'Amérique* (1912), was published in French.

Les démocraties latines de l'Amérique covers a broad range of economic, sociological, political, demographic, and historical problems. Unlike Bunge, García Calderón does not make the study of racial psychology the obvious keystone of the essay's organization, yet he clearly reveals that the "race problem" is uppermost in his mind. One must read some three fourths of the book before finding a forthright statement of the importance of race in the over-all analysis of Latin America's problems:

> The race question is a very serious problem in American history: it explains the progress of some nations, the decadence of others; it is the key to the incurable malady which is lacerating America. Finally, many other secondary phenomena depend upon it: general wealth, industrial organization, the stability of governments, and the steadfastness of patriotism. It is necessary, therefore, that the continent have an unswerving policy, based on the study of the problems posed by race, just as there is an agrarian policy in Russia, a protectionist policy in Germany and a policy of free-trade in England.[55]

For García Calderón as for so many of his contemporaries, there was little problem in deciding whether the non-European element was inferior; rather he addressed himself to the question of whether cultural forces could unify and elevate a people admittedly debilitated by the malignant effects of mixed blood: "This complexity of castes, this mixture of different blood has given rise to numerous problems. For example, is the formation of national consciousness possible amidst such disparate elements? Is it possible that democracies so heterogeneous in nature can resist the invasion of superior races? In short, is South American miscegenation absolutely incapable of culture and organization?"[56]

55. Francisco García Calderón, *Les démocraties latines de l'Amérique* (Paris, 1912), p. 327.
56. *Ibid.*, p. 328.

The answer to this question is never made perfectly clear. Agreeing with the late nineteenth-century Argentine anthropologist, Lucas Ayarragaray, García maintains that the first generation mestizo is "superior" to the pure Indian but "inferior" to the pure European.[57] This position has an appealing simplicity about it; the more European "blood" bred into the mestizo, the better will be the resulting product. In many cases little distinction is made between the various types of racial mixtures; the use of the more generalized French term *métis* may explain why García Calderón so frequently speaks of *mulato, mambo,* and *mestizo* as if they were simply one group. Thus, when he discusses the contradictory forces at work in the psyche of the *métis* he will say: "There are many *métis* who are unfortunately disturbed by two races which are antagonistic by heredity. The strangest characteristics, the sensualism of the Negro, the sadness of the Indian, give this new race a spirit full of contradictory hues. . . ."[58] García Calderón's fundamental evaluation of the mestizo is best observed in his analysis of Latin American political structure. The progress of Argentina, Uruguay, Chile, certain states of Brazil, and Peru (an inclusion motivated by a bit of jingoism, no doubt) is described as a "result of the purification of the race, of the great amount of virile immigration, of the development of industrial activity."[59] Similarly, of the unequal political development of the Central American nations, he states that "race explains the differences which we observe in the broad field of political experience. . . ."[60] The Peruvian essayist's fears extend even to the United States, where "the national heritage is threatened by the invasion of Slavs and Orientals, by the fecundity of the Negroes; a foreboding uneasiness clouds the future of the race."[61]

Despite his interest in the problems posed by miscegenation in North America, García Calderón is no Yankeephile. Rather, he feels that the Anglo-Saxon disdain for the colored races leads to an irreducible enmity between the two halves of the New World and that Hispanic America would do well to recognize this situation. He observes that in North America's superficial friendship toward her sister republics "there is contempt . . . in her policies there is the

57. *Ibid.,* p. 333.
58. *Ibid.,* pp. 236-37.
59. Francisco García Calderón, *La creación de un continente* (Paris, 1913), pp. 256-57.
60. García Calderón, *Les démocraties,* p. 204.
61. *Ibid.,* p. 207.

ambition to dominate. It is the inevitability of blood—stronger than political affinity or geographic proximity."[62]

Throughout this discussion, and also in many other contexts, García Calderón uses such phrases as the "Latin Spirit," the "Anglo-Saxon Spirit," and the like. These terms, ambiguous as they are, may shed light upon his basic view of race. His remarks concerning the "Latin Spirit" versus the "Anglo-Saxon Spirit" indicate that he has in mind a parallel action of both race and culture; thus, in describing this conflict he speaks of an "enmity and divorce between the two races *and* the two traditions"[63] (italics mine). Occasionally, as at the very beginning of *Le Pérou contemporain*, he seems to reject the race concept entirely in favor of culturally or environmentally formed traits: "There is a Latin civilization; a Latin spirit; there is no Latin race. And the Latinity of France and of Spain, and of the South American republics, if one understands by that term the persistence of Roman blood, is a false notion, an obsolete anthropological concept."[64] In *Les démocraties* too, he rejects the biological concept of race. Taking note of the large amount of non-Latin blood in Spanish America, and of the many non-Anglo-Saxon elements in North America's population, he maintains that only "two moral heritages" will remain after the English and Spaniards vanish.[65]

On the basis of such statements García Calderón apparently held to the view that cultural forces are all-powerful in creating and modifying national or group character. However, he also believes that the cultural force itself, be it the "Latin Spirit" or the "Anglo-Saxon Spirit," cannot exert complete control over these traits. His concept of these culture-souls is essentially mystical: they are composed of the traditions, language, and customs of a people plus an undefined and irreducible quality which would, for example, make the "Saxonization" of the Latin impossible: "This spirit of a New America is irreducible. Contact with Anglo-Saxon civilization may alter it to some extent; but the complete transformation of the peculiar genius of these nations will never take place."[66] Granted that the Anglo-Saxon "National Soul" cannot radically alter peoples dominated by the *Âme Latine*, may the non-European peoples of

62. *Ibid.*, p. 289.
63. Francisco García Calderón, *Le Pérou contemporian, étude sociale* (Paris, 1907), p. 242.
64. *Ibid.*, p. 33.
65. García Calderón, *Les démocraties*, p. 261.
66. *Ibid.*, p. 265.

Spanish America be in any way modified by the forces of European culture? Can the "Latin Spirit" operating within Hispanic America herself elevate or transform the Indian, Negro, and person of mixed blood—groups which are obviously considered inferior by this essayist? Apparently not, for García Calderón never presents the National Soul as an active agent; rather it is simply the expression of an irreducible set of characteristics.

In one of his few major essays written in Spanish, the *Creación de un continente* (1913), he attempts to solve the problem of transforming Latin America in a different manner. In this work the emphasis is placed upon a more general "forming force" of the New World, rather than upon the more restricted "Latin Spirit."

> The continent has revealed its tremendous forming force. Detailed North American statistics prove that the most irreducible races respond to the action of the American environment. The head of the Jew slowly changes form. . . . In the North and in the South, in the United States and in Argentina —huge racial laboratories—the same transformation may be observed; the German becomes a Yankee, the Italian becomes 'Argentinized.'[67]

Statements such as these do not, however, qualify García Calderón as a liberal, for he never clearly admits that the environment might erase the biological "inferiority" of the non-European. When he seeks an explanation for Spanish America's political instability, he reverts to his racistic mentors: [Spanish America's] agitated history demonstrates that ideologies, equalitarian prejudices, and romantic liberalism are all sterile. It confirms the psychological laws formulated by Dr. Gustave Le Bon: "the depressive effect of miscegenation, and the inability of institutions to transform the soul of peoples. A policy based upon the study of race may redeem these disorganized nations. Their future greatness will depend upon their willingness to submit to inflexible laws."[68]

In summing up García Calderón's ideas on race, one is struck by the eclecticism of his position. Despite his fundamentally racistic view, the rigid scientism of, say, Carlos Octavio Bunge, is to a degree counterbalanced in his essays by a greater appreciation of cultural forces, by the concept of the National Soul, and by a similarly mystical notion of environmental influence—the "forming force"— of the New World. Certain facts of García Calderón's life—his long

67. García Calderón, *La creación*, p. 60.
68. *Ibid.*, p. 260.

residence in Europe at a period in which the revolt against scientism and positivism was gaining momentum, and his association with the Spanish American group (the *arielistas*) representing a similar reaction—account in part for his peculiar position. Like many Latin Americans of his day, García Calderón felt that in order to be a full-fledged citizen of the Western World it was necessary to be European, to speak (and write) French, to look upon one's native land and her primitive, "atavistic," mixed-blooded masses through the works of Europe's leading social scientists and philosophers. Yet the very primitiveness, the uniqueness, and the grandeur of America could not be ignored. There is, particularly in his *Creación de un continente*, an inkling of that profound sensitivity to the destiny and possibilities of the New World which was soon to become a major theme in the work of some of the most distinguished essayists of the present century.[69] Significant, too, is the fact that García Calderón's deviations from the scientism of his European mentors are found in his later writings, while his racism is most frequently encountered in his early work.

In 1912 García Calderón founded and directed an important literary review: the *Revista de América*. Published in Paris, the *Revista* became a sounding board for Spanish Americans living in Europe as well as for overseas contributors. The journal reflects many of the opposing intellectual currents that will be observed in the Spanish American essay of the period: "New Worldism" (*novo-mundismo*) versus Europeanism; Bergsonian thought versus positivism; and racism versus indigenism. José Ingenieros (1877-1925), a contributor to the *Revista* and one of Argentina's most prolific essayists was often in the thick of the magazine's polemics. Ingenieros had much to say on a wide range of subjects: sociology, criminology, socialism, ethics, philosophy, psychology, and, of course, race.[70] Since Ingenieros was an active Socialist one would expect him to explain "racial" characteristics on the basis of economic forces and historical materialism. But, like many of his contemporaries, he could

---

69. See below, Chapter IV, pp. 59-67, 80-101.
A further corroboration of García Calderón's Americanist sympathies may be seen in his rebuttal of Ortega y Gasset's condescending attitudes toward the New World. See his article, "Ortega y Gasset y nuestro tiempo," *Repertorio Americano*, XX (1930), 147.
70. In addition to the essays considered below, Ingenieros' abundant bibliography includes the following items: *La criminología* (1911), *La evolución de la antropología criminal* (1911), *La simulación en la lucha por la vida* (1909), *Principios de psicología biológica* (1913), *El hombre mediocre* (1913), *Hacia una moral sin dogma* (1917), *Ensayos filosóficos* (1917), *Proposiciones relativas al porvenir de la filosofía* (1918), and *Las fuerzas morales* (1923).

not resist the "scientific" attraction of social organicism. Since Ingenieros was a moderate rather than a radical, he found Spencerian ideas quite compatible with the evolutionary socialism he professed. And so, in his attitudes towards race, as in much of his sociological thought, the influence of Darwin and Spencer is much more striking than that of the Marxists.

Ingenieros repeatedly asserts his belief in the innate superiority of the white man. This attitude is evident in an article published in the *Revista de América*, critical of Ricardo Rojas' Indianist theories;[71] in an extensive essay, *Sociología argentina* (1910); and in the collection of informal memoirs, *Crónicas de viaje* (1919). He feels it is an accepted fact that history proves the superiority of the white man,[72] that the Indian's defeat by the European is evidence of the white man's superior level of development; and that the Negroes are "closer to anthropoid monkeys than to civilized whites."[73] Ingenieros believes, moreover, that the "inferior races" will never develop upward and so lose their inferior status; rather, they will simply vanish in the struggle for life. It follows that an effort to "uplift" such races would be in vain, or more exactly, "anti-scientific": "Whatever we do in favor of the inferior races is anti-scientific; at the most, we could protect them in order that they destroy each other without undue cruelty; [we could also] facilitate the provisional adaptation of the few exceptional cases."[74] Ingenieros carries his reasoning to some surprising extremes; he doubts that men of colored races should be considered politically and juridically the equal of whites, and he even goes as far as justifying the institution of slavery as "the legal and political sanction of a purely biological reality."[75] The strong current of jingoism evident in his *Sociología argentina* is based, to a great extent, upon an exalted evaluation of the nation's racial stock. Ingenieros sees Argentina ("finally free . . . of inferior races") as the dominant force in a continent which has been debilitated by Indian and Negro blood.[76] He feels that the temperate zone is the natural home of the European and that the nonwhite's inability to adapt to this environment is another proof of his "inferiority."

71. José Ingenieros, "Nacionalismo e indianismo," *Revista de América*, II (May/August, 1913), 185-94.
72. José Ingenieros, *Obras completas*, revisadas y anotadas por Aníbal Ponce (Buenos Aires, 1939), VIII, 40.
73. José Ingenieros, *Crónicas de viaje* (Buenos Aires, 1919), p. 163.
74. *Ibid.*, p. 165.
75. *Ibid.*, p. 163.
76. Ingenieros, *Obras completas*, VIII, 87.

However, the fact that the European is not adaptable to a tropical environment is never considered a sign of *his* inferiority.[77]

Ingenieros' manipulation of the race concept, his acceptance of a vague environmentalism, and his frequent recourse to economic determinism lead only to confusion. The following statement is typical: "race is not an abstract factor: each race, together with its environment, expresses itself by specific customs and institutions, its clearest exponent being the economic system."[78] Virtually all of the crucial terms in this passage are ill-defined. Ingenieros does not make clear whether "environment" refers to the physical environment or whether it includes "customs and institutions"; and the precise meaning of the term "exponent" is equally diffuse. If Ingenieros means that a given physical enviroment produces a given complex of institutions, and that one of these, the economic organization, merely "explains" the basic nature of the society then economics would be relegated to a decidedly insignificant position. Yet on other occasions Ingenieros says that economic forces play a "preponderant role in the over-all orientation of social changes."[79] On one occasion, he dismisses the entire problem by stating, "It is sufficient that we know, in general, that all civilized peoples, through a process of successively building-up and breaking-down, have had to go through various stages from savagery and barbarism, this series of steps being determined by different forms of economic organization. . . ."[80] These occasional references to the role of economic forces in the creation of a group or racial character certainly do not make Ingenieros an economic determinist, his adherence to Marxism notwithstanding. The statement of one critic that Ingenieros "makes economics the omnideterminant factor and the key to the entire process of social evolution"[81] fails to take into account the racistic irreductionism that pervades his view of society and culture.

The question "Why are we sick?" is answered by Bunge, Arguedas, García Calderón, and Ingenieros in unequivocal terms: we are sick because of our bad blood, because of the preponderance of "inferior" non-European races in our midst. If a cure for the continent's malady is sought, these writers prescribe virtually the

77. *Ibid.*, pp. 17-18.
78. *Ibid.*, p. 42.
79. *Ibid.*, pp. 185-86.
80. *Ibid.*, p. 39.
81. Alberto Zum Felde, *Indice crítico de la literatura hispanoamericana: Los ensayistas* (México, 1954), p. 262.

same medicine: European immigration, absorption of the colored races, education, and "utilization" of the nonwhite within the restricted limits of his abilities.

In contrast to the diagnosticians of the sick continent, more recent essayists have focused their attention upon questions of essence—"*What* are we?" rather than "why" are we one way or another. The first question, aside from its logical priority, calls for a self-contained, reflective answer; while the second question immediately suggests an *external* cause, an explainer. In the specific writers whom we have been analyzing, this external factor is race. Others have used similar "explanations" of Spanish American character and society, based upon climate, geography, or even upon nutrition.[82] As with the raciologists, the technique involves the detailed scrutiny of the society—viewed as an impersonal mass of data—using concepts, terminology, and hazily understood methods borrowed from the natural sciences. As later essayists pointed out, the failure of scientism in general, and of raciology in particular, lay not only in the fact that many of their "scientific" tenets have been proved erroneous, but in that their approach to man and his society left unanswered the great human questions of values, goals, and aspirations. They shed little if any light on man's emotional life, his creativity, or his aesthetic sense.

However, not all the essayists of the period shared the views of a Bunge or an Arguedas. During the 1880's and 1890's the godfather of radicalism in the Andean region, González Prada, was proclaiming the falseness of the "inferior race" theory as applied to the Indian and mestizo, while Mexico's Justo Sierra, despite his association with the *científicos* of the Díaz regime, was reluctant to accept an exclusively scientific view of man. He maintained, moreover, a consistently open view of race.[83] During approximately the same period Cuba's José Martí—a figure whose stature as a writer and as a man is impossible to overestimate—wrote that questions of race were pointless, simply because "there are no races: there are only modifications of man,"[84] and that those who speak of races are deluding themselves with something that is simply a bookish

82. A notably unfortunate example is Francisco Bulnes' *El porvenir de las naciones latino-americanas* (1899). See below, Chapter IV, p. 60.

83. For a discussion of Sierra's role in the general rejection of scientism, see below, Chapter III, pp. 44-46. Regarding details of his raciological liberalism see the author's article, "Indigenism and Racism in Mexican Thought, 1857-1911," *Journal of Inter-American Studies I* (Oct., 1959), 405-23.

84. José Martí, "La verdad sobre los Estados Unidos," *Obras completas* (La Habana, 1946), I, 2035.

fantasy—"Sickly thinkers, those who work by lamp light, string together and mull-over races that exist only on paper."[85]

Martí's tolerant humanism, Sierra's liberalism, and González Prada's fervent love for indigenous America are important exceptions to the general spirit of pessimism and resignation which pervaded much of the Spanish American essay during the waning years of the nineteenth century. These atypical writers were in a real sense precursors of a substantial change in the continent's intellectual outlook. Although positivism and racism continued to hold a firm grip on the minds of some of Spanish America's most widely read —though not in all cases most profound—essayists, as the new century passed through its first decade younger writers were beginning to chafe under the restraint of scientism's straight-jacket. The old gods—Comte, Darwin, Spencer—were challenged; more important, new questions were phrased and new ways of looking at Spanish America's realities were suggested.

85. José Martí, "El Partido Liberal," *Obras completas*, II, 112.

III / THE REVOLT

AGAINST SCIENTISM

The memories of my adolescence are linked chiefly with the masters of positivism. Renan, Guyau, Herbert Spencer, August Comte; I read them almost as a child and they took hold of me profoundly.... For many years I actually thought that I would never be able to rid myself of them ... it saddened me, for as far as I was concerned, this was a gloomy confinement. Body and soul rebelled secretly against the conclusions of positivism (in) that nothing but a strictly biological interpretation for the higher phenomena of human life was admitted....[1]

This fragmentary confession by one of contemporary Argentina's finest philosophical essayists, Carlos Alberto Erro, might well sum up the intellectual autobiography of a host of present-day Spanish Americans. It would be difficult to establish the date when this "gloomy confinement" was broken, for the general reaction to positivism varies substantially from one writer—or group of writers —to another.[2] It is almost as difficult to characterize this revolt.

1. Carlos Alberto Erro, *Diálogo existencial* (Buenos Aires, 1937), pp. 13-14.
2. This reaction is most evident during the first two decades of the twentieth century; however we have already noted (in the previous chapter) that Positivism was under attack by some writers even at the height of its vogue in the 1880's and 1890's. Paul Groussac, who by virtue of his French birth and rather peripheral relationship to Argentine letters will not be discussed above, was one such critic. His eloquent words of 1896, however, bear repetition in the context of the present chapter: "La comparación de una sociedad humana con un organismo es más antigua que Spencer, Bacon, y el mismo Aristóteles.... Puede que los sociólogos modernos se excedan en su cotejo de la circulación comercial con la vascular, o de la administración nacional con el sistema nervioso.... Pero, no debe echarse en olvido que estas aproximaciones son metafóricas y provisionales; sobre todo, conviene no abusar del paralelo...." He continues by attacking the concept of "economic man" in terms which are remarkably like those which Spanish Americans—Antonio Caso, for example—were to use some twenty years later: "El ser humano dotado de existencia real es el que ... produce y conserve materialmente, sin duda alguna, pero que siente, además, medita y cree, sobordinando en horas decisivas su producción y su consumo a sus creencias y pasiones...." The foregoing in his article, "La paradoja de las ciencias sociales," *La Biblioteca*, II (Oct., 1896), 309-13.

When a rigid idea is attacked from a number of quarters, the rebels seldom affirm a single well-defined position. Several general tendencies of the movement, however, do stand out in retrospect. As we see in the quotation from Erro, a clear rejection of the notion that natural science could be the sole indicator of ethical, political, or aesthetic routes for man to follow underlies the spirit of the times. The affirmative side of this reaction against positivism in particular and scientism in general can be found in what, for want of more precise terms, may be called the appeal to idealism, to things of the spirit, to those areas of man's nature which are motivated by "disinterest" (the Spanish word *desinterés* retains more of the original force of the expression). Closely related to these tendencies is a deep-seated rejection of the apparent benefits of late nineteenth-century material progress: physical comforts, the products of industry and technology, and in a wider sense, the entire well-ordered, self-satisfied world of the *petit bourgeois*. Of course, a good deal of this reaction is simply a reflection of certain European modes of expression: parallels with attitudes typical of the English Decadents or French Symbolist poets are obvious here.[3] The fact that neither material progress nor the growth of a large middle class were very evident in Spanish America of the late nineteenth century would appear to lessen the authenticity of this "rejection." However, it is not the physical comforts and the material progress themselves that the new generation of essayists attack; their target is rather the attitude toward these things. The very fact that a "typically bourgeois" outlook existed in Spanish America *without* the corresponding material advances makes the attack of our essayists the more justifiable. From its inception this movement was led by writers of widely divergent beliefs. In some cases they were partisans of the theory that only an intellectual aristocracy could redeem a society corrupted by a vulgar "mesocracy." Others—the Marxists, for example—saw the rightful renovators of a decadent world in the Indian and rural proletariat.

One of the earliest—and most clearly defined—manifestations of the "New Idealism" emerged from the essayists who found a focus for their thought in the writings of the young Uruguayan, José Enrique Rodó (1871-1917). Even before the turn of the century, in his essay "El que vendrá," Rodó expressed Spanish America's need

3. In Spanish American poetry and prose fiction of this period much of the same attitude appears—explicitly or implicitly—in the work of the writers who have come to be known as the *Modernistas*: Rubén Darío, Leopoldo Lugones, *et al.*

for new literary gods to replace the aging masters of French naturalism, Zola in particular.[4] Rodó amplified the desire for a new intellectual mentor in a widely read series of essays beginning with *Ariel* in 1900. Rodó's essays have, with justification, come to be considered classics of the genre; and the group of writers who found inspiration in his ideas have been called *arielistas*, after Shakespeare's "aeyrie spirit" employed by the Uruguayan writer to symbolize the best of Latin character.

Ariel itself has been commented upon at length by critics of Spanish American letters.[5] Briefly, the framework of Rodó's essay is the teachings of an aged man, Próspero, who instructs "youth" (read Hispanic America's young intellectuals of 1900) by developing the contrast between two symbolic figures: Ariel and Calibán. Ariel epitomizes all that is spiritual, the realm of the aesthetic, human creativity, imagination, etc., while the unattractive, gross Calibán stands for material appetites and activities. Rodó makes use of this duality to discuss the national character of various groups, particularly Latins and Anglo-Saxons. He clearly indicates that both spirits exist among all peoples; however, he also feels that the "Ariel" qualities have been, in the past, highly cultivated by Latin nations and that it is the mission of the Latins of the New World to bring this spirit to even greater fruition. Rodó's criticisms of North America are generously interlaced with this theme: he does not hate the United States, nor does he feel that the spirit of Ariel is completely uncultivated in the North. However, he believes that Calibán's utilitarianism does dominate North American life. His critique is specific and often well taken: when discussing the Yankee's aesthetic sense he notes that the North American does not appreciate a work of art for itself, but rather as an "acquisition," a symbol of his economic power (Rodó's North American contemporary, Thorstein Veblen, was saying much the same thing at roughly the same time). The United States' educational system is another major target of Rodó's criticism. He felt that this system gave a great number of

4. José Enrique Rodó, "El que vendrá," *Obras completas*, compilación y prólogo de A. J. Vaccaro (Buenos Aires, 1948), I, 112-17. The article was first published in 1897 in the *Revista nacional de literatura y ciencias sociales*, a journal to which Rodó made several contributions early in his career.

5. A few representative views of the essay are the following: Alberto Zum Felde, *Índice crítico de la literatura hispanoamericana: Los ensayistas* (Mexico, 1954), pp. 291-301; and by the same author, *Proceso intelectual del Uruguay* (Montevideo, 1941), pp. 223-50; Robert G. Mead, Jr., *Breve historia del ensayo hispanoamericano* (Mexico, 1956), pp. 74-75; and Gonzalo Zaldumbide, *José Enrique Rodó* (Madrid, 1919), pp. 36-56.

people superficial learning but failed in identifying and selecting the necessarily small, but influential intellectual elite. One of his basic criticisms is that in the United States no aristocracy—with its all-important sense of *noblesse oblige*—exists. Rodó, of course, thinks of an aristocracy in the sense of a respected, highly talented "aristocracy of merit," not unlike the group of "experts" which Plato placed at the directive apex of the society described in the *Republic*. But Rodó's most profound criticism is directed at a certain fundamental incomprehension of human values and human destiny which he finds in North America: "Her prosperity is as great as her inability to satisfy even a middling concept of human destiny. . . . Lacking the orientation afforded by well-established traditions, this nation has not discovered how to substitute the inspiring idealism of the past with an elevated and disinterested vision of the future."[6]

By contrast it is in the tradition of the Latins—the cultivators of Ariel—to recognize the value of material things in their proper role of providing the conditions for the free exercise of such essentially human activities as artistic creation and philosophic seeking. Rodó believed that the Latin concept of education, properly understood and uncorrupted by a narrow utilitarianism, leads to the development of that kind of an intellectual elite required for the proper functioning of any society. In short, Rodó envisioned a very specific role for Spanish America: that of the torchbearers of the best of the Greco-Roman humanistic tradition in the New World. There is, however, an undeniably strong "Americanist" spirit in Rodó. The very fact that he was so intent upon bringing his message of new faith in the Latin genius to Spanish America at a time when the great northern powers—England, Germany, and the United States—were pushing Latin Europe into a position of economic and political "inferiority," suggests that he felt that the role of Hispanic America's neo-Latins was not simply that of transferring European culture, but of surpassing it, of bringing it to fuller fruition.

Rodó's later essay, *Los motivos de Proteo* (1909), is in some respects similar to *Ariel*. As in the earlier work a symbolic figure—ever-changing Proteus in this case—serves as a focal point for his theme. In the *Motivos*, Rodó's emphasis is on the necessity for modern man to avoid the narrow specialization towards which present-day technology drives him. Like the many-sided individual of the Renaissance, he should have broad interests and varied talents.

6. José Enrique Rodó, *Ariel* (Buenos Aires, 1947), p. 94.

Throughout the essay Rodó directs his attention toward the individual, rather than toward the collectivity. This simple fact is
significant, for it indicates a trajectory which has been followed by
many—and perhaps the best—of Spanish America's intellectuals
and artists of the present century. Even writers who have pressed
for sweeping reforms of society have shown a deep-seated conviction
that changes must be effected in the individual as well as in the
structure of social institutions. The "socio-economic orientation"
of Spanish American literature, so frequently noted by its historians,
can be very misleading. The fact is that the de-personalized,
abstract treatment of man—implied by this generalization—has
been quite alien to the best of contemporary Spanish American
writing. Rodó's emphasis on the value of the individual bears this
point out, as does the work of a great number of the essayists whom
we shall examine. In this context Rodó's fervent exhortation to the
individual that he guard his own integrity and permit it to flourish is
particularly noteworthy.

The diffusion of Rodó's ideas throughout Spanish America did
not come about by chance. For one thing, the continent was certainly
ready for the kind of appeal he was to make. Moreover, Rodó
himself had a rare sense of the timeliness of his message; and he
made a conscious effort to spread his ideas through personal contacts
as well as through the leading journals of the day. An example may
be seen in an open letter to the Venezuelan writer, César Zumeta,
published in the widely read Caracas review *El cojo ilustrado*. Speaking of the book which he was about to publish (*Ariel*, of course, since
the letter is dated August, 1900) Rodó states: "It is, as you will see,
something like a manifesto directed toward the youth of our America.
. . . I should like this work of mine to be the starting point for a
propaganda campaign that will continue to spread among America's
intellectuals. . . ."[7] Rodó's desire was certainly fulfilled. During the
first decade of the century—roughly the period between the publication of *Ariel* and the *Motivos de Proteo*—his influence grew steadily
throughout Spanish America. A series of articles on "Liberalismo y
jacobinismo," dealing with highly volatile problems of church and
state, led to a sharp polemic with other important essayists;[8] the
leading Spanish critics of the day, recognizing that Rodó's defense
of Latinism was also a much needed defense of Hispanic culture, ap-

7. José Enrique Rodó, "América," *El cojo ilustrado*, IX (Aug. 15, 1900), 526.
8. See especially Pedro Henríquez Ureña's critique and plea for complete separation
of church and state in his review of these essays, "Marginalia: José Enrique Rodó,"
Revista Moderna, IX (Dec., 1907), 240-42.

plauded his writings;[9] and important literary reviews, *El cojo ilustrado* of Caracas and *Nosotros* of Buenos Aires, published and discussed his work frequently. A Mexican critic reported in 1908 that far to the North, Bernardo Reyes, the governor of the border state of Nuevo León prepared a special gift edition of *Ariel* for private distribution among his friends.[10]

The work of a number of essayists of this period bears a clear similarity, both stylistically and thematically, to Rodó's writings. In Uruguay itself, Alberto Nin Frías (1882-1937), a co-worker in the vineyard of *arielismo*, was virtually a disciple of Rodó, as were Carlos Arturo Torres (1867-1911) of Colombia and Manuel Díaz Rodríguez (1868-1927) of Venezuela. Francisco García Calderón, despite the scientism, racism, and frequent positivistic lapses of his earlier writings, reveals a good deal of the spirit of Rodó. In addition to its impact upon these few writers—a kind of "inner circle" of *arielistas*—Rodó's influence was felt indirectly throughout the continent. By the end of the second decade of the century, book-length studies of his work began to appear,[11] and upon his death in 1917 the very important journal *Nosotros* dedicated an entire issue to him.[12] The exact nature of the *"arielista* movement" has occasioned no little controversy. Its defenders as well as its attackers have, I think, attempted to define *arielismo* in an overly generalized manner. As Zum Felde observes, there are really only a few common denominators for the movement.[13] One of these, however, would certainly be the broad emphasis upon humanism. Specifically, manifestations of the *arielista* spirit may be seen in the great value given the realm of the nonutilitarian—art, philosophic contemplation, etc.—as definitively human activities; in the relegation of science to its proper limits; and in the conviction that any well-organized society must be hierarchical in structure.

Other characteristics commonly ascribed to the movement, are more difficult to isolate. The rather pedantic, somewhat pompous

9. See the collection of laudatory articles compiled by Hugo D. Barbagelata, *Rodó y sus críticos* (Paris, 1920). Among the many Peninsular writers who acclaim Rodó in this volume, the most distinguished are Unamuno, Leopoldo Alas, and Juan Valera.

10. Francisco Monterde, "Nueva salida de Ariel," *Cuadernos americanos*, I (May-June, 1942), 101-106. Bernardo Reyes, incidentally, was the father of the renowned humanist and essayist, Alfonso Reyes.

11. See above, note 5 for Zaldumbide's study. Also see Victor Pérez Petit, *Rodó* (Montevideo, 1919); A. Andrade Coello, *Rodó* (Quito, 1917); and Max Henríquez Ureña, *Rodó y Ruben Darío* (Habana, 1918).

12. *Nosotros*, No. 97 (May, 1917).

13. Zum Felde, *Indice crítico*, p. 311.

style considered typical of *arielista* writing, the penchant for classical allusions, the long, intricate sentence structure, and the over-all tone of *afrancesamiento*,[14] are all quite general in Spanish American letters of the time. It would seem reasonable, therefore, not to speak of a specific *arielista* style. Similarly, the link between the *arielistas* and the "anti-Yankee" trend in the Spanish American essay is very tenuous. Had Rodó never lived, I think it certain that essayists like Manuel Ugarte or Rufino Blanco Fombona would have produced their sharp criticisms of the Colossus of the North. The expansionist policies of the United States, her political intervention, and her economic penetration of Latin America elicited in these writers a kind of reaction quite different from Rodó's analysis of cultural contrasts between the Latin world and North America. Thus Ugarte, writing as a Socialist, analyzed the United States' inroads in Spanish America in terms of the interplay of "natural" economic forces; despite his fervent desire to awaken his countrymen to these dangers, there is little human involvement in his writing; in short, his tone is hardly *arielista*.[15] Although anti-Yankeeism coincides with the diffusion of Rodó's ideas and although there is a current of fear, suspicion, and even hostility toward the United States among some of his followers, the inclusion of *yánquifobia* in the definition of Arielism clouds the issue.

Much of the criticism of the *arielistas* has come from writers who are partisans of *indigenismo* and who tend to place great value upon literature having overt social content.[16] For such critics, the fine distinction drawn by Rodó between the aristocracy of merit and the ordinary notion of "aristocracy"—i.e., simply the upper classes—is of little consequence. Thus, they feel that the *arielista* emphasis on natural hierarchy has merely provided a justification for the status quo; that the traditionally wealthy and powerful classes could claim to be this aristocracy of merit which Rodó described. The *arielistas* are also accused of being slavishly European—of either forgetting or deprecating the indigenous American and his cultural contributions.

14. The most striking example of the Francophile tendency among these writers is that of Francisco García Calderón, who as we noted in Chapter II wrote most of his major books (including his general study of American life, *Les démocraties latines de l'Amérique*) in French. Moreover, as virtually all of the commentators have pointed out, Rodó himself was strongly influenced by French writers—notably Renan and Guyau.

15. Note, however, Zum Felde's inclusion of Ugarte among the writers of "*la promoción arielista.*" See *Indice crítico*, pp. 313-16.

16. See especially Luis Alberto Sánchez, *Balance y liquidación del novecientos* (Santiago, 1941), pp. 15-36; and Fernando Diez de Medina, *Sariri: Una réplica al Ariel de Rodó* (La Paz, 1954), pp. 12-16. For a discussion of *indigenismo*, see below, Chapter IV, pp. 60-67.

Perhaps what annoys the anti-Arielist most is the similarity of much of this writing to the affected prose of certain *modernistas*. The assumption is made that the *arielista* is an ivory tower aesthete; that he is so involved in his own world of verbal elegance and philosophic meditation that he cares little for his fellow man (particularly if this fellow man is less talented, a member of the lower classes, or an Indian). Although there is a grain of truth in these assertions, those who condemn Rodó and the *arielistas* may be guilty of losing perspective and of judging the movement by its least representative members. The *arielistas* were certainly not revolutionaries in the ordinary sense of the word, and their cultivation of the individual tended to keep them from attacking specific social or political problems. This disinclination to deal with the world of marketplaces, governments, exploited Indians, and the like does not necessarily mean that the *arielistas* approved of what today would be called "the establishment." It could be argued that the flight to the ivory tower, motivated by a deep disgust with the milieu, is the first step on the path to revolution. The artist—the man whose greatest reward and greatest punishment come from within—is a threat to the powers that be. He is not a cog in a wheel, and he cannot be easily manipulated. In this sense, Rodó's movement toward the cultivation of the self can lead to a profoundly radical position.[17]

Perhaps the critics of *arielismo* are on firmest ground when they attack the followers of Rodó rather than the master himself. As is often the case with literary schools or "generations" the initiator of the movement is usually a writer far superior to the coterie which gathers about him. The mediocrity of many *gongoristas* compared with the brilliance of Góngora himself, or the contrast seen in the clichés of the *rubendarianos* compared with Darío's best pages are cases in point. Similarly, the empty and often pompous verbosity of some *arielistas* is more typical of the disciples than it is of the master. Rodó, even in the florid style of his youth would hardly

17. While Rodó could hardly be called a "radical" on religious questions, here again his emphasis on the personal rather than the institutional sets him apart from the conservatives with whom the anti-*arielistas* tend to associate him. For one thing, the heterodoxy of Renan lay behind much of Rodó's religious thinking; in the controversial essays on "Liberalismo y jacobinismo," the objection to the removal of crucifixes from public hospitals is made not because Rodó felt that ecclesiastical privileges must be respected, but rather because he thought of Christ as "a model of charity" for believer and nonbeliever alike. And at least one writer of the inner circle of *arielismo*, Alberto Nin Frías, professed Protestant inclination to the extent that he considered Hispanic catholicism "El cáncer de la raza latina." See Nin Frías' "Ensayo sobre la raza latina, el catolicismo y el protestantismo" in his *Ensayos de crítica e historia* (Valencia, 1907).

have been responsible for a sentence like the following from C.A
Torres' *Idola fori*:

> In the elegant and corrupt Italian courts which Pinturicchio
> has shown us with a richness of color and detail that would be
> sought in vain in any other chronicler or historian, the pagan
> spirit makes its re-appearance; combining at this moment of its
> reincarnation, in the powerful and diabolical personage of Caesar
> Borgia, all the refinement of Athens with the most sinister arts
> of the assassins crowned by imperial Rome.[18]

Torres is also guilty of the worst sort of name-dropping; in his com-
pulsive urge to say a word about virtually every philosopher, sociologist, and intellectual of his day he will commit such blunders as
grouping Bunge and Ingenieros as representatives of the reaction
against positivism.[19] Many other details of Torres' writing reveal
a confused eclecticism; examples may be seen in his desire to reconcile
such questions as the Great Man theory of history versus the power
of the masses; in his praise of Spencer *and* of the "idealism" found in
the new philosophy of Bergson, Boutroux, and Nietzsche; and in his
condemnation of socialism, on the one hand, and his praise of ex-
periments in state controls of commodity prices, on the other.[20] In
his desire to achieve a breadth of viewpoint and a reconciliation of
opposing positions, Torres became a veritable caricature of Rodó's
Proteus. Once again the superiority of the master over the disciple is
very apparent.

The *arielistas'* view of social structure and their emphasis on a
natural aristocracy of merit certainly imply a kind of snobbery.
Significantly, Rodó himself seldom deprecates those levels of society
which are below the intellectual élite. There is a marked freedom
from bitterness and invective in his criticisms of the *vulgo*; moreover,
he often stresses the reciprocal nature of the various strata of society.
Here again, the attitude of some of his followers differs substantially.
Francisco García Calderón—if we include him among the *arielistas*—
reveals one of the most pernicious forms of snobbery: racism.[21] And
Rodó's compatriot, Alberto Nin Frías, is little better when, in his
enthusiasm for the racial exclusivism of Anglo-Saxon countries, he
states: "Of all the nations of America, the ones that have the greatest

18. Carlos Arturo Torres, *Idola fori*, (3ᵉʳᵃ ed., Bogotá, 1935), p. 70. The first
edition appeared in 1910.
19. *Ibid.*, p. 160.
20. *Ibid.*, pp. 193-96.
21. See above, Chapter II, pp. 25-29.

intrinsic value are Argentina and Uruguay: this is so because they have almost completely gotten rid of the autochthonous race."[22]

One of the most interesting examples of *arielista* snobbery is seen in the work of Manuel Díaz Rodríguez who combines an effete cultivation of the European decadents (in his own words, "the gentle and delightful mysticism of certain Pre-Raphaelite paintings and the poetry of Wilde and D'Annunzio"[23]) with a stinging attack upon "Don Perfecto"—the typically dull, pedantic, positivistic critic.[24] Perfecto is vain without having any nobility or inner pride; he is a slavish imitator of "scientific" criticism; he has no understanding of originality; and he "explains" things by recourse to "the most rancid of metaphysics under the guise of the subconscious."[25] Although the stodgy European critic Max Nordau is singled out as a typical Don Perfecto, the general tone suggests that people closer to the Venezuelan literary scene of 1908 were under fire.

Despite his snobbery and despite the sharpness of his personal attacks, one must admit that Díaz Rodríguez was a fine writer. A good example of his skill as an essayist is his treatise on pride in the *Camino de perfección*. In some twenty-five pages of carefully polished prose he weaves a classic essay on the theme: the entire gamut of positions—from the humility of a St. Francis to the blatant vanity of a Don Perfecto—is analyzed in an attempt to develop a distinctively *arielista* concept of the term.[26] Also to Díaz Rodríguez' credit is his sharp refutation of scientism, of writers who assign scientific "fact" an absolute value.[27] An important aspect of this critique is his rejection of racism and particularly of the racistic explanation of cultural achievement.[28] In this regard, Díaz Rodríguez' views are in marked contrast to those of García Calderón and Nin Frías. On balance, Díaz Rodríguez' "snobbery" is not entirely unattractive: in his impatience with mediocrity and superficiality he is perhaps the closest of the *arielistas* to Rodó himself.

Although Rodó and his followers had serious reservations regarding the ability of science to provide a basic orientation for human existence, their attack on the bastion of scientism was more a flanking engagement than a frontal assault. In fact, Rodó himself

22. Nin Frías, *Ensayos de crítica e historia*, p. 197.
23. Manuel Díaz Rodríguez, *Camino de perfección* (Caracas, 1942), p. 100. The first edition of these essays appeared in 1908.
24. *Ibid.*, pp. 24ff.
25. *Ibid.*, p. 71.
26. *Ibid.*, pp. 24-49.
27. *Ibid.*, pp. 71ff.
28. *Ibid.*, p. 110.

accepted a good deal of Comte's political and social thought. In *Ariel* he notes with approval that the founder of positivism viewed democratic equality as simply "a transitory dissolvent of old inequalities" and that he shared Rodó's own belief in a natural social hierarchy.[29] The *arielista* attention was not directed toward undermining the foundations of positivism, but rather toward the critique of what were felt to be the outgrowths of the system: the worship of material progress, the cult of mediocrity, and the mortal effects of specialization on the human spirit. It is true that these writers were aware of the revolutionary philosophies of Boutroux, Bergson, and even the North American James;[30] they certainly were on familiar terms with the voluntarism of Nietzsche. However, Rodó and the *arielistas* apparently did not have a sufficient grasp of these newer ideological currents to ally themselves unequivocally with such powerful forces.[31] Had they done so, their importance in the intellectual history of Spanish America would have been much greater.

At about the same time that *arielismo* was attracting the intellectuals of the South American continent, to the North, in Mexico, other important events in the turning of the tide against scientism were taking place. One of the most dramatic of these events occurred on the evening of March 22, 1908, in Mexico City's Arbeu Theater. On that occasion, the cream of Mexico's intellectual élite gathered to hear Justo Sierra—respected, mature, former Minister of Education, and a key *científico*—deliver an oration commemorating the fiftieth

29. Rodó, *Ariel*, p. 70. Note also that Zum Felde in the *Indice crítico* discusses Rodó and the *arielistas* under the general heading of *El imperio del positivismo científico*.

30. A few isolated articles dealing with these thinkers appear in Spanish American journals during the first decade of the century. E. Duprat, in a routine report of French philosophic activity for the year 1907, reviewed briefly Bergson's *Creative Evolution* in "La filosofía francesa en 1907," *Nosotros* II (Oct., 1908), 156-60. In September of 1908 García Calderón participated in a philosophic congress in Heidelberg; a paper which he delivered was printed in a French philosophical journal and was subsequently translated into Spanish (by Pedro Henríquez Ureña) as "Las corrientes filosóficas en la América Latina," and was published in the *Revista Moderna* XI (Nov., 1908), 150-56. García Calderón discusses Bergson in this paper, although he does not attempt a critical evaluation of Bergson's philosophic impact. "Las corrientes filosóficas..." was also included in his collection of essays, *Profesores de idealismo* (1908).

31. Rodó, like García Calderón was aware only of the superficialities of irrationalist thought. He did not, for example, see the broad implications of Bergson's concept of "creative evolution," although critics have attempted to link this Bergsonian notion with the ideas in *Motivos de Proteo*. See Mead, *Breve historia*, p. 75; and Enrique Anderson Imbert, *Historia de la literatura hispanoamericana* (Mexico, 1961), I, 439. Bergson's work *L'evolution creatrice* was only published in 1907, though students of Rodó agree that the material in the *Motivos* was composed in the three years preceding this date (1904-1907). Moreover, neither Rodó nor the other *Arielistas* ever came to grips with such basic Bergsonian concerns as human freedom, the nature of intuition, etc.

anniversary of the introduction of positivism into Mexico by Gabino Barreda. What Sierra's audience heard was not quite the superficial panegyric which was commonly accorded the intellectual mentor of the Díaz era. Rather, Sierra suggested that the very nature of science was such that blind faith in absolute, undebatable truth was untenable. What he called for was a degree of "scientific" skepticism:

> Let us doubt: in the first place because if science is nothing more than the systematic knowledge of that which is relative, if things in themselves can not be known, if we can only know their constant relationship, if all this is genuine science, then must it not be in perpetual discussion, in perpetual conflict? What great fundamental truth of science has not been discussed or is not under discussion at this time?[32]

Sierra substantiated this view by citing a lengthy and quite sophisticated list of basic scientific theories which were then undergoing fundamental revision. He even quoted Nietzsche's belief that "science is always based on a metaphysical position, our faith in science."[33] One other point underscored by Sierra in this speech could easily pass unnoticed today; but considering the frame of mind of his audience, its effect must have been great:

> "... we all know that science has extinguished the light of heaven and has filled space with suns and worlds—among which ours is but an atom—and has worked out laws for the marvelous equilibrium of the universes which fill the infinitude. It has reduced these laws to a single one which we poets might call the very word of God, beyond which we glimpse only a sea of mystery, on whose shores science, quaking with aspiration and impotence, extends its arms. The founder [i.e., Comte] never denied that an intelligence ruled over the universe; what he always denied was that this could be a matter of scientific discussion. . . ."[34]

The speech in the Arbeu Theater, with its ringing repetition of the exhortation "Dudemos" ("let us doubt"), is certainly a remarkable example of Spanish American oratory. As an essay it was published in the *Revista Moderna*, an influential journal through whose pages a new generation of artists and intellectuals was emerging. Several of these writers—José Vasconcelos (1881-1959), Antonio Caso

32. Justo Sierra, "Discurso en el Teatro Arbeu," in José Gaos, *Antología del pensamiento de lengua española de la edad contemporánea* (Mexico, 1945), pp. 801-2.
33. *Ibid.*, p. 808.
34. *Ibid.*, p. 809. For a further discussion of Sierra's earlier breaks with Positivist orthodoxy, see the author's "Indigenism and Racism in Mexican Thought: 1857-1911," *Journal of Inter-American Studies*, I (Oct., 1959), 405-23.

(1883-1940), and Pedro Henríquez Ureña (1884-1946)—soon became the leading spokesmen of the century's new spirit, rekindled enthusiasm, and reborn humanistic faith. Sierra's relationship to the *Ateneo de la Juventud* (Athenaeum of Youth)—as this group came to be called—was established in other ways. It was through his efforts that the modern National University of Mexico came into being. Throughout the nineteenth century, the institution enjoyed a shadowy existence as a loosely knit group of professional schools. Sierra, however, saw the need for a unifying central unit, the school of Higher Studies, which would eventually become the heart of the University, the Faculty of Arts and Letters. It was through this significantly "impractical" unit of the university that certain writers of the *Ateneo de la Juventud*, particularly Antonio Caso, came to exercise a decisive influence upon the intellectual development of contemporary Mexico.

In addition to Sierra's invitation to re-examine the basic tenets of positivism, the *Ateneo* writers were stimulated by the essays of Rodó and his disciples. Pedro Henríquez Ureña, the only non-Mexican of the group, played an important role in the diffusion of *arielista* thought through his *Revista Moderna* articles on Rodó and García Calderón.[35] Even earlier, before leaving his native Santo Domingo, Henríquez Ureña had produced a short but penetrating study on the Uruguayan mentor and the movement which he had initiated.[36] At least one *arielista*, García Calderón, was a frequent contributor to the *Revista Moderna* during the early years of the century.[37] Of course, there was much in these writings which the *Ateneo de la Juventud* group could not accept. While Henríquez Ureña could laud Rodó's faith, hope, enthusiasm, and vigor,[38] he took sharp issue with him on the religious questions aired in "Liberalismo y jacobinismo."[39] The Mexican group clearly shared the *arielista* critique of scientism, their humanistic spirit, and their general idealistic tone; but the emphasis on the role of the aristocracy and on the hierarchical social structure seem alien to the *Ateneo's*

35. Henríquez Ureña, "Marginalia: José Enrique Rodó," *Revista Moderna*, 240-42; and Pedro Henríquez Ureña, "Profesores de idealismo," *Revista Moderna*, XIV (June, 1910), 213-16.

36. Pedro Henríquez Ureña, "Ariel" in *Obra Crítica* (Mexico, 1960), pp. 23-28. The original article is dated 1904.

37. García Calderón published at least five pieces in the *Revista* during the period 1904-1909. The most important of these, "Las corrientes filosóficas en la América Latina," is discussed in note 30 above.

38. Henríquez Ureña, *Obra crítica*, p. 25.

39. See note 8 above.

thinking. The attitude of snobbery and the pose of the haughty aesthete noted in some of the *arielistas* are likewise quite absent in the writings of the Mexican group.

There is little doubt that the intellectual revolt of the *Ateneo* is far more radical than that of the *arielistas*. Instead of the mild eclecticism which Rodó inherited from Guyau and Renán, the Mexican group grounded its viewpoint on the Germans—Schopenhauer, Nietzsche, and Stirner—in addition to Boutroux and Bergson. From about 1906, when the group collaborated on its short-lived journal, *Savia Moderna*, until 1910, when they presented the important lectures of the *Ateneo*, their intellectual position was in the formative process. In the 1910 lectures, however, a fairly clear picture of the group's underlying philosophy begins to emerge. José Vasconcelos is particularly eloquent in describing the group's development: "the schools . . . where positivistic morality is still taught, are not where we might receive illuminating inspiration, where we might hear the strains of a deeper music, the mysterious voice of contemporary sensibility bearing renewed and abundant vitality. This new feeling was brought about by our own desperation; the mute pain of contemplating life without hope or nobility."[40] The obstacle which was to be overcome before a genuinely new philosophic position could be established was seen with remarkable unanimity by the members of the group: it was the problem of human liberty set against a world dominated by necessity and by a suffocating mechanistic chain of events; a world in which there was, in effect, nothing new under the sun. This "new sensibility" of which the *Ateneo* group writes, was at odds with the tradition of Kant ("the synthetic chief of intellectualism," in Ureña's words) which leads, they felt, to both Hegelianism and positivism. They even commented fearfully on Mill's highly theoretical view that if we could know everything at one given moment in time, it would be possible to predict with accuracy the entire subsequent history of the universe.[41] The writers of the *Ateneo* were striving to give man a chance to act as a free agent, to act creatively and disinterestedly. If human beings were simply cogs in a machine, freedom becomes an illusion; creativity can always be explained away by showing pre-existing influences (Taine's race, historical moment, and milieu, for example); and the concept of a disinterested act becomes meaningless.

40. José Vasconcelos, *Obras completas* (Mexico, 1957), I, 43-44.
41. Henríquez Ureña, *Obra crítica*, p. 69.

The ideas of the *Ateneo*, however, were not crystallized without considerable probing and hesitancy. Henríquez Ureña, despite his very solid comprehension of European intellectual currents chose merely to describe rather than criticize,[42] although his grasp of Nietzsche, Schopenhauer, Bergson, and even of the North Americans Peirce and James was at the time probably superior to that of the other members of the group. He was, perhaps by temperament, an observer and an analyzer rather than an intellectual activist. As for Caso, his writing at this time still lacked the spirit of personal involvement of his later works; he was sampling philosophic wares and had not as yet taken a stand. Vasconcelos, by contrast, plunged into the philosophic problems of the "new sensibility" with youthful abandon: one of the best presentations of the *Ateneo's* intellectual position is found in his essay of 1910, "Don Gabino Barreda y las ideas contemporáneas." Vasconcelos takes as his point of departure the all-important problem of knowledge, which he finds "unsolvable within the limits of reason."[43] By this he means that "things in themselves"—the real world of the Kantian noumenon—cannot be known; that our knowledge is limited to their "representation," the phenomena. In the perceived world, the realm of the phenomena, the laws of causality of course hold sway; everything that happens is part of a determined chain of events. Like many other thinkers of the nineteenth and early twentieth century, Vasconcelos would like to reserve this phenomenal or "representational" world for matter, substance. If human existence could in some sense be thought of as nonsubstantial, it would fall outside the realm of cause and effect; man, in a word, would be free: "Is it not preferable to search the universe for some power which would not be reducible to the laws of representation? Something contradictory to the very law of the phenomenon. . . ?"[44] A possible solution is offered by the voluntarism of Schopenhauer. Vasconcelos states the philosopher's famous dictum, "the world is my will and my representation," and then notes that philosophy has traditionally concerned itself with "representation" (i.e., the physical world as perceived by men), but that now *"the thing in itself* was also going to be interpreted by the philosopher, with universal data, with the aid of religions, with the aid of literature, art, and of life as it is lived."[45] Although Vas-

42. See, for example, Henríquez Ureña's article of 1908, "Nietzsche y el pragmatismo," *Obra crítica*, pp. 73-78.
43. Vasconcelos, *Obras completas*, I, 44.
44. *Ibid.*, I, 46.
45. *Ibid.*, I, 44.

concelos considers that the will-representation polarity of Schopenhauer contains "the germ of the entire modern age," he seems dis-
satisfied with the implied equation of *the thing in itself* with the will;
he feels that the attempt to establish such an equation will lead to
only a vague, uncommunicable mysticism which cannot serve as a
guide for mankind.[46]

He then turns to Bergson and vitalism as a more fruitful method
of establishing man's autonomy from the mechanistic world of
matter: "life is a reaction . . . [an] impulse which tends to free itself
of being controlled by material laws. . . ."[47] The very core of the
vitalist position, Vasconcelos notes, lies in the problem of the genesis
of life. Following Bergson, he feels that this must not depend
upon any "phenomenon of energy," for energy tends to dissipate
itself, to "run down" while life perpetually increases.[48] He then
suggests that the life force is given as "the disinterested act, because
such an act is only produced in violation of all the laws of the material
realm."[49] He concludes by adding that it is "the only miracle of
the Cosmos." Vasconcelos did not attempt the arduous task of
deriving a complete and consistent world-view (or even the lesser
task of formulating a philosophy of values) on the basis of vitalism
and voluntarism. Moreover, his summation of the "new sensibility"
which stems from these currents lacks the rigor of professional
philosophic writing. Vasconcelos' impatience, his desire to translate
these ideas into meaningful terms, dominates his expression:

> Our age lives as if it imagined that there was at work in the
> universe a power whose laws are different from those of the
> phenomena, and when people think seriously about this, they
> will discover within themselves the germ of this indestructible
> power; they will find it in their conscience, which is capable of
> self-denial and is therefore more powerful than everything else
> in the universe. . . . The generous act in the midst of universal
> self-interest is the strangest contradiction of factual reality. . . .[50]

That Vasconcelos speaks here as a popularizer rather than as a
professional philosopher does not detract from his importance. One
wonders how much influence a Kant or a Bergson might have had
had their works been accorded only "professional" attention. In
the specific case of Spanish America, for better or for worse, the

46. *Ibid.*, I, 45.
47. *Ibid.*, I, 48.
48. *Ibid.*
49. *Ibid.*, I, 49.
50. *Ibid.*, I, 51.

popularizers have exercised a crucial influence. A case in point is Antonio Caso, whose impressive essay, *La existencia como economía, como desinterés y como caridad* (1919), attests the impact of Vasconcelos' earlier popularization of Schopenhauer and Bergson.

If 1910 was an auspicious year in Mexican intellectual history, it was no less auspicious in Mexican politics. Although the *Ateneo* group cannot be considered the literary instigator of the Revolution of 1910-17, it certainly played an important part in shaping the new Mexico that arose after the military phase of the revolt had ended. The group itself gradually disbanded during the chaotic years of factional strife. Henríquez Ureña left Mexico in 1914 to pursue a distinguished career as a teacher and literary critic in Argentina and in the United States. The youthful Alfonso Reyes (1889-1959) published a valuable collection of essays on aesthetics, *Cuestiones estéticas* (1911), but left for Europe shortly afterward. Vasconcelos, after considerable direct involvement in the Revolution, was forced to spend a number of years as an exile in Europe, South America, and the United States. During the decade of post-Revolutionary consolidation—the 1920's—he returned to Mexico to serve in the important post of Minister of Education. His activities of this period will be discussed in a later chapter.

Antonio Caso, by contrast, remained in Mexico, cultivating the basic themes of the *Ateneo* group throughout the Revolution. His earliest statement of these themes appears in a series of essays written during the years immediately preceding the conflict. His piece on Nietzsche, in the *Revista Moderna* of August, 1907, is basically explanatory, though he does show a marked dislike for the German thinker.[51] Caso's first lectures in the *Ateneo* were characterized by an overestimation of Barreda's importance and by some reticence to attack positivism directly. The lectures were sharply criticized on both these points by Pedro Henríquez Ureña.[52] Caso's 1908 *Revista Moderna* article on Max Stirner, however, gives a better hint of his future development. Caso approves of Stirner's vigorous attack on Hegelism; but what appeals most to the young Mexican is the emphasis on an instinctive, concrete ego and the general tone of "personalism" in Stirner's work. Caso warns, however, that the

51. Antonio Caso, "Nietzsche, su espíritu y su obra," *Revista Moderna*, VIII (Aug. 1907), 348-58.

52. Antonio Caso, "Conferencias sobre el positivismo," *Revista Moderna*, XII (July, 1909), 301-10. Reprinted in *Horas de estudio* as "El positivismo de Comte"; see Henríquez Ureña, *Obra crítica*, pp. 52-53.

excess of voluntarism evident in Stirner and other thinkers like him must be balanced by love.[53]

Caso's article of 1909, "Perennidad del pensamiento religioso y especulativo" is particularly significant for its clear attack upon positivism and also for its emphasis on religious experience. He states that to deny either the scientific or the religious explanation of reality "is to mutilate humanity and explain the most glorious part of its past with fantasies and chimeras stripped of universal value."[54] His remark that like science religion bases truth on experience—spiritual experience—merits attention, for the theme continues as a *leitmotif* in his later work. In 1914, when Caso's essay "La filosofía de la intuición" appeared, Spanish American intellectuals knew relatively little about Henri Bergson. Caso was the first Mexican to discuss the French philosopher at length; and he may well have been one of the first Spanish Americans to do so.[55] His essay was a clear, though brief, exposition of the Bergsonian concept of intuition and of Bergson's relationship to such key movements as Boutroux's philosophy of contingency and the newer, less rigid scientific thinking of Mach, Ostwald, and Poincaré. Caso repeatedly underscores the profoundly human orientation of intuitionist thought: "It is not idealism, as people often term it, but humanism . . ." he explains; for the new philosophy is "a restoration of the spiritual ... of that which is essentially and genuinely human."[56] The extent to which philosophic anti-intellectualism had taken hold of his thinking is dramatically summed up in his view that "whatever does not reflect one iota of our will, of our intelligence, of our activity, is nothing . . . that which is absolutely dissimilar to humanity, does not exist. . . ."[57]

La existencia como economía, como desinterés y como caridad is a fitting climax to this period of Caso's career and to the work of the *Ateneo*. Though published in 1919, the essay grew out of Caso's 1915 lectures at the Universidad Popular Mexicana, an institution which virtually owed its existence to the efforts of the *Ateneo* group.

53. Antonio Caso, "Max Stirner," *Revista Moderna*, X (March, 1908), 80-84.
54. Antonio Caso, "Perennidad del pensamiento religioso y especulativo," *Revista Moderna*, XIII (Oct., 1909), 68.
55. Note, however, Vasconcelos' familiarity with Bergson, discussed above. Also note the *arielistas'* awareness of Bergson: see above, p. 44, note 30. Robert G. Mead's statement that "Caso es el primero en introducir en su patria las ideas de Bergson sobre la intuición y la evolución creadora," *Ensayo hispanoamericano*, p. 101, must be qualified by these considerations.
56. Antonio Caso, *La filosofía de la intuición* (Mexico, 1914), p. 4.
57. *Ibid.*

Caso frames his essay on the basis of two opposing concepts of life. The first of these, life in the "economic" sense, may be described by the phrase "the maximum benefit with the minimum effort." The second concept, life as "sacrifice," as "disinterest," or as "charity," is described as "the maximum effort with the minimum benefit."[58] Human existence, when viewed from the standpoint of the "economic" concept, remains irretrievably enmeshed in the determinism of natural forces. Man, as a producer and consumer of goods is simply another natural object, simply a "thing" in a material world. The human will may, however, liberate man from the realm of material necessity. Caso implies—and here the exact formulation of the problem is my own—that the will, ego, or humanized life-force, call it what we will, can pursue *either* self-interested (i.e., "economic") ends, or it can pursue certain completely "irrational," not self-interested, and even un-directed ends. We have already noted that in the pursuit of "economic" ends, the will functions merely as an instrument of economic forces and hence man remains simply another determined object in nature. When, however, the will—or the formalizing force, as Caso occasionally terms it—pursues that which is "disinterested," man assumes his distinctive, free, human character. In short, it is not simply man's will which liberates him, but his will directed toward acts of disinterest, charity, and love. Caso's attitude toward the voluntaristic philosophies of Schopenhauer and Nietzsche is consistent with this viewpoint. He acknowledges a great debt to the former for having pointed out the "disinterested" and liberating nature of art and similar activities,[59] but he rejects the Nietzschean concept of will with its accompanying moral code.[60] Caso objects particularly to the equation of the "lamb morality"—the code of the weakling—with Christianity. He points out that sacrifice and charity require great strength of character and a kind of nobility which surpasses the "lion morality" of which Nietzsche was so fond.[61] Caso even ventures to analyze the disturbance that eventually forced the German philosopher to an asylum: Nietzsche's madness, he feels, represented the frustrated attempt of the weakling striving for strength.[62] Much of what Caso wrote in *La existencia* had been

58. Antonio Caso, *La existencia como economía, como desinterés y como caridad* (Mexico, 1943), p. 154.
   59. *Ibid.*, pp. 50-53.
   60. *Ibid.*, pp. 156ff.
   61. *Ibid.*, pp. 155-56.
   62. *Ibid.*, p. 157. Caso's interpretation of Nietzsche is fairly typical of his period and of several decades after. An appealing and different contemporary view of the Nietzschean ethic appears in the work of Walter Kaufman, who notes that "The

written before, both by himself and by others. His debt to Vasconcelos' work of 1910 is, for example, abundantly clear. But in this essay Caso writes with a warmth and conviction found neither in his own earlier works nor in those of his compatriots. Perhaps the conditions under which it was produced, conditions of strife and chaos which must have brought acts of self-interest and disinterest into dramatically sharp focus, influenced the essay's general tone. *La existencia como economía, como desinterés y como caridad,* though based substantially upon Caso's earlier thinking on voluntarism and on Bergsonian vitalism, points the way toward even newer intellectual horizons. For example, Caso speaks of the "culminating" nature of the then current, but still little known philosophic school of phenomenology. He views its chief exponent, Husserl, as representing a kind of dialectical "synthesis" of Hegel and Comte, who are seen in terms of a thesis-antithesis relationship.[63] Caso stresses that the value of Husserl's method lies in the fact that phenomenology uses "intuitional" data without becoming metaphysical.[64] Although he does not discuss phenomenology at great length, Caso's very early acquaintance with Husserl—a thinker who contributed in no small measure to twentieth-century existentialism—is noteworthy.[65]

The victory of the anti-Positivist forces was incomplete even after two decades of sustained activity. A number of widely read essayists could see nothing but chaos in the growing trend toward voluntarism and vitalism. Interestingly, their defense of their own position points up the weaknesses of positivism rather than those of the newer intellectual currents. Two such men are the Chilean philosopher Enrique Molina (1871-?) and a writer whom we have

highest type, to Nietzsche's mind, is the passionate man who is the master of his passions, able to employ them creatively without having to resort to asceticism for fear that his passions might conquer him." See Kaufman's "How Nietzsche Revolutionized Ethics" in his *The Owl and the Nightingale* (London, 1959), pp. 190-99.

63. Caso, *La existencia como economía*, pp. 88-90.

64. *Ibid.*, pp. 90-91.

65. The work of Rodó, the *arielistas* and the *Ateneo de la juventud* group represents an important expression of the idealistic—or to take Caso's suggestion—the "humanistic" reaction against scientism. The essayists were not, however, alone in their desire to rejuvenate Spanish American thought and attitudes. The work of many different kinds of writers—poets, prosists, and pure philosophers—could be discussed in the context of these tendencies. Of particular importance was the work of the philosophers. In the *rioplatense* region, Carlos Vaz Ferreira and Alejandro Korn show, if not a clear rejection of positivism, newer viewpoints which go well beyond the rigidities of nineteenth-century scientism; while Peru's Alejandro O. Deústua, drawing first upon the German neo-idealist Krause, and later upon Bergson, developed a philosophical position quite similar in many respects to that of Caso.

already met, Argentina's José Ingenieros.[66] Both seem tempera-
mentally unable to accept the kind of thinking demanded by irrationalism; both exercised great influence in their respective countries
through high academic and editorial positions;[67] and both were
fundamentally reformers rather than radicals. The ideas of these
two essayists are shaped by the typically nineteenth-century dilemma
of the thinker who accepts a deterministic position (in this case
social organicism), but who nevertheless wishes to improve and act
upon his society. Faith in social meliorism, in reform, and activism
is thus constantly corroded by a deep-seated conviction that man is
merely a bystander, capable only of observing the "unfolding" of
pre-determined forces of the growth of autonomous organisms.

Enrique Molina, for example, cannot bring himself to say that
man may act independently of the laws of causality; however, he
holds that causality and determinism should not be equated with
"fatalism." In his *Filosofía Americana* (1914), he makes the point
that it is only through a recognition of scientific determinism—the
law of cause and effect—that man can work effectively and scien-
tifically on his environment, and thus achieve freedom.[68] Molina
was actually more concerned with developing a social philosophy—or
social technology—than he was with solving the theoretical problems
suggested by these ideas. Accordingly he found much to admire in
the work of the North American social philosopher, Lester F. Ward.
In Ward's "sociocracy" Molina saw an ideal state, one in which the
masses, the "little man," could have a truly representative voice,
but one which nevertheless would not "suffocate" men of genius.[69]
Throughout his *Filosofía Americana* Molina stresses that under a
"sociocratic" organization society could pursue its "ideals" without
fear of statism, since people are capable of controlling their own
destiny through the proper employment of social techniques. Molina
seldom discusses the crucial question of just what society's ideals
are or how they are evolved, but one would assume that the Chilean
thinker held a vaguely defined, deep-seated belief in utilitarianism.
The general tone of his work, as well as his frequent and specific
criticisms of Bergsonian irrationalism,[70] indicate a marked reluctance

66. For a discussion of Ingenieros' race thinking, see above, Chapter II, pp. 29-31.
67. Molina was until 1957 editor of the highly respected journal of letters and ideas,
Atenea; while Ingenieros edited the important *Revista de Filosofía* from 1915 until his
death in 1925.
68. Enrique Molina, *Filosofía americana* (Paris ,1914), pp. 1-65.
69. *Ibid.*, p. 242.
70. As late as 1925 Molina was critical of Bergson. His article "José Ingenieros,"
Atenea, II (Nov., 1925), 411-18, praises his Argentine colleague warmly for having

on his part to leave the comfort and security of nineteenth-century positivism.

Ingenieros—whom, incidentally, Molina admired greatly[71]—was even less suited by temperament to accept the ideas of the irrationalists. One of his commentators noted that he lacked "pity, sympathy . . . and love." Alejandro Korn, the philosopher, felt that when Ingenieros was confronted by anything "mystical" or "metaphysical," he was like a person without any "ear" who vainly tries to appreciate a delicate musical passage.[72] And Ingenieros himself, in speaking of the mystique in the North American ethical movement admits that his admiration notwithstanding, "For those of us who do not have a mystical temperament, this naturalistic mysticism will always be a bit disconcerting."[73] Like Molina, Ingenieros was interested in social reform. He felt, however, that the betterment of society depended in great measure upon the recognition of "ideals" and the derivation of an ethcial system from these. In his philosophic essay *Hacia una moral sin dogmas* (1917), subtitled "Sobre Emerson y el eticismo," he attempts to tackle the difficult problems of establishing an ethical code without recourse to religious dogma, metaphysics, or anything "supernatural." In typically Spencerian jargon he views this "morality without dogmas" as "a better adaptation of humanity to the environment in which it exists."[74] However, Ingenieros abandons biologism by inserting another term in his argument: the "ideals" which are to serve as guideposts for the ethical code. He takes pains to have his readers understand that "idealism" is quite different from "ideism," a designation which he reserves for the metaphysical notion of the "idea" as used in Hegelian or Platonic philosophy. "Ideals," as the Argentine essayist envisions them, arise when the imagination can "foresee" or anticipate experience:

> Ideals . . . are natural formations: they appear when the thought process reaches such a state of development that the imagination can anticipate experience. They are not mysterious entities that

---

fought the good fight against the "filosofía intuicionista." Molina's appreciation of the irrational trend increased somewhat in his later writings. See especially his "Concepción filosófica," *Atenea*, XVIII (Dec., 1941), 281-317; and "La filosofía en Chile en la primera mitad del siglo XX," *Atenea*, XXVIII (Sept.-Oct., 1951), 213-77.

71. See note 70 above.

72. Cited by Leon Dujovne, *La obra filosófica de José Ingenieros* (Buenos Aires, 1930), pp. 120-21.

73. José Ingenieros, *Hacia una moral sin dogmas: Lecciones sobre Emerson y el eticismo* (Buenos Aires, 1917), pp. 193-94.

74. *Ibid.*, p. 74.

appear by chance; they are formed like any phenomenon capable of being observed, they are effects coming from causes . . . they are induced on the basis of vast experience, upon which the imagination fixes itself in order to foresee the direction which Humanity will take. . . .[75]

Ingenieros, in effect, bases his ethical code on a typically deterministic notion of the unfolding of a pre-existing pattern; man, through his "imagination," can only glimpse the direction toward which this process is moving; he may then plan, organize, and direct his future accordingly. As a good Socialist, Ingenieros would like to see man improve his lot and reform his society. He does not, however, feel that the naturalistic determinism to which he adheres will necessarily impede human efforts toward these ends. "Improvement" and social betterment are in his none-too-logical view "natural" phenomena, since "altruism is as innate and as natural as egoism."[76] Drawing upon Emerson, he further refines this viewpoint by stressing that "evil," though natural, represents "moral pathology . . . a monstrosity or sickness."[77]

Ingenieros' best known essay, *El hombre mediocre* (1918), is grounded on the same concept of idealism. The superior individual forges the great ideals of his time, while the lower levels of society follow—or should follow—the lead of the superior. As Rodó pointed out before, and as Ortega was to point out later, the great problem of modern society was that the masses failed to recognize their true leaders, and that therefore genuinely superior ideals were not heeded. Again the underlying contradictions in Ingenieros' thought may be seen: his attacks on the egocentrism of the Nietzschean ethic are frequent,[78] and yet he will build an entire essay around an idea which is, in some respects, similar to the German philosopher's glorification of the superman.

Ingenieros made a desperate effort to put the newer intellectual currents of vitalism and irrationalism in their "philosophic place." The essays already discussed attempted to do this indirectly, while his more technical *Proposiciones relativas al porvenir de la filosofía* (1918) was a direct attack on all philosophies which deviated from

75. *Ibid.*, p. 175.
76. *Ibid.*, p. 181.
77. *Ibid.*, p. 198.
78. For further discussion of Ingenieros' ambivalence regarding Nietzsche, see Dujovne, *La obra filosófica*, p. 11. A typical critique of the German thinker appears in the *Hacia una moral*, p. 146, where Ingenieros includes Schopenhauer and Stendhal as other representatives of a "dangerous tendency towards moralistic individualism."

what he considered the only path toward knowledge, empiricism.[79] In the *Proposiciones* he discusses the relationship of "metaphysics" to knowledge in a manner analogous to his treatment of "ideals" and social progress. Just as "ideals" are previews of what the future holds for society, "metaphysics" anticipates what science will later show to be empirically true. By virtue of his "imagination" the superior man, be he idealist or scientist, is in some way attuned to these future developments. Ingenieros skirts the crucial matter of just how the "imagination" glimpses that which is to come. Though he does not acknowledge it, he was in effect using a term perilously akin to the "intuition" of the Bergsonians and others whom he opposed. In short, the *Proposiciones* may be of some use in developing a philosophy of science or in establishing a framework for sociology, but as an over-all philosophic world-view it is deficient, inconsistent, and totally lacking in concern for the human condition.

Despite the efforts of writers such as Molina and Ingenieros, the revolt against scientism in general and positivism in particular continued to gain momentum. Virtually everything which will be discussed in the chapters to follow may be looked upon as an outgrowth of this general trend. The flowering of a revitalized sensitivity to all America—what writers to the south have called *novomundismo* (New Worldism)—is one such outgrowth. Without the liberating effect of the revolt against scientism this "rediscovery of America" might never have come about; certainly its distinctively humanistic fervor and faith in man's creativity would have been less intense.

79. For a critical discussion of Ingenieros' antivitalist position, particularly his misunderstanding of Bergson and Ortega, see Julio Endara, *José Ingenieros y el porvenir de la filosofía* (Buenos Aires, 1922).

IV / AMERICA REDISCOVERED

SINCE THE MOMENTOUS DAYS OF DISCOVERY AND CONQUEST, the New World—the land, the people, the very air—has fascinated speculative writers and especially essayists. European views regarding the Americas run the gamut of awe, picturesque interest, hope, and at times, disdain. The native Americanist expresses as wide a range of attitudes, but the persistent matter of viewpoint makes his task more difficult and often more dramatic. His problem is not unlike that of the autobiographer. Shall he look into the mirror of his experience and consciousness describing what he finds, or shall he try to gain the objectivity of the outside observer? Shall the cosmopolite of Buenos Aires or Mexico City attempt a reflective analysis of himself and his ethos by means of a mirror of his own making, or shall he formulate this analysis using the intellectual instruments of the general European culture? And just what is the significance of a "different," an American, viewpoint? Is the American simply a product of the Old World who merely happens to live geographically removed from the centers of this culture, or is he something quite unique? And why establish a sharp distinction between Europe and the New World? If a dividing line is in order could it not be drawn horizontally rather than vertically: Doesn't the Latin of the Western Hemisphere have more in common with Mediterranean Europe than he does with North America? Finally, is the entire question of one's relationship to other cultures or to a "universal" culture a valid one? Is it really possible for a writer to achieve that vantage point which enables him to judge these matters with any degree of objectivity? Although such questions have figured prominently in the Spanish American essay throughout the genre's history,[1] they have become particularly pressing during the contemporary period.

Students of Spanish American culture have often noted that the first few decades of the twentieth century are characterized by a marked spirit of Americanism and nativism. It is a time when the continent attempts to replace European social, political, and aesthetic models by social institutions, political structures, and artistic creations of her own making. It is not difficult to explain why this reaction against Europe came about. As the century progressed it became increasingly evident that European culture might not be as worthy of emulation as was once thought. The possibility that war, depression, and totalitarianism might thoroughly exhaust the traditional centers of Western civilization gradually became quite real. But aside from these external factors, the intellectual changes occurring in Spanish America herself had a profound effect in stimulating the new spirit of Americanism. The repudiation of scientism with the concomitant exaltation of humanistic values and of man's creativeness could not fail to make Spanish Americans assess their own potentialities with increasing optimism. In a world whose most valued goals were technical progress, material abundance, and a "rationally" ordered middle class society, Hispanic America might well feel inferior; but the essayists whom we are about to consider saw that these typically nineteenth-century values were in retreat. Hence they write of the new America in tones of hope and confidence.

1. If a broad definition of the essay is accepted, the roots of the Americanist concern may justifiably be traced to the writings of the sixteenth-century *cronistas*: Bernal Díaz del Castillo, Alvar Núñez Cabeza de Vaca, Father Bartolomé de las Casas, Father Bernardo de Sahagún, Father José de Acosta, and others. Later in the colonial period the Mestizo chronicler, Inca Garcilaso de la Vega wrote his *Comentarios reales* (1608-1616), perhaps the first "essay" in which a distinctly Americanist viewpoint prevails. The eighteenth centur saw much essayistic activity centered about the growing desire for political and cultural independence. The most impressive work of the period is that of the Jesuit humanists and various lay writers of Spanish America's Enlightenment. For an excellent study of this movement see Mariano Picón Salas, *De la conquista a la independencia* (Mexico, 1950). Of the early independence period, the most noteworthy contribution to the development of the Americanist concern would be the speeches, letters, and miscellaneous essayistic writings of Simón Bolívar, especially his *Carta de Jamaica* (1815) and the *Discurso al Congreso de Angostura* (1819). Although nationally oriented essays seem to predominate during the nineteenth century, several transcend local concerns and must be considered in any outline of the Americanist preoccupation: the essays of Argentina's greatest prosist of the century, Domingo Faustino Sarmiento, *Facundo* (1845) and *Conflicto y armonía de las razas en América* (1883); the works of Chile's anti-Spanish liberals, Francisco Bilbao, author of the *Evangelio americano* (1864), and José Victorino Lastarria, *La América* (1867); and finally the writings of Cuba's great José Martí whose devotion to the American ideal is evident in dozens of essays scattered throughout the some seventy volumes of his complete works.

A long-forgotten polemic between two very different Mexican writers will perhaps illustrate the spirit of the younger generation of *novomundistas* (New Worldists). When Antonio Caso wrote, in the early twenties, of the glorious future of the New World, he was sharply criticized by Francisco Bulnes, then rector of the National University. Caso's view of America's destiny in the article "En América dirá su última palabra la civilización latina" ("In America Latin Civilization Will Say Its Final Word") was typical of his enthusiastic, creative attitude toward the future. Bulnes, who had been one of the prominent *científicos* of the Díaz period, had written a lengthy, inconsistent essay, *El Porvenir de las naciones latino-americanas* (1899), which stressed the notion that Latin America had little hope of achieving any greatness since the corn-based nutrition of the masses could only produce an "inferior" human product. Caso's reply to Bulnes' pessimism is an eloquent expression of how remote the world of the *científicos* was from that of the younger generation: "Señor Bulnes, as the only opposing argument, takes off and exhibits his historic high-buttoned shoes which he wore during those remote pseudo-scientific nineteenth-century soirées when he read, in preparation for what might be called his general culture, the acid works of Mr. Gustave Le Bon and those of the great and unbending Herbert Spencer.[2]"

An important manifestation of the new Americanism in the essay may be seen in the growth of indigenism. A brief working definition of the term itself might be that indigenism is a sympathetic awareness of the native American. This awareness may vary in intensity from a mild, "picturesque" interest to fervent devotion to the cause of reforming New World culture on an indigenous pattern. Aside from the many versions of indigenism found in the essay, contemporary Spanish American art and social science have reflected the same interest. But exactly who is the native American—the *indígena* —as used in our definition? The answer will vary. One writer will restrict its meaning to the biologically "pure" Indian, assuming for a moment that the concept of racial purity is meaningful; another will include the Indian's half-brother, the mestizo; others equate *indígena* with virtually any native-born American of non-European stock; and finally, many writers abandon biology and genetics completely. The *indígena*, they say, must be culturally defined: he who lives as an Indian *is* an Indian; he who has a "mixed" culture,

2. Antonio Caso, "El enemigo de la tierra," *Repertorio Americano*, IV (1922), 172.

is a mestizo, etc. In one form or another, this last attitude is the most characteristic of the more recent essayists. Modern indigenism, following the broad lines of the rejection of scientism, tends to refute not only the prejudiced, pessimistic "classical" racism, but even the race concept itself.

Although the essayists who have contributed most significantly to this glorification of nativism write from a particular national viewpoint, the nature of the subject tends to make political frontiers fade into the background. The writers of Peru and Bolivia—Manuel González Prada, Franz Tamayo, or Fernando Díez de Medina, for example—have a regional outlook rather than a national one. And some of the most celebrated essays in this tradition, Vasconcelos' *La raza cósmica* and *Indología* or Ricardo Rojas' *Eurindia*, are clearly continental in orientation. Even the usual divisions of Spanish America into "white" or "European" regions versus "Indian" regions tend to disappear in the *indigenistas'* desire to point out the distinctively autochthonous nature of New World culture.

Indicative of the continental nature of this interest is the fact that one of the first essayists to stress indigenism in the twentieth century,[3] Ricardo Rojas (1882-1957), was from Argentina, often considered the least "Indian" and most European nation of Spanish America. His work, moreover, is particularly interesting as it reveals not only the positive side of indigenism, but also some of the pitfalls and excesses of the nativist position.[4] Rojas' earliest treatment of the Indian is frankly romantic and sentimental. In a speech of 1905 he recalls his youthful desire to saturate himself in everything native: "Everything told us of the renovation which had already begun, and having witnessed it from a distance, I wanted to plunge myself into the native forests, to take by surprise the last avatars of the spirit of the race, to save from oblivion their most genuine creations . . . the ballads, the folk dances, and the ingenuous

3. There are, however, important antecedents of contemporary indigenism in the nineteenth century. Examples may be seen in the ideas of the Peruvian radical Manuel González Prada (see below, Chapter V, pp. 109-11) and in a number of Mexican writers of the Díaz period. Regarding these, see the author's "Indigenism and Racism in Mexican Thought: 1857-1911," *Journal of Inter-American Studies,* I (1959), 405-23.
4. See Alberto Zum Felde, *Indice crítico de la literatura hispanoamericana: Los ensayistas* (México, 1954), pp. 447-54. See also the penetrating criticisms of Rojas' general Americanism by Luis E. Soto, "Ricardo Rojas y la Americanidad," *Revista Iberoamericana,* No. 46 (julio/dic., 1958), 317-33; and the similarly oriented article of Bernardo Canal Feijóo, "Sobre el americanismo de Ricardo Rojas," *Revista Ibero-americana,* No. 46 (julio/dic., 1958), 221-26. This entire issue (No. 46) of the *Revista,* a homage to Rojas, contains several other relevant studies.

customs. . . ."[5] Much of Rojas' work during the early decades of the century was devoted to a revitalization or, as he himself called it, a "restoration" of Argentine nationalism. Although he is often thought of as an inveterate jingoist,[6] it is seldom stressed that the one element which distinguishes his "restored" nationalism is his emphasis on an all-pervading Indian spirit in Argentina. Thus, in one of his best-known essays, *Eurindia* (1924), he attempts to answer the objections of his countrymen of pure European stock who feel that as such they have nothing in common with Indians or mestizos: "Race . . . is a spiritual phenomenon, collective in meaning, determined by a language and a territory, or perhaps by an ideal. Accordingly, individuals, regardless of their native origin, perform as a function of an historical group. . . ."[7] Here, as in many other instances, Rojas gives great weight to the physical environment in shaping national or group characteristics. The character of the native of any given place thus becomes, to some degree, a product of what Rojas calls the *genius loci*:

> National territory is not only a political jurisdiction, but a retort of cosmic forces that shapes the race, giving it a regional character, transcending man or history. . . .
>
> . . . . . .
>
> Race is not only a matter of the scientific ethnos, but also the collective conscience of a people confirmed by a territorial emotion and by a common historical experience.[8]

The "territorial emotion" and "common historical experience" then, link even the white Argentine cosmopolite to the Indians that once inhabited the coastal Pampas; similarly, the modern dwellers of the Andean plateaus would have much in common with the Argentines of the Northwest (the region, incidentally from which Rojas comes). It might appear that the great weight assigned by Rojas to physical environment could lead to a determinism as rigid as that invoked by the racists. Geographic determinism has often gone hand in hand with the typically quasiscientific thought which Rojas and his generation were attempting to combat. However, the "force of the land," as viewed by Spanish American essayists of the twentieth century, differs substantially from the rigid, "scientific" environmentalism of an Ellsworth Huntington. For many, Rojas

5. Ricardo Rojas, *Obras completas* (Buenos Aires, 1924), VI, 278.
6. See the criticisms indicated in note 4 above, especially the article by Soto.
7. Rojas, *Obras completas*, V, 69.
8. *Ibid.*, p. 332.

included, it is an almost mystical adoration of nature, a kind of inter-relationship between man and the land which liberates rather than constrains. He who comprehends nature, who is sensitive to the land and its elemental forces is more genuine, more authentic than the overcivilized city dweller.[9] This rather romantic exaltation of nature is intimately related to the glorification of the *indígena*; for it is the native who is closest to the land. In certain essayists, as we shall see, the city—as a symbol of everything artificial, European, and materialistic—is mercilessly attacked, while the country, the natural realm, is greatly praised. The values of Sarmiento's celebrated formula of 1845 describing American reality in terms of "civilization and barbarism" are thus reversed.

An interesting example of an early indigenist viewpoint, and one that illustrates many of the trends noted above, appears in an important, but little-known essay of Bolivia's Franz Tamayo (1879-1956): *La creación de la pedagogía nacional* (1910). Tamayo's vigorous rejection of scientism might well have been analyzed in the previous chapter: his succinct observation, "In the laboratory everything is known except knowledge,"[10] is as good a summation of his position as one would wish to find. Although science is helpful in a limited sphere, it has not solved problems of human existence and motivation: "It is necessary to search somewhere else for the unalterable source of our actions."[11] Tamayo refutes Haeckel, Buchner, and the social Darwinists roundly, and he terms historical determinism "a naive error of Comtians and Taineans."[12] The affirmative side of Tamayo's thought rests solidly on his belief that only a kind of "vital energy" and the will can explain the nature of human events both present and past: "Energy . . . is the ultimate word and also the ultimate explanation for life . . . . All that remains is the will, undebated and undebatable, the soul of empires, the master spring of all history. . . ."[13] In a very Nietzschean tone he calls for Bolivian youth to concentrate on the full development of their vital energy: in effect, he exhorts them to become "little savages."[14]

9. This theme has been very evident in contemporary Spanish American literature. The romantic primitivism of the poet Pablo Neruda (as seen in his *Residencia en la tierra*) illustrates this trend particularly well. We shall also note, in later chapters, that such writers as Ezequiel Martínez Estrada and Octavio Paz have dealt at some length with the general theme of man's alienation from the natural realm.

10. Franz Tamayo, *La creación de la pedagogía nacional* (La Paz, 1910), p. 207.

11. *Ibid.*, p. 210.

12. *Ibid.*, p. 207.

13. *Ibid.*, p. 211.

14. *Ibid.*, pp. 212-13.

Tamayo feels that the inexhaustible supply of energy upon which national development depends is to be found in the Indian masses: "the Indian is the true depository of national energy."[15] The racistic, "surgical" attitude of writers like his compatriot, Alcides Arguedas (whom Tamayo does not specifically mention), is vigorously refuted: "Bolivia is not sick of anything except the illogicality and absurdity of granting power and superiority to those who do not really possess these qualities, and of denying the eternal rights of power to its legitimate representatives."[16] The apparent victory of the whites during the conquest was only temporary and superficial; the pure European can only survive by miscegenation with the native American. "Interbreed or perish" is the only choice for the white man, for "energy is not on his side."[17] The Indian's energy, his vital force, is not what, in terms of nineteenth-century scientism, would be called a "racial" trait, for Tamayo denounces the "scientific" study of races as "an insoluble maze, completely entangled by contradictions."[18] Earlier in his essay he even speaks of concepts such as race as "paper façades behind which there does not exist a physically real or logically valid entity."[19]

From what source, then, does the vital energy of the *indígena* come? Apparently to a great extent from the land itself. Tamayo, like Rojas, gives great importance to what he calls "the force of the land and the spirit [*genio*] of the place."[20] These concepts are at times phrased in mystical terms ("the land has its own spirit which gives life to the germinating tree and to man who flourishes upon the earth's surface"[21]), and at other times in fairly specific, scientific terms, as when it is stated that the chemical salts in the food and water of the Andean Indian are responsible for his strength.[22] Like the massive Andes which surround him, the Indian's soul "seems to be made of granite."[23] This rock-like solidity is the native's "difficulty as well as his greatness." The nation's great educational problem, as seen by Tamayo, lies in preserving the "granitic" strength of the Indians: the whites and mestizos must be educated to appreciate this native force, and the Indian must be "prophy-

15. *Ibid.*, p. 58.
16. *Ibid.*, p. 60.
17. *Ibid.*, pp. 62-63.
18. *Ibid.*, p. 144.
19. *Ibid.*, p. 20.
20. *Ibid.*, p. 163.
21. *Ibid.*, p. 161.
22. *Ibid.*, p. 162.
23. *Ibid.*, p. 138.

lactically" indoctrinated in order that while gaining modern knowledge he will not lose his natural energy and vigor.[24] The idea that city life—always associated with the European—is decadent, corrupting, and inferior in comparison to country life (considered, of course, typical of the Indian) underlies Tamayo's thought. This profound indigenism, linked physically and spiritually with the land, is the defining characteristic of his Americanism. His primary concern for Bolivia notwithstanding, Tamayo's attitudes imply a very basic *novomundista* viewpoint, for he clearly believes that the New World and its original inhabitants exercise a powerful formative influence on all contemporary Americans. His remark that even "in the native Yankee, despite all appearances, the redskin is resuscitated"[25] is a good expression of what could be called this radically Americanist position.[26]

The most impressive flowering of Spanish American indigenism is, in all probability, that of Mexico of the 1920's; and its most outstanding spokesman is José Vasconcelos.[27] The course of Mexican indigenism has been rather different from that of the South American continent. Although the Indian and his culture had been almost forgotten during the Díaz regime, it is difficult to encounter markedly racistic, anti-Indian feelings in the essay of that period. Despite the fact that he had been economically exploited by the upper classes and generally ignored by creative artists, the Indian of nineteenth-century Mexico was surprisingly well appreciated by a number of important writers, including at least one major figure in the Díaz circle, Justo Sierra.[28] But with the Revolution and its emphasis on land reform led by popular, pro-indigenist chieftains such as Emiliano Zapata, a tremendous vindication of everything native took place. Vasconcelos, from his important position as Minister of Education in the Obregón regime (1920-25), was not only an interpreter of this movement, but also played an impor-

24. *Ibid.*
25. *Ibid.*, p. 162.
26. A polemic between Tamayo and the Spanish essayist Ramiro de Maeztu further illustrates the Bolivian's profound Americanism. In an article titled "Carta de Americanos para Americanos," *Repertorio Americano* XIII (1926), 177-80, Tamayo criticizes the Spanish for fostering an exclusively pan-Hispanic movement which didn't take into account the unique spirit of the New World. For the Spanish side of the question, see Ramiro de Maeztu, "El mito de la raza," *Repertorio Americano*, XV (1927), 214-15.
27. Regarding Vasconcelos' important early work in collaboration with the *Ateneo de la Juventud* group, see above, Chapter III, pp. 48-50.
28. For a resumé of Sierra's indigenism see Stabb, "Indigenism and Racism," *Journal of Inter-American Studies*, pp. 405-23.

tant role in directing its course.[29]   His great nationalistic fervor notwithstanding, Vasconcelos' two major essays on the indigenist theme, *La raza cósmica* (1925) and *Indología* (1926) are clearly continental in scope.

These two works of Vasconcelos, while representative of a rather glib, rhetorical Americanism, have been widely read. Perhaps the title of the first essay has had the appeal of a motto; when the interested reader goes beyond the first chapter, however, he may well be disappointed, for the major portion of the book deals primarily with the author's travel experiences throughout the continent. Even the more important first chapter is marred by Vasconcelos' fanciful revival of the Atlantis myth and by a rather outmoded concept of race. The main point of the essay, the idea that the destiny of America is the amalgamation of all the "races" of the world into one great "cosmic" race of the future,[30] rests upon a simplistic concept of "pure" and "mixed" races. It is true that Vasconcelos, unlike the racists, looks upon this future mixture with great optimism, for such a people would combine all the best of its contributing groups. The value of *La raza cósmica* and the similar *Indología* is lessened, however, by a grandiose vision of a future tropical American paradise which Vasconcelos fails to relate to the realities of his time.[31] Despite this weakness and despite his later conservatism, Vasconcelos certainly played an important role in the diffusion of a broadly conceived Hispano-Americanism both in Mexico and indirectly in other countries.[32] As Minister of Education he made it possible for Pedro Henríquez Ureña to undertake a cultural mission to Argentina in 1921; at about the same time, Gabriela Mistral, the budding Chilean poetess (and ardent Americanist in her prose) was invited by him to teach at the summer school

29. Among some of Vasconcelos' specific acts as a promulgator of indigenism are the following: the establishment of a government supported program in the graphic arts (the *Dirección de dibujo* and the *Revolutionary Syndicate of Technical Workers Painters and Sculptors*) having a distinctly nativist orientation; the setting-up of the "Cultural Missions" which sent volunteer teachers to the backlands in order to educate the Indians and yet preserve much of their folk-culture; and the support of periodicals such as the review *El Maestro* which stressed doctrines of Americanism and nativism among the growing ranks of postrevolutionary school teachers.

30. José Vasconcelos, *La raza cósmica* (Barcelona, n.d.), p. 16.

31. See the critique of Zum Felde, *Indice crítico*, p. 426.

32. Vasconcelos on occasion even expressed his Americanist faith in the United States, a nation which he frequently attacked bitterly. His speech before the Chatauqua Society on Mexico's educational program is a fine expression of liberal racial thought and confidence in the future of the New World. The speech is reprinted as "La educación en Mexico," *Repertorio Americano*, V (1922), 376-78 and 386-89.

of the National University,[33] and finally his encouragement of the widespread university reform movements of the early twenties was warmly praised by student leaders throughout the continent.[34]

The first phase of indigenism is rough-hewn, hastily conceived, and very susceptible to attack. It was often propagandistic and journalistic. Rojas' glib reduction of Argentine, and by extension Spanish American, cultural history to two trends, "Indianism" and "exoticism," cannot withstand careful analysis. Tamayo's Nietzschean worship of force leads to certain logical inconsistencies as well as to a perilous emphasis on authoritarianism. Vasconcelos' verbosity—what Spanish American critics often call "tropicalism"—led him to create fantasies that are often completely untenable. But the ideas of the three essayists certainly served as points of departure for further—and more fruitful—investigation of the basic questions of the new Americanism. Before examining some of the more recent essays devoted to this theme, the catalytic effect of several writers from outside Spanish America must be considered.

It would be difficult to find two men as different as José Ortega y Gasset (1883-1955) and Waldo David Frank (1889-1967). Yet both exercised, in dissimilar ways, a profound influence upon the contemporary essayists of Spanish America. Ortega, modern Spain's best-known philosopher and essayist (with the possible exception of Miguel de Unamuno) visited Spanish America in 1916 and again in 1929. Stemming from these visits, and from his own meditations on the New World, are several important essays: "Carta a un joven argentino que estudia filosofía" (1924), "Hegel y América" (1928), and "La pampa . . . promesas"-(1929). Although these works gave rise to a good deal of comment in Spanish America, Ortega's greater contribution to the continent's intellectual and literary development was undoubtedly his work as a disseminator of European thought through the medium of his excellent journal the *Revista de Occidente*.

33. Gabriela Mistral expressed her fervent Americanism often during this period (the early twenties). Her remarks on the occasion of the close of classes at the summer school were particularly eloquent. This speech, directed incidentally at a student body which included many North Americans, was printed first in the newspaper *Excelsior* and then as "Mexico y los Estados Unidos," *Repertorio Americano*, IV (1922), 365. Earlier she expounded her Americanism in even more eloquent terms: "¡América, América! ¡Todo por ella, porque todo nos vendrá de ella . . . Haz amar la luminosa meseta mexicana, la verde estepa de Venezuela, la negra selva austral. . . .'" ("El grito," *Repertorio Americano* IV [1922], 45.)

34. The various university reform movements not only aimed at giving students a greater voice in choosing faculty, but also were often oriented toward political radicalism. Several of the writers under discussion began their literary careers as leaders of such movments. An outstanding case is that of Peru's Haya de la Torre (see below, Chapter V, pp. 124-27).

Furthermore, Ortega's own vast general writings on literature, philosophy, and history cannot be discounted in the shaping of present-day Spanish American thought. Waldo Frank, in contrast to Ortega, never enjoyed wide acclaim in his own country. I do not think it would be an exaggeration to say that he was better known and perhaps more appreciated in Latin America than he was in the United States. Frank, however, traveled much more extensively in Spanish America than Ortega, and his contacts with Latin writers and intellectuals seem to have been warmer and on a more personal level. At a time when Spanish American writers were struggling to define their relationship to Europe and North America and to clarify a number of vexing problems within their own culture, the observations of these and other foreigners (those of Jacques Maritain and Count Keyserling, for example) provided new perspectives and fresh idealogical leaven.

Ortega, educated in pre-World War Germany, was, to put things bluntly, dazzled by German philosophy and the German spirit. The burden of one of his most celebrated essays, *España invertebrada* (1922), is that the weakness and backwardness of modern Spain can be traced to the relatively minor role Germanic peoples played in her formation. Among the works translated into Spanish by his *Revista de Occidente* publishing firm, modern German masterpieces figure prominently. These include Spengler's *Decline of the West* (1923), Hegel's *Philosophy of Universal History* (1928), and later, important works of Dilthey, Husserl, and Brentano.

To characterize the complex philosophy of Ortega in a few lines would be fruitless: several major themes would, however, stand out in any over-all view of his thought. Vitalism, historicism, and in his later works, existentialism, have frequently been ascribed to him.[35] His celebrated "vital reason" (*razón vital*) takes as its "radical reality," "life," which is in turn defined as "what we do and what happens to us." In the key phrase "I am myself and my circumstance," Ortega further clarifies this "radical reality." "Circumstance" has a literal connotation of *circum stantia*, (i.e., "that which surrounds me"), and life is a kind of interaction between the ego and the *things*

35. Of the many studies dealing with Ortega's fundamental ideas see especially Julián Marías, "Ortega y la idea de la razón vital," in his *El existencialismo en España* (Bogotá, 1953); Hugo Rodríguez Alcalá, "Existencia y destino humanos en José Ortega y Gasset y Jean-Paul Sartre," in *Ensayos de Norte a Sur* (México, 1960); José Ferrater Mora, *Ortega y Gasset: An Outline of his Philosophy* (New Haven, 1957); Paulino Garagorri, *Ortega, una reforma de la filosofía* (Madrid, 1958); and Francisco Romero, *Ortega y Gasset y el problema de la jefatura espiritual, y otros ensayos* (Buenos Aires, 1960).

which surround it. As Ortega's thought is developed, activism characterizes this relationship: life is then defined as what I do with those things which make up my "circumstance." Ortega stresses that this action upon "that which surrounds us" must not be haphazard or undirected; rather one chooses a "mission," a "project," a destiny. The amount of freedom enjoyed by the individual to act within his "circumstance" is a nice question, but one which would carry this discussion far afield.[36] Life—the radical reality—is in Ortega's view a project, a "doing"; it must be thought of as a verb rather than as a noun. This position—formulated as early as the 1920's—has a decidedly existential flavor; however, the exact nature of Ortega's relationship to the mainstream of existentialism is an involved problem and one which has been studied at length elsewhere.[37]

Ortega's view of reality bears closer analysis in any attempt to relate his thought to Spanish America. If the radical reality—life —is looked upon as an interaction between the individual and his circumstance, then the path to reality becomes a very personal, individual process of first recognizing the authentic circumstance, and subsequently acting upon it. Following this line of thought, it can be seen that an Argentinean or a Mexican may approach the radical reality—by analyzing his circumstance and then acting upon it—just as effectively as one of Ortega's famous mentors at Marburg. Carrying the logic of the position a bit further, the Argentinean or Mexican is virtually *condemned* to seek reality in terms of interaction with his own circumstance; for him to pursue it through bookish "universal" philosophic systems, evolved in terms of a very different "circumstance," would be unthinkable. As early as 1910 Ortega himself stated that he was seeking "the Spanish interpretation of the world."[38] The implications of Ortega's fundamental position were tremendous in the context of the Spanish American intellectual scene of the 1920's. Budding philosophers could take heart in the knowledge that their efforts now had a validity undreamed of a few years earlier; and the careful investigation of the "circumstance"—in all its aspects—acquired fresh significance and greater urgency.

Ortega's actual contact with Spanish America antedates his Argentine visit of 1916. Alfonso Reyes speaks of his acquaintance

36. See especially Rodríguez Alcalá's discussion of this question in his study cited above, note 35.
37. See José Sánchez Villaseñor, *Ortega y Gasset, Existentialist* (Chicago, 1944).
38. Cited by Marías, *El existencialismo*, p. 46.

with Ortega in Europe during 1914.[39] In the same year Ortega published an important article "La voluntad del barroco" in the *Revista de América*, a journal whose significance we have already noted. This article, though written before the young philosopher had worked out his theory of *la razón vital*, complements the analysis of Spanish American intellectual development presented in the previous chapter, for in it Ortega comes out clearly for "overcoming determinism, that is, the materialistic determinism ... of the physical realm."[40] The 1916 visit itself made a deep impression on the writers of the Río Plata region. One critic has suggested that it was this onslaught of Orteguian ideas which induced that staunch defender of positivism, José Ingenieros, to attempt the reconciliation of science and metaphysics in his *Proposiciones relativas al porvenir de la filosofía* (1918).[41] Years later, Alejandro Korn called Ortega's coming "an event," and there is evidence that Korn's own philosophic trajectory was altered substantially at about this time.[42]

Ortega seemed particularly skillful in passing out left-handed compliments to Spanish America. In his 1924 piece, "Carta a un joven argentino que estudia filosofía," he praises the vigor, freshness, and vitality of America; but he also chastises Argentineans (and Americans in general) for not having enough intellectual discipline.[43] In his more extensive "Hegel y América" he restates the German philosopher's basic distinction between the "True State" and "Nature". In the "True State" historical development (the manifestation of *Spirit*, to use Hegel's peculiar terminology) takes place, and thus events follow each other as part of a meaningful pattern. In "Nature," however, events simply are repeated, and often identically; there is no development, no trajectory—in short, history does not exist.[44] Since Hegel felt that the "True State" could only be found in areas which had a relatively dense population and which had already reached a certain degree of civilization, it is clear that in the Hegelian view America must be relegated to the ahistoric world of Nature.[45] Another point which Ortega apparently accepts is that

39. Alfonso Reyes, "Treno para Ortega y Gasset," *Cuadernos Americanos*, XV (Jan.-Feb., 1956), 65-67.
40. José Ortega y Gasset, "La voluntad del barroco," *Revista de América*, IV (June-July, 1914), 89.
41. See Julio Endara, *José Ingenieros y el porvenir de la filosofía* (Quito, 1921).
42. Zum Felde, *Indice crítico*, pp. 429-30. See also the article by Alejandro Korn, "Filosofía argentina," *Nosotros*, LVII (1927), 52-65.
43. José Ortega y Gasset, *Obras completas* (4th ed.; Madrid: Revista de Occidente, 1957), II, 350.
44. *Ibid.*, p. 568.
45. *Ibid.*, pp. 569-70.

when a European comes to dwell in the wilds of the natural realm, in this case America, he reverts to a kind of primitive.[46] Ortega interprets these ideas rather optimistically: the primitivism of the New World is vigorous and virile; Americans may be likened to the Germanic barbarians who roamed Europe 2,000 years ago.[47] In short the future belongs to the Americas.[48] The problem of how the transition from the natural realm to that status which permits true historical development to occur is, however, not discussed. In this same article, Ortega seems to agree with another curious Hegelian viewpoint; namely, that the flora and fauna (including the human stock) of America were weak or "frail."[49] This point is not developed in any detail, nor has it, to my knowledge, been taken up by Ortega's Spanish American readers.

The natural realm, especially the influence of the land, is the point of departure for the Spanish thinker's third essay on New World themes. In "La pampa . . . promesas" Ortega offers the interesting view that Argentine character has been deeply affected by the presence of an ever-receding, ever-"promising" horizon.[50] This situation leads to a constant projecting forward, to a constant existence "outside of oneself" and, in retrospect, to a profound sense of frustration and emptiness.[51] When a European speaks with an Argentinean he feels this as a kind of absence: "his intimacy is not present. What we see is, then, a mask. . . . To sum up, we note a lack of authenticity."[52] The falseness or insincerity is further aggravated by the Argentinean's defensiveness. Unlike the European, the Argentinean is incapable of "giving himself" completely to anything; he goes around within a shell of fear, perhaps brought on by the constant challenge of the newly arrived immigrant coupled with a deep-seated sense of his own hollowness: "he doesn't devote himself wholly to anything, he hasn't irrevocably submerged his existence in the service of something outside himself."[53] Ortega even suggests that if one were to examine the sexual life of the typical Argentinean he would likely find this same inability to "give oneself" completely (*entregarse*).[54] By far the most interesting point made in

46. *Ibid.*, p. 575.
47. *Ibid.*, p. 576.
48. *Ibid.*
49. *Ibid.*, p. 571.
50. *Ibid.*, pp. 637-38.
51. *Ibid.*, p. 640.
52. *Ibid.*, p. 650.
53. *Ibid.*, p. 658.
54. *Ibid.*, p. 659.

the essay is closely related to the earlier matter of authenticity. Ortega finds in Argentine life an endemic "narcissism" which is doubly pernicious since the image that is contemplated is hazy and poorly defined. Nevertheless the Argentinean remains infatuated with this fuzzy reflection of his true self.[55] Ortega closes his essay with the plea that a select minority of intellectuals lead the nation toward a recognition of her true image and "authentic" nature. If this is not done, Argentina's narcissism will keep her living in an unreal, hollow world; ". . . the serious thing about narcissism isn't that it disregards others, but that it tends to make one take no notice of his own real person. . . ."[56] Reaction to these specific essays and to the general lines of Ortega's thought abound in the writing of many of Spanish America's most outstanding essayists. Alfonso Reyes declared "his trip to America has given a new direction to this 'discovery of one's self' to which Ortega is commited,"[57] while the lesser-known, but extremely interesting Peruvian essayist, Antenor Orrego, has considered the concept of *razón vital* as a major advance in transforming philosophy from a dry, bookish discipline to a living instrument for probing reality.[58] Further echos of Ortega's impact in Spanish America will become apparent as our study progresses. At this point, however, the role played by another foreign visitor, Waldo Frank, must be examined.

Waldo David Frank was part of a North American literary and critical reaction which in certain respects was similar to that initiated by Rodó and the *arielistas*. Frank himself marks the genesis of this new era of "cultural criticism" by the publication, in 1909, of Herbert Croly's essay, *The Promise of American Life*.[59] Although Croly's "fidelity to atrophied instruments for transformation" had only

55. *Ibid.*, pp. 660-62.
56. *Ibid.*, p. 663.
57. Alfonso Reyes, "José Ortega y Gasset," *Cuba contemporánea*, XVI (Jan., 1918), 53.
58. Antenor Orrego, "¿Cuál es la cultura que creará América?," *Amauta*, II (April, 1928), 3-4. Further indications of Ortega's decisive influence in Spanish America abound. Leopoldo Zea has stated ". . . la aportación de Ortega a la América Ibérica . . . dió a esta preocupación por la realidad americana la dignidad de una filosofía, la dignidad de una ciencia; la de la ciencia europea, la ciencia occidental. . . ." This statement appears in his article "Ortega el Americano," *Cuadernos Americanos*, XV (Jan.-Feb., 1956), 138. This entire number of the *Cuadernos* is a homage to Ortega and includes several other valuable pieces on his impact in Spanish America. Even more recently Juan Carlos Ghiano has written, "En la Argentina de los últimos treinta años, el ensayo ha sido por lo general la forma expresiva de aplicados y casi siempre deslumbrados lectores de Ortega y Gasset. La influencia orteguiana ha amparado a ensayistas de los más diversos temas, en actitudes ampliadas y renovadas en los últimos años." Ghiano, "De ensayistas," *Ficción*, No. 27 (Sept.-Oct., 1961) p. 88.
59. Waldo Frank, *The Re-discovery of America* (New York, 1929), p. 314.

slight appeal, the lyricism in the movement and the emphasis on "the person" attracted Frank considerably. A more radical culture critique, that of Van Wyck Brooks, was more to his liking.[60] The appearance of the review *The Seven Arts* in 1916, edited by Brooks, Frank, and James Oppenheim provided Frank with a vehicle for what he himself calls his "literary polemics." A number of important collaborators contributed to *The Seven Arts'* "groping and experimenting in an aesthetic life": John Dewey, Theodore Dreiser, H. L. Mencken, Louis Untermeyer, and Sherwood Anderson. The group's efforts according to Frank, "converge into a national program after Whitman, by which America shall become a creative focus in the modern world."[61] *Our America*, Frank's book of 1919, grew out of the preoccupations of the *Seven Arts* group. The work, the author claims, "stem from Whitman and Brooks: it begins also with the attempt to form a usable past and from the analysis of the background to distill an energy for the future. Dynamically, it is a drama and a call."[62] Frank himself admits that his book was "theoretical," "diffuse," and that "it rested at the verbal level."[63] In it he analyzes the wide gap between American idealistic aspirations and the actual facts. Though the book called for a profound revolution, the precise nature of such a revolt was unclear; and the chief accomplishment of the work was to spread American discontent, at least among Frank's sympathizers.

Frank's interest in and fascination with Hispanic peoples dates from a visit to Pueblo, Colorado, in 1917. Here he was struck by the economic and cultural poverty of the Mexican-Americans living in a typically modern, dreary industrial town. Coming from a Jewish background, Frank has consistently shown a good deal of sensitivity to minority problems. However, his interest in minorities involved more than the usual "liberal" concern over their being the victims of social and economic prejudice; it was the loss of cultural identity which most disturbed him. In his *Re-discovery of America* (1929) the metaphor of American culture as a "symphony orchestra" all playing the same theme on different instruments and having distinctive timbres frequently appears.[64] It is in this manner that each individual group—the Negro, the Irish, the Mexican, the Jew, etc.—is part of the one national "integration" and yet retains its

60. *Ibid.*, pp. 316-17.
61. *Ibid.*, p. 318.
62. *Ibid.*, p. 319.
63. *Ibid.*, p. 320.
64. *Ibid.*, pp. 259-60.

ethnic tonality. When Frank speaks of the New World as a greater integrated Whole (this word, and many others are accorded the capital letter in his rather inflated style) the Indian, the mestizo, and the European immigrant are similar units within the totality. Frank's visits to Europe were undertaken first in response to his deep interest in French literature, and then later, in response to his fascination with Spain. Aside from the immediate fruits of his European experience—his book *Virgin Spain* (1926)—Frank notes that it was through his intimate contact with the Old World that his ideas regarding America were greatly clarified. This process, incidentally, is clearly paralleled in the European experience of a host of Spanish American essayists. Vasconcelos, Rojas, Reyes, José Mariátegui, and more recently, Octavio Paz, have found in the Old World a valuable vantage point from which to reshape their views of America.

In 1921 the Mexican writer, J. J. Tablada while in the United States representing his government, happened to read *Our America*. Struck by Frank's sympathetic attitude toward the Mexicans of Colorado, Tablada translated a portion of the work for publication in the Mexican daily, *Excelsior*. Shortly afterward, in March of 1922, his translation was reprinted in one of the major literary vehicles of Spanish American unity, the review *El Repertorio Americano*. Appended to the translation was Tablada's remark, "we deem very important . . . a new attitude on the part of North Americans as regards our universal values."[65] In the mid-twenties, while in Spain gathering material for *Virgin Spain*, Frank became friendly with a number of important Spanish Americans. Alfonso Reyes, then in Madrid, recalls his early acquaintance with this atypical North American: "It seems to me that our successive meetings, fused in a symphony of friendship, are becoming more and more meaningful for us both, at least in our conception of the American destiny. . . . We are forging plans regarding better mutual understanding among our respective literary colleagues. The dream of two writers has come to be an unquestionable human need."[66] It was at this time that Frank, distressed at the deteriorating relations between the governments of the United States and Latin America, composed a "Message to the Intellectuals of Hispano-America" which he en-

65. Waldo Frank, "México en Norteamérica: como se juzga nuestra cultura," trans. J. J. Tablada, in *Repertorio Americano*, III (1922), 406.
66. *Obras completas de Alfonso Reyes* (Mexico, 1956), XI, 139-40. Subsequent citations from Reyes will be from this work and will be noted as *Obras*.

trusted to Reyes for personal delivery. The burden of this message was simply that the writers of Anglo America and Hispanic America must become friends.[67] Frank added that faith must be placed in the "minority" of both Americas and that the intellectuals were fighting a "common enemy." The message was published in various places, including the widely circulated *Repertorio Americano*, where it appeared as the "Mensaje a los escritores mexicanos."[68]

Frank's associations with the Hispanic world increased markedly in the period following. His views on Spanish history and character were aired in a *Revista de Occidente* article of 1925;[69] soon afterward Ortega's publishing house put out *España virgen*, a translation of the North American's popular book. The great Peruvian Leftist, José Mariátegui, wrote of Frank in the mid-twenties, and the two were destined soon to become close friends. In 1927 the influential organ of Peruvian radicalism, *Amauta*, published translated selections from a series of magazine articles which were to be incorporated in his crucial book, *The Re-discovery of America*.[70] Thus, in 1928 when Frank was invited to Buenos Aires by the Argentinean publisher and writer, Samuel Glusberg, he was already a familiar figure to many.

Just what did Waldo Frank represent in the eyes of the audience which greeted him in his Spanish American tour of 1929? Here was a man, they felt, who was the spokesman of the "other" North America; the North America of the intellectual minority, of Whitman, Emerson, and Poe; rather than that of the politicians, the generals, and the bankers. Here was a man who might well be a Yankee Rodó; a man who could praise, in the dedication of his *Re-discovery of America*, "the view of America as a democratic nation led by an aristocracy of spirit. . . ."

The essence of what Frank said to Spanish America (in dozens of speeches, lectures, and personal contacts) may be found in the *Re-discovery* and in a work published shortly after his return to the United States, *America Hispana: A Portrait and a Prospect* (1931). In the earlier work, Frank begins with an analysis of the crucial matter of the Old World's relationship to the New. The discovery of America, he feels, is misunderstood and misjudged. In the fifteenth century Europe discovered not a new land, but *the Ocean*

67. See the discussion of Frank's message in M. J. Bernardete (ed.), *Waldo Frank in America Hispana* (New York, 1930), pp. 82-90. This volume is a collection of varia, chiefly articles and speeches dedicated to Frank by Spanish Americans. The translations presumably are by Bernardete.
68. Waldo Frank, quoted in *Repertorio Americano*, VIII (1924), 305-6.
69. Waldo Frank, "El español,." *Revista de Occidente*, X (1925), 39.
70. See *Amauta*, No. 14 (April, 1928).

". . . the antithesis of the Latin sea" which was "uncharted (and) led to limitless lands."[71] The contrast between what he calls the "old Way" (i.e., Europe and the Mediterranean world) and the "new" or "Atlantic Way" bears careful examination:

> Men's thoughts and dreams had bridged the Mediterranean. For ages, east and west, south and north, the littorals had mingled. Europe came of this. Now, parabola-wise, men's dreams move to the Ocean and Europe begins to die. The conquest of World power, by arms and science; the political crumbling of the Catholic state; the religious vagrancies that follow Luther—all the modern shifts in value and in power, are traits of Europe's dislocation. And they are traits, as well, of the New Way—the Atlantic. . . Europe bleeds seaward, into soils unknown.
>
> And the old Mediterranean dies. Into the Atlantic flows its death: the new search of man, the new earthwise boundlessness.[72]

The "dislocation" of Europe is virtually synonymous with the shattering of Europe's "wholeness," the concept of which is basic in Frank's thinking: "Wholeness is no mere desired goal; it is the origin and the end of all our creative being. Wholeness must be both personal and social, in order to be either. Individual man cannot achieve his health unless he live, consciously, within a Whole that holds all life."[73] Implied throughout Frank's writings is the idea that a new "Whole" must be created in America—and in broader terms—in the Americas. To do this, great "dislocative" forces must be overcome, not the least of which is the self-interested Will and its creation, the Machine, "the most perfect symbol of personal desire."[74] Frank repeatedly underscores the idea that the will (as expressed in egoism, jingoistic nationalism, etc.) is the destroyer of the desired unity: "We come to have a world where men were willful atoms—atoms of will—dissolved from what had been a spiritual Whole."[75] "Power," frequently contrasted with "love" in Frank's thinking, is equated with blindly imposed brute force. He who exercises "power" (as so defined) lacks true self-awareness and a "sense of the whole." Moreover, the personal will is "chaotic" and often ineffective, for it cannot fuse with a "synthesis greater than itself."[76] The "creative act"—love—be it sexual, intellectual,

71. Frank, *Re-discovery*, p. 18.
72. *Ibid.*
73. *Ibid.*, p. 19.
74. *Ibid.*, p. 44.
75. *Ibid.*
76. *Ibid.*, p. 79.

social, aesthetic, or mystic, transcends the individual ego, and though 'more Powerful than Power," is its antithesis.[77] Frank considers the worship of the machine and the use of machine methods to be examples of "power ill-used." As such they are constantly working at cross purposes with love which has as its goal the unity or "integration" of American society: "America is a herd longing to become a true society—frantically longing—It is . . . a potential Whole, and it must reach its organic health or rot and die. It strives to achieve this goal of Unity. . . . Our purpose is good. . . . But since the means we use is Power—child of chaos—we perpetuate our chaos."[78]

But Frank's pessimism is balanced by faith in what he calls "the peculiar energy of the American world—the forming life of our land which makes us all, Nordic and Negro, American. . . ."[79] This same mystique of the "American world," together with the continent's peculiar relationship to the Old World,

> relates us more essentially with the Indian or the Peruvian, than with our blood-brothers of Europe. This energy tends towards a passioned restraint; it is plastic, cruel, darkly exalted. It made the culture of Maya and Pueblo: it is already inscrutably at work within us and without: transfiguring our unconscious spirit, plotting the straight structure of our streets. It is so wondrously atune with our mystique tradition that one is almost ready to believe in an Atlantis. . . .[80]

Although both North America and "America Hispana" are profoundly united by this "peculiar energy of the New World" and the "longing" for the realization of an harmonious Whole, there are differences between the two cultures: "In one place (North America) there is order that lacks life, in the other, there is life that lacks order."[81] This lack of order is further aggravated by an anomaly which, though evident throughout the New World, is particularly pronounced in Hispanic America: the Spanish American, Frank feels, "is forced, by his young and deliberate world to live in a time to which he is essentially alien. This . . . leads, again, to pathos—the pathos of the man abiding forever in strangeness. All these affinities

77. *Ibid.*, p. 80. Note the parallelism in Frank's love-power polarity and the opposition of love and will in Caso's thought, as discussed in Chapter III, pp. 50-53.
78. *Ibid.*, p. 83.
79. *Ibid.*, p. 229.
80. *Ibid.*, p. 230.
81. Waldo Frank, *America Hispana: A Portrait and a Prospect* (New York, 1931), p. 340.

have, then, a minor key. All have lostness or longing or tragedy within them."[82]

Much of what Frank said struck a responsive chord among his audience. For one thing the very style of his speeches, articles, and books had a certain indefinable Latin flavor. English speakers might well consider his writing wordy, diffuse, and perhaps pompous: yet his verbal display and his penchant for the *recherché* term were obviously appreciated in Hispanic countries. The fact that he loved the Spanish language and spoke it rather well also added immeasureably to his popularity. His warm friendship for Spanish America, his outspoken criticism of North American power politics, his passionate nature, and his fervently humanistic approach to philosophic questions, all served to endear him to his audience. His emphasis on certain ideas—albeit already "in the air" in Spanish America— helped a number of Spanish American essayists to crystallize their own thoughts. Among the many Frankian themes most frequently reflected in Spanish America are the following: the belief in a mystical, all-encompassing American spirit; the recognition of a profoundly erotic element in man; the view that ideally society should be an integrated, but not homogenous, whole (i.e., the "symphonic" image); the feeling that the present-day American inhabits an alien or unnatural world; the conviction that modern technological society is in effect a "machine jungle"; and finally, the idea that genuine self-awareness (cf., Ortega's "authenticity") is necessary before the individual or group can become fused into the desired whole.

That Frank was very well received on his 1929 tour of the southern continent is eloquently confirmed by a glance at the many articles, editorials, and reprints of speeches which subsequently appeared in Spanish America's leading journals and newspapers.[83] His eulogists were many and distinguished while his detractors were few and obscure. In some instances entire issues of journals were dedicated to him, as is the case of the Cuban Leftist magazine *Avance* or the important Argentine review *Síntesis*.[84] The editors of the journal *Crítica* considered Frank to be "among the first Americans who have existed; that is to say, he is the American of both North and South who will be the future man of this continent." In Mexico, where Frank lectured at the University's summer school, the critic Julio

82. *Ibid.*, p. 337.
83. A handy compendium of these writings may be found in Bernardete, *Frank in America Hispana.*
84. See *Avance*, No. 42 (Jan., 1930); and *Síntesis*, No. 29 (Oct., 1929).

Jiménez Rueda seconded earlier expressions of Mexican friendship toward the North-American writer by praising Frank warmly in the influential journal *Contemporàneos*.[85] The leading Cuban essayist, Jorge Mañach, gave him a glowing eulogy on the occasion of his speech before the Instituto Hispano-Cubano de Cultura;[86] and the Peruvian, Luis Alberto Sánchez, was similarly generous in his praise when Frank was awarded an honorary doctorate by San Marcos.[87] A list of the Argentine writers who received Frank's message sympathetically would include some of the most illustrious literary figures of the day: Leopoldo Lugones, Alfredo Colmo, Alberto Gerchunoff, and Ezequiel Martínez Estrada were among the leaders in this chorus of praise.[88] Leon Dujovne and Coriolano Alberini, both philosophers rather than creative writers, discussed Frank in his relation to contemporary intellectual movements. Alberini analyzed in considerable detail the *Re-discovery of America* for the Argentine audience,[89] while Dujovne contrasted Frank's profound optimism, his lack of jingoism, and his emphasis on cultural unity with Spengler's pessimistic views regarding the decline of occidental civilization.[90] One of Frank's most fruitful personal associations in Buenos Aires was with Victoria Ocampo, who had many conversations with the North American preparatory to her founding, in 1931, of the great Argentine review *Sur*. Years later Ocampo fondly recalled discussing with Frank in Buenos Aires and in New York plans for establishing a new "ecumenical" journal, one that would include ". . . toda la América . . . la de Waldo como la de Gabriela Mistral, Alfonso Reyes, Germán Arciniegas, Jorge Amado, Pedro Henríquez Ureña, Juan Marinello."[91] Ocampo, whose position as an intellectual leader of Spanish America should not be underestimated, has stated of Frank that he was "the first North American with whom I had been able to speak of our problems."[92]

85. Julio Jiménez Rueda, "La visita de Waldo Frank," *Contemporáneos*, IV (1929), 357-58, reprinted in *Repertorio Americano*, XIX (1929), 202.
86. See Bernardete, *Frank in America Hispana*, p. 72.
87. *Ibid.*, pp. 110-27.
88. Of particular interest is the poem "A Waldo Frank" by Martínez Estrada. Published earlier in the magazine *Vida Literaria* it is reprinted by Bernardete, *Frank in America Hispana*, pp. 236-37.
89. Coriolano Alberini, "Waldo Frank en la Facultad de Filosofía y Letras," *Síntesis*, No. 29 (Oct., 1929), pp. 117-25.
90. Leon Dujovne, "Waldo Frank y Spengler," *La Vida Literaria*, No. 15 (Oct., 1929), p. 7. The same article also appeared in *Síntesis*, No. 29 (Oct., 1929), pp. 159-69.
91. Victoria Ocampo, "Waldo Frank en Buenos Aires," *Sur*, No. 92 (May, 1942), p. 75.
92. Victoria Ocampo, "Carta a Waldo Frank," *Sur*, No. 75 (Dec., 1940), p. 13.

Frank and Ortega, despite many differences in personality and in intellectual orientation, drew Spanish America's attention to certain basic themes which have contributed substantially to the essay of the past three decades. Both visitors exhorted Spanish Americans to "know themselves," to seek "authenticity," or self-awareness. Both professed a rather mystical or "poetic" belief in the power of the land to shape the destiny of man and society; yet both felt that life was an active project over which man could exercise a fair measure of control. Both were fascinated by the native American: Ortega, with characteristic aristocratic condescension, tended to consider him a promising primitive, while Frank implies that the Indian, by dint of his receptivity to "the peculiar energy of the American World," was more of a blood brother to "white" Americans than to the racially similar European. Both writers shared a deep fear of the tendency of modern civilization to make of man a thing, a cog in a vast social machine: Ortega wrote often of the perils of *"deshumanización,"* while Frank's description of twentieth-century American society as a "mechanical jungle" was insidiously appealing.[93]

The parallel between these two thinkers may not, however, be carried too far. Frank's influence cannot be compared with that of Ortega when we consider the role of the Spanish essayist as a disseminator of European thought. And Frank's impact as a contributor to the English language *New Republic* was likewise less than that of Ortega, the editor of the widely read *Revista de Occidente.* On the other side of the ledger, however, Frank's personal appeal to Spanish Americans was apparently far greater than Ortega's. The North American, as a representative of an intellectual and ethnic minority, could be thought of as an underdog—a role whose universal appeal seems particularly strong in Hispanic America. The Spaniard, on the other hand, represented the sophisticated mother country which tended to look upon the New World as a mere colonial upstart. Furthermore, there were certain intellectual circles —principally the very substantial radical Left of the 1920's and 1930's—which found a kindred spirit in Frank but which could find little common ground with the more conservative Ortega.

The quest for a new Americanism was certainly enriched by the contributions of Frank and Ortega. Along with other foreign writers and visitors they helped Spanish Americans refine the rather ingenuous nativism of earlier essayists such as Rojas, Vasconcelos,

93. See Dujovne's article (note 90 above) for a Spanish American appreciation of this point.

and Tamayo. Thus, by the third decade of the present century, this quest becomes noticeably more complex and more sophisticated. Of great significance too is the fact that the theme of America's rediscovery became a truly hemispheric concern. Typical of this later phase of this preoccupation is the work of Alfonso Reyes, Mexico's most distinguished essayist. An important link between the *Generación del Ateneo* and present-day writers, Reyes touched upon this theme frequently during his long career. His essays "Discurso por Virgilio" (1933) and "Posición de América" (1942) are particularly good examples of his Americanist views. Reyes' close friend and collaborator in the *Ateneo*, Pedro Henríquez Ureña, has shown a similar interest in broad questions of Americanism. Although a Dominican by birth, Henríquez Ureña's activities as writer, educator, and literary historian have brought him to Argentina, to Mexico, and to the United States. Such essays as his *La Utopía de América* (1925) and *Seis ensayos en busca de nuestra expresión* (1928) attest the sincerity of his *novomundismo*. The somewhat narrower indigenist trend, the earlier development of which has already been discussed, has been continued by several writers, particularly by essayists of the Andean region such as José Uriel García, Guillermo Francovich, and Fernando Díez de Medina. Of interest also are the Peruvian radicals whose Americanist concern has been inextricably linked with questions of basic political philosophy: José Carlos Mariátegui, Antenor Orrego, and Victor Raúl Haya de la Torre. Considering the great importance of these writers as radical thinkers, their work will be discussed in a later chapter. The interest in Americanist themes has continued unabated in a number of fine essays of the more recent past. This is evident in the work of Colombia's Germán Arciniegas; in the prolific writings of Peru's Luis Alberto Sánchez, the author of *¿Existe América Latina?* (1945); and in the provocative essay of the naturalized Colombian, Víctor Frankl, *Espíritu y camino de Hispanoamérica* (1953). A number of writers to be discussed in later chapters are clearly Americanists, though their work has other facets upon which our attention will be centered: thus, such essays as *El pecado original de América* (1958) by Argentina's H. A. Murena, or *América en la conciencia de Europa* (1955) by the Mexican Leopoldo Zea could justifiably have been included at this point.

The unifying thread which binds these essays together is the recognition that there exists a problem, or group of related problems, which must be solved if Spanish America is to fulfill its destiny. Our analysis of this more recent phase of the rediscovery of America begins rightfully with the work of Waldo Frank's message-bearer to Hispanic America, the late Alfonso Reyes. To attempt to isolate one theme—or even one cluster of related themes—in the work of Mexico's most prolific essayist is no simple task. Some of Reyes' most penetrating views on broad matters of *novomundismo* are found in rather unlikely places, as in his "Discurso por Virgilio" (1933). True to the classical tradition, Reyes is quick to point out that man's social and individual nature show a remarkable constancy across vast realms of time and space. Thus, he can relate a plan of the Mexican government to develop local viniculture and cottage industries with similar motifs in Virgil's *Georgics*. It is in this essay on the Virgilian theme that Reyes expresses his own broad Americanist faith, born of a profound love for classic literature and for his native Mexico. The great literary works of the western European tradition—and especially those of Greece and Rome—are not "foreign" or "exotic" to the American scene, he tells us. Properly appreciated, they are means by which our own indigenous world can be better revealed: "I wish that the Humanities (be) the natural vehicle of expression for everything autochthonous."[94] In the context of Mexico's vigorous but often superficial indigenism of the 1920's, Reyes' comments on the relationship between nativism and Old World culture were extremely timely. First of all he wisely observed that what is genuinely autochthonous will manifest itself in the work of a writer, painter, or thinker of its own accord. Since *lo autóctono* is part of the very make-up of the person one need not be deliberately "nativist": "this instinctive tendency (nativism) is so evident that to defend it with sophisms is to deprive it of its greatest virtue: its spontaneity."[95] He then warns his countrymen not to deceive themselves, for although "the autochthonous element (is), in our America an enormous lode of raw material, of artifacts, of forms, of colors and sounds,"[96] only the barest fragments of the world of the pre-Columbian is known today. Therefore Reyes holds that any return to the primitivism of the Aztec would be unthinkable. By contrast, he stoutly maintains that "until now the only waters which have bathed us are . . . Latin waters."[97] Though Reyes does not carry his metaphor any further, it is not unreasonable to view these "Latin waters" as the agent by which the gold of the autochthonous

94. Reyes, *Obras*, XI, 160.
95. *Ibid.*, p. 161.
96. *Ibid.*
97. *Ibid.*

mineral lode is revealed in all its purity, washed clean of its dross. Reyes' view of what he calls "the hour of America" is decidedly ecumenical: he frequently states that the mission of the New World is to overcome the divisive effects of racism and of cultual jingoism. Support for such a program may be found, he notes, in Vasconcelos' vision of an amalgamated "Cosmic Race" and in Waldo Frank's deep humanistic faith.[98]

In the "Discurso por Virgilio," Reyes touches upon a theme which has figured prominently in a number of Spanish American essays—the city as opposed to the country. He finds the basic terms of this polarity to be quite simple: in the city the "social act" dominates, the fundamental relationship being that of man with man; while in the country the relationship involves man with the land.[99] Reyes feels that human life, virtually by definition, is "a continuous reference to the natural ambience, an unending journey between man and external nature."[100] City life, though not actually attacked, is viewed as a kind of artificial creation, a setting up of barriers against the natural order of man's life. Country life, particularly that of the modest, hardworking landholder, is seen as "The balsam (that) soothes the wounds of politics."[101] More concretely, it is a means for the absorption of immigrants into the national life. Throughout Reyes' discussion of the city versus country theme, this Virgilian attitude toward the land dominates; it distinguishes his telluricism from that of many of his Spanish American contemporaries who view the "force of the land" in terms of the mystical, romantic adoration of nature's primal forces. In one of Reyes' earlier works, the beautifully wrought essay "Visión de Anahuac" (1917), he notes that this more romanticized feeling toward nature may be justified in much of the New World, (in the jungle, for example) but that his own Mexican plateau is characterized by "sparse and stylized vegetation, an organized landscape, an atmosphere of extreme clarity. . . ."[102] In short, he finds a distinctly "classic" spirit pervading the countryside of his beloved Anahuac. Although it would be misleading to consider Reyes a believer in rigid geographic determinism—the very antithesis of the classically humanist view of nature—we have seen him speak of man's "continuous reference to the natural ambience." Thus, in the "Visión de Anahuac" he

98. *Ibid.*, XI, 172.
99. *Ibid.*, p. 175.
100. *Ibid.*
101. *Ibid.*
102. *Ibid.*, II, 16.

suggests that there is a real link, disregarding all questions of blood, between the Mexican of today and the pre-Columbian Indian. This link exists since both peoples had the same natural environment with which to contend, and since "the everyday emotion produced by the same natural object" engenders a common spirit.[103] As we have seen, substantially the same view was professed by Reyes' Argentine contemporary, Ricardo Rojas, and by Waldo Frank when he wrote of "the forming life of our land."

Reyes has developed his idea of what I have called the New Americanism in an impressive number of essays, historical studies, articles, and speeches. Two of these, "Notas sobre la inteligencia Americana" (1937) and "Posición de América" (1942), merit special attention in that they present Reyes' profoundest meditations on the important theme of the relationship of the Old World to the New. In a sense the second essay is a clarification of the first. In 1936 Reyes participated in a series of conferences, held in Buenos Aires under the auspices of the *Instituto Internacional de Cooperación Intelectual,* dealing with the theme "Present-day relations between European and Latin American cultures."[104] George Duhamel initiated the meeting stating the European viewpoint; Reyes presented the first statement for Latin America. In the "Posición de América" he notes that this paper, "Notas Sobre la Inteligencia Americana," was in part misunderstood by some of the distinguished Europeans present. Reyes spoke of an American cultural synthesis which would involve two elements: "a unique balance between our understanding of intellectual activity as public service and as cultural responsibility," and a fusion of autochthonous elements with the "intellectual instruments" of Europe.[105] The product of such a synthesis would be, moreover, greater than the mere sum of its parts. At the Buenos Aires conference Reyes expressed the hope that this distinctive American culture would fulfill the utopian dream of a New World—a dream which formed part of Europe's literature and folklore even before Columbus' voyage. Referring to the Europeans' misunderstanding of his term "cultural synthesis" at this meeting, he states:

> Some of those present remained sadly convinced that we were trying to reduce the function of the American mind to the mere

103. *Ibid.,* p. 34.
104. *Ibid.,* XI, 82. Some of the distinguished Europeans present were George Duhamel, Jacques Maritain, Emil Ludwig, Jules Romains, Stefan Zweig; among the Spanish Americans, Baldomero Sanín Cano, Perdo Henríquez Ureña, and Francisco Romero.
105. *Ibid.,* XI, 86.

organizing of compendiums of European culture. Above all, we would not have recourse only to the European tradition, but to the entire human heritage. . . . Lastly, in this synthesis we do not envision a compendium or resumé just as hydrogen and oxygen on combining in the form of water do not produce a mere sum of the parts but a new substance, possessing, as does any true synthesis, new powers and qualities.[106]

In these two essays Reyes constantly emphasizes that the fulfillment of the American destiny is a responsibility to Europe ("If the European economy has come to have need of us, so ultimately will the European *inteligentsia* have need of us"[107]) or, in broader terms, a responsibility to humanity. Retaining the fervent activism of his early association with the *Ateneo de la Juventud* group, Reyes has been more concerned with the ability of the New World to meet this obligation than with the problem of "choosing" between universalism and nativism. As we have seen, for Reyes there is really no problem of a choice here. Whether he employs the metaphor of the "autochthonous mineral lode" noted previously, or the interesting analogy of culture and a series of concentric circles—as in the "Posición de América" [108]—his message is clear: the Universal and the Particular have a complementary relationship; they "nourish" each other; and a society based solely on what he terms "alternatives and peculiarities" would be unthinkable, just as would be a purely "Universal" culture. A final note regarding Reyes' concept of the American cultural synthesis is in order. Several times in these essays he states that although he is restricting himself to Latin America, there are broad grounds for cultural fusion with Anglo-Saxon America: "We do not feel that one may speak seriously of unsurpassable barriers to cultural synthesis. . . ."[109] At the conclusion of the "Posición de América" he looks upon the American synthesis in broad philosophical terms. Drawing from the rich thought of one of the Spanish American intellectuals' favorite sources, Max Scheler,[110] Reyes notes that one of the great problems to be resolved before this synthesis may be achieved is that of reconciling three basic types of knowledge: the Hindu knowledge of salvation through psychic and bodily self-

106. *Ibid.*, p. 265.
107. *Ibid.*
108. *Ibid.*, XI, 257.
109. *Ibid.*, p. 269.
110. Max Scheler (1874-1928) is perhaps better known to Spanish Americans than he is to North Americans. A German philosopher, academician, and at times, a freelance writer, he was introduced to the Hispanic world through Ortega's *Revista de Occidente* in the mid-1920's. The English titles of some of his best-known works are *The Nature of Sympathy, Man's Place in Nature, On the Eternal in Man,* as well as

control; the wisdom (*saber culto*) of ancient Greece and China; and finally the scientific, practically motivated, knowledge of the western European tradition. Citing Scheler directly he notes, "the time has come to open the way towards an assimilation, and at the same time, towards an integration of these three partial tendencies of the human spirit."[111] The "integration" called for by Scheler is precisely what Reyes would wish America to achieve. The continent, if it is to accomplish its mission, must not develop one of these types of knowledge at the expense of the others:

> Pure knowledge of salvation will convert us into prostrate peoples, into thin, mendicant friars; pure knowledge of culture, into sophists and mandarins; pure knowledge of technique, into scientific barbarians which, as we have seen, is the worst kind of barbarism. Only a balance of all these will insure our loyalty to heaven and earth. Such is the mission of America.[112]

Pedro Henríquez Ureña has, in his *Seis ensayos en busca de nuestra expresión*, investigated the specific question of whether original cultural contributions are even possible in Hispanic America. The fact that a common history has been shared with Europe does not preordain the failure of the New World's attempts at original expression. He feels that the Old World's tradition determines to a great extent the "forms" of American culture, but that "the unique character of a people comes from its spiritual depths, from its native energy."[113] The method by which original and authentic expression may be attained is one of deep probing involving considerable effort: ". . . there is but one secret here: work at it deeply, make every effort to obtain pure expression by descending to the very roots of the things we wish to say, to refine, to clarify. . . ."[114] As in the case of many contemporary Spanish American essayists, Henríquez Ureña maintains that the writer or artist of the New World should, if he truly desires to attain authentic cultural achievements, embark upon a profound search of his own "spiritual depths." He does not carry this view further, as others will do. He does not, for example,

---

several more technical volumes in ethics and axiology. For a good resumé of his philosophic position, see the "Translator's Introduction" to *Man's Place in Nature*, trans. Hans Meyerhoff (New York, 1961), pp. ix-xxxv. Meyerhoff views Scheler as a follower of Husserl's phenomenology who has also incorporated, but never fused, divergent "philosophies of life" (Nietzsche, Bergson, and Dilthey) into his general world view.
111. Reyes, *Obras*, XI, 270.
112. *Ibid.*
113. Pedro Henríquez Ureña, *Obra crítica* (Mexico, 1960), p. 251.
114. *Ibid.*

suggest that this kind of intensive analysis of the self yields not only authenticity and genuineness, but that it is, in effect, the only possible method for grasping reality.

In his later writings Henríquez Ureña has distinguished himself as a literary and cultural historian of great breadth. His work as a teacher of Hispanic literature in some of the hemisphere's greatest universities—including our own Harvard—encouraged him to write two invaluable works, *Literary Currents in Spanish America* (1945) and the posthumously published *Historia de la cultura en la América Hispánica* (1947). Although it is probably true that Henríquez Ureña's major contributions as an original thinker date from his very early association with the Mexican writers of the *Ateneo*, rather than from this later period of activity, his role as a highly skilled synthesizer and as a devoted Americanist cannot be overstated.

The delicate interrelationship of indigenism and universalism in the work of an Alfonso Reyes or the breadth of viewpoint of a Pedro Henríquez Ureña are not always evident in contemporary Americanist essays. There are good reasons why this "narrowing of the focus" should occur but to consider these now would anticipate the problems to be attacked in our final chapters. Writers of the Andean region—where interest in the Indian and the land on which he lives tends to dominate a good deal of the literary production—often display this somewhat more restricted view of Americanism. Nevertheless their work, in essays such as José Uriel García's *El nuevo indio* (1930), Guillermo Francovich's *Pachamama* (1942), and F. Díez de Medina's *Thunupa* (1947) and *Sariri* (1954), illustrates important facets of the *novomundista* concern. In their efforts to define the Indian and his place in Hispanic American culture, these writers attempt to clarify fundamental problems which though touched upon by Rojas, Vasconcelos, and Tamayo are as yet not completely resolved.

Telluricism—in the sense of a powerful, mystic force which the land exerts upon its inhabitants—is the dominant theme in the work of José Uriel García (1884——). Typical of many contemporary *indigenistas*, he feels that this force, rather than the biological determinants, molds man. The Indian is thus defined as "everyone whose inner being responds upon contact with the incentives that American nature offers and who feels that his spirit is rooted in the land."[115] And anyone, regardless of physical type, who comes to

115. José Uriel García, *El nuevo indio. Ensayos indianistas sobre la sierra superuana* (2ª edición corregida; Cuzco, 1937), p. 6.

the sierra, "open-hearted" and willing to saturate himself in the environment, may justifiably be called an "Indian."[116] Uriel García is intrigued by the indigenous folklore of his native Peru, and especially by the ancient Indian notion of *apu*, a kind of local spirit which may be embodied in a physical feature (a mountain or river) or in an animal totem. The *apu* is a unifying element in Indian life: although he calls for no reversion to indigenous superstition, Uriel García feels that a serious study of the *apu's* symbolic role would yield valuable insights into the political and social needs of the region.[117] Uriel García—not unlike Reyes in his criticism of the superficial, sentimentalized Indianism of the period—distinguishes carefully between the *incaismo* or antiquarian's interest in an ancient civilization, and *indianismo* which he defines as a "problem to be resolved."[118] Thus, though he may be fascinated by the communism of the Indian landholding system—the *ayllu*—he does not call for a return to this institution, despite the fact that he considers it "fresh and vigorous like everything primitive."[119] Like so many of the writers whom we shall discuss, Uriel García sees in the awakening of the Indian an effervescence, a brimming over of powerful primitive forces—"barbarism in ebullition, culture in germination," as he calls it. Paralleling Tamayo's Nietzschean attitudes and Ortega's love of the virile barbarian, he holds that the "redemption" of the Indian must be achieved while this wonderful vitality is retained. Although the Indian must be educated, economically elevated, and incorporated into the modern world, the indigenous spirit, the force of the sierra ("that wonderful retort of the New America's spiritual chemistry"[120]) should be conserved as a tremendous "reservoir" of energy. The intellectual, the educated indigenist, what Uriel calls the "nucleus," has the "moral obligation to open new channels for the outflow of this vast reservoir. . . ."[121]

Guillermo Francovich (1901———), one of Bolivia's leading *indigenistas*, has, in his dialogued essay *Pachamama*, analyzed a number of problems relating to the general theme of nativism and universalism. The essay is constructed as a conversation between a group of young Bolivians discussing the problem of the possible cultural autonomy of Spanish America. Several European writers

116. *Ibid.*, p. 8.
117. *Ibid.*, pp. 10ff.
118. *Ibid.*, p. 81.
119. *Ibid.*, p. 24.
120. *Ibid.*, p. 95.
121. *Ibid.*, p. 192.

are mentioned in support of the idea that through the catalytic action of European culture, a great new civilization will evolve in the New World. Max Scheler's concept of the fusion of Orient and Occident is introduced, as are similar ideas of Duhamel and Keyserling. Waldo Frank's thought figures prominently in the essay, as when one of the young men, in describing the desired new culture uses an "orchestral" figure very similar to that employed by the North American writer: "a kind of magnificent spiritual orchestration would come about, one in which each group of people would strike its own distinctive notes—notes which though different, would be complementary of each other."[122]

One of the most interesting clashes in the dialogue occurs when telluricism, or what one of the discussants calls *geofilosofía* is debated. The theme is introduced when it is recalled that Frank once said that the Andean natives were "children of the rocks,"[123] and that Keyserling on occasion commented that the American native was a "mineraloid" being.[124] Another member of the group suggests that there is, in effect, a deep cosmic subconscious in all men which is "formed by the forces of the natural environment."[125] It is further explained that the Indians, dimly aware of its existence, attributed this cosmic subconscious to man's common descent from the goddess Pachamama, whose very name is equivalent to "earth-mother." The idea is then developed that by probing this cosmic subconscious an inkling of a metaphysical realm of "a vast and higher reality" may be obtained.[126] Though it is not explicit, a decidedly Jungian note is struck in this discussion. The error of older philosophies, the essay continues, lies in attempting to discover this ultimate reality by use of reason: "it is not by means of our intelligence, it is not our reason which gives us the basis of its existence, but rather it is our body. . . ." The "ultimate reality" itself is mystically equated with "the land, the natural support of our life."[127] Interestingly enough this irrational viewpoint is roundly attacked by "Carlos," the speaker who is presented as having the soundest opinions of the group, and who perhaps represents the author's own position. Carlos relegates this *geofilosofía* to the category of untenable ideas

122. Guillermo Francovich, *Pachamama: diálogo sobre el porvenir de la cultura en Bolivia* (Asunción, n.d. [1942]), p. 16. Cf. Frank, *Re-discovery*, pp. 259-60.
123. Francovich, *Pachamama*, p. 31.
124. *Ibid.*, p. 46.
125. *Ibid.*, p. 54.
126. *Ibid.*, pp. 64-65.
127. *Ibid.*, p. 70.

which, like racism and Marxism, ignore the fundamentally autonomous nature of the human spirit.[128] Attacking both irrationalism
and the "antihumanist" determinism of Marx and Spengler, Carlos
calls for Spanish America to adopt a position which would be based
on "the idea of personality as the expression of the spirit and granting
reason domain over instinct and the irrational."[129] This position,
however, is in turn attacked when another discussant points out
that the supposedly "universalist" attitude has been responsible for
Bolivia's—and by extension, for Spanish America's—cultural sub-
ordination to Europe. Carlos defends and qualifies his argument
by pointing out that, on the one hand, "all cultural process is the
adoption by one group of the values discovered by others," and, on
the other, that a profoundly nationalistic search for one's own
"distinctive nature" will lead to a true universalism.[130] This search
must be concentrated upon internal elements in the culture rather
than upon superficialities of local color, picturesque nativism, etc.
In short originality must not be pursued as an ultimate objective,
but rather as an instrument for the deeper understanding of "human
universality."[131] This process is only suggested in Francovich's
essay; however, as we shall see in a later chapter, it has come to
occupy a central position in the very recent work of some of the continent's most distinguished writers.

A frequent contributor to Spanish America's leading journals, an
active nember of the Bolivian revolutionary movement which
triumphed in 1952 (*Movimiento Nacional Revolucionario*), and an
ardent student of Indian lore, Fernando Díez de Medina (1908———)
has been a vociferous, and often controversial, spokesman of Andean
indigenismo. Many of his articles, as well as his books *Thunupa*
(1947), *Sariri* (1954), and *Fantasia coral* (1958), are characterized
by a curious mélange of generous Americanism and personal prejudice. In the first of these works, his attitude is rather negative:
Aside from presenting a picture of the Kolla deity Thunupa (a
symbol of noble primitivism, a doer of good deeds, and a defender of
the just), he devotes himself principally to invective. The targets
of his attack include the United States, whose intellectual and
political paranoia is sharply criticized, and Alcides Arguedas, whose
racistic theories of the *pueblo enfermo* are roundly refuted. A good

128. *Ibid.*
129. *Ibid.*, p. 86.
130. *Ibid.*, p. 81.
131. *Ibid.*, p. 86.

many pages of the book are devoted, unfortunately to a personal squabble with his compatriot, Franz Tamayo. Though many of the criticisms in *Thunupa* are valid, the collection of essays makes few, if any, affirmative points.

By contrast, in "Sariri," the essay which serves as a title piece to his 1954 collection, Díez de Medina speaks in more substantive terms. Subtitled "An answer to Rodó's *Ariel*," the essay calls for Próspero to be replaced by a new Spanish American mentor—Sariri, the Indian traveler and teller of legends, who by his very nature "cannot remain silent and indifferent."[132] What obviously displeases Díez de Medina most about Rodó's attitudes is the "egoism of the man of erudition," the "excess of verbal jewelry," and the "lack of collective sensibility."[133] In short, Rodó strikes him as being effete, overly concerned with matters of style, aristocratic, and lacking in militancy. Whether Díez de Medina's estimate of Rodó is justified or not is less important than his contrast of the "humanism" of 1953 with that of 1900: "the cultured, cold, haughty, and exclusivistic humanism of 1900 is yielding to the social, warm, and frank humanism of 1953—an openly militant humanism, in search of a philosophy of reintegration, a philosophy that would be idealistic and at the same time capable of organizing the material realm. . . ."[134] This newer concept of the term "humanism" will, as we shall see, come to play an increasingly important role in shaping contemporary Spanish American attitudes, especially among the essayists of the Left.

Paralleling Rodó's masterpiece, Díez de Medina begins his essay by having Sariri introduce two opposing deities: Makuri, a decidedly Calibanesque figure, and Thunupa, the great activist, defender of the weak, and ameliorator of suffering. The fact that Thunupa represents the practical virtues rather than the vague idealism of Ariel is stressed repeatedly. The burden of the essay is presented in the simple tale of a struggle between the two gods. The maleficent Makuri slays Thunupa, whose spirit, however, continues to live on in the forces of the land: "He speaks with the voice of thunder, he flashes his warning with lightning, he chastises with thunderbolts."[135] Thunupa represents duty: the duty of Spanish America to work out her own destiny in a practical, honest manner without

132. Fernando Díez de Medina, *Sariri: Una réplica al Ariel de Rodó* (La Paz, 1954), p. 9.
133. *Ibid.*, p. 14.
134. *Ibid.*, p. 12.
135. *Ibid.*, p. 23.

attempting to take flight in vague, ethereal idealism. Díez de Medina suggests—at least in this essay—that Hispanic America should not blame all her troubles on external forces, such as the policies of the United States. North America, he notes parenthetically, is not all bad; she has a great "moral tradition" and a notable literature.[136] Díez de Medina prides himself on his practicality; his essays have a down-to-earth approach which is at the same time their strength and weakness. He can, for example, sketch out a definite plan for a Bolivian national economy based upon small independent land holdings,[137] but his analysis of the problems posed by the issue of nativism versus universalism is certainly less impressive than that of the other *indigenistas* we have examined. And more often than not, his indigenism is little more than thinly veiled nationalism, as when in the rather disconnected later essays of *Sariri*, he emphasizes the antiquity and achievements of the Bolivian Kolla Indians, at the same time implying that the accomplishments of Peru's Incas have been overrated.

The intellectual development of Venezuela's leading essayist of the twentieth century, Mariano Picón Salas (1901-65), rather closely parallels that of Henríquez Ureña, Reyes, and the *Ateneo* group. His earliest works, such as the essays in *Buscando el camino* (1920), show a typical anti-Spencerian, vitalistic viewpoint. Like many a Spanish American of the day, he looks upon nineteenth-century life as dull and self-satisfied; he considers the philosophy of the century, dominated as it was by fatalistic scientism, equally unattractive.[138] These very early essays are characterized by a typical mélange of *arielista* sentiment, fascination with Nietzschean paganism, and rejection of the French decadent poets. His thought is further enriched by a deep concern for a Spanish American rejuvenation through a "responsible philosophy capable of arousing dormant spirits."[139]

In the 1920's Picón Salas, seeking a less repressive intellectual climate than that afforded by dictator-dominated Venezuela, journeyed to distant Chile where he remained for many years as a teacher, student, and journalist. In Santiago he frequented the lively *tertulia* of the novelist Eduardo Barrios; here, incidentally, he had the opportunity of hearing a strange new poetry, solemnly declaimed, he re-

136. *Ibid.*, pp. 33-34.
137. *Ibid.*, p. 44.
138. Mariano Picón Salas, *Buscando el camino* (Caracas, 1920), pp. 143-44.
139. *Ibid.*, p. 144.

calls, by "a lanky awkward youth who had a melancholy voice and whose name was Pablo Neruda."[140] But what struck the young Venezuelan emigré most in his new environment was the spirit of Spanish American solidarity and of commitment to the quest for a continental ideal. He noted this particularly among the students and younger teachers at the University: "we hopefully thought, in those years of the twenties, that the impetus of university reform which had spread throughout the continent . . . not only would make us wiser and better, but that it would also change the harsh realities of tyrants and foreign intervention. . . . Never, as in those days, did we have the desire to be more generous. We thought that a new generation of patriots would have to come forth, to re-establish the unity of our shattered continental destiny."[141] Whether university reform should be considered a cause or an effect of the reawakened Americanism of the period is difficult to determine, but there is no question that the leaders of the two movements were often identical: Vasconcelos in Mexico, Mariátegui and Haya de la Torre in Peru, as well as Picón Salas in his second homeland, Chile.

It is not surprising then, that one of Picón Salas' early expressions of Americanism was presented as a lecture to an academic group at the University of Concepción in 1931. The speech, published subsequently as *Hispano-América, posición crítica*, though necessarily brief, is rich in ideas. Picón Salas' point of departure may be taken as a veritable *leitmotif* for the times: "There exists in our times, and with great justification in our new countries . . . an ardent desire for definition."[142] He warns, however, that "definitions" based on ready-made, borrowed patterns are dangerous, particularly as they often reflect the narrowness of a single viewpoint. Beware of the "man who reads only one book," he tells his audience. It is because of this type of thinker that Spanish America has servilely copied foreign forms, and it is to "the man who reads only one book" that the continent owes her incapacity to come face to face with reality.[143] An even broader criticism of the failings of the continent's intellectuals and artists is made when Picón Salas points out that the Spanish American pursues a "chimerical and bookish" kind of learning rather than genuine culture. He views *arielistas* like Rodó and Francisco García Calderón as writers whose cultivation of verbal

140. Mariano Picón Salas, *Regreso de tres mundos* (México, 1959), p. 78.
141. *Ibid.*
142. Mariano Picón Salas, *Hispano-América, posición crítica* (Santiago de Chile, 1931), p. 5.
143. *Ibid.*, p. 6.

ornament and affected cosmopolitanism barely disguises an innocuous, mediocre personality. In his comments on the Andean radical writers, especially González Prada, he stresses the point that the truly great intellectual not only must be deeply rooted in his milieu, but must also be an activist, if not a revolutionary.[144] Art and literature of the purely "ornamental" sort are not in keeping with the "American attitude." He singles out the paintings of Diego Rivera, the writings of Prada, and the work of the then emerging Mexican thinker, Samuel Ramos, as pointing the way toward a genuine New World culture. Such a culture, he notes should be thought of as a particular "modality" within a "general" western European tradition. Attacking from a slightly different quarter, he calls for the use of European technique and method for the exploration of the New World's "own peculiar destiny."[145] In an article written some years later, "Americanismo y autóctonismo" (1937), he again deplores mechanical imitation of foreign art and literature, while he stresses the need for the "conscious adaptation" of Western culture to American reality. Although he may praise the efforts of a González Prada or a Diego Rivera, Picón Salas would not have the desire for an independent, uniquely American culture lead to ridiculous extremes. Like Alfonso Reyes, he is quite aware that the great emphasis placed on nativism throughout Spanish America during the present century could easily produce a sentimentalized, romantic, and utterly false art. He even suggests that the exuberant *indigenista* of the day would do well to study the rather conservative view of the Indian which Simón Bolívar had expressed over a century before.[146]

In later years Picón Salas continued to probe the American reality in formal as well as in informal essays. His well-documented and well-written historical study *De la conquista a la Independencia* (dedicated, incidentally, to Alfonso Reyes, with whom he admits sharing "a common hope in America") has become a classic in the field of colonial cultural history. The essays collected in *Europa-América: Preguntas a la esfinge de la cultura* (1947), while dealing specifically with the author's impressions of various aspects of European culture, are united by an underlying preoccupation with the problem of America's relationship to the Old World. Much of

144. *Ibid.*, p. 24.
145. *Ibid.*, pp. 18-19.
146. Mariano Picón Salas, "Americanismo y autoctonismo," *Atenea* No. 144 (June, 1937), pp. 254-60.

what Picón Salas writes in this work is an amplification of earlier ideas on the same theme: "The finest spirits of both Americas . . . discovered the American essence by introducing as a first assumption European methods and technique."[147] He does, however, suggest an interesting way of re-stating the basic problem: perhaps Europe may be equated with a formalizing concept of "Culture," while America may be thought of as "Nature"—youthful, unformed, but vibrantly alive. The integration of "Culture" and "Nature," as he defines these terms, would be Picón Salas' ideal American synthesis. When "Culture" loses contact with the natural realm, "it becomes cold intellectualism, calculating, abstract, and inhuman." Likewise, "Nature" without "Culture" is equally barren: "Nature without Culture is the hazy and haphazard realm of instinct—a region of terrifying surprises, of lustful cruelty, of sheer panic occasioned by ignorance."[148] Just as there is no opposition between "Culture" and "Nature" there is no real opposition between America and the Old World. As with Reyes, at the root of Picón Salas' thinking lies a classical concept of man and nature; nature must be controlled, ordered, and made rational by human effort; by so doing man may take his vital sustenance from her. In a more recent work, the warmly semi-autobiographical collection of essays *Regreso de tres mundos* (1959), Picón Salas again underscores his fundamental belief that it is only through the utilization of the experience and wisdom of the Old World that America will discover herself. It is significant that he considers one of the New World's great neoclassicists, Andrés Bello, a writer who succeeded in grasping this truth at the very dawn of American independence: "Perhaps the secret—as an educator of the stature of Andrés Bello has already guessed—lies in utilizing the methods, forms and experiences received from older cultures, to define that which is intrinsically ours."[149]

It is not surprising that the lands bordering the Caribbean, a region whose colorful past and ethnic complexity are unrivaled in the hemisphere, should produce essayists whose work is dominated by a passion for history. Picón Salas' interest in Colonial Spanish America is a case in point; the writings of his Colombian contemporary, Germán Arciniegas (1901——) perhaps bear even more eloquent testimony of the fascination which the past may exercise. Arciniegas' love of history is complemented by two other loves: that

147. Mariano Picón Salas, *Europa-América: Preguntas a la esfinge de la cultura* (México, 1947), p. 10.
148. *Ibid.*, p. 27.
149. Picón Salas, *Regreso de tres mundos*, p. 140.

of America, in the widest sense, and that of the little man, the *Don Nadie*. These themes have lent his work a vibrancy and warmth which are often lacking in the typical historical essay. Whether he is writing a highly personal, tongue-in-cheek piece such as "La academia, la taberna y la universidad,"[150] the memoirs of early student days, *El estudiante de la mesa redonda* (1936), a serious (though never pedantic) investigation such as *Este pueblo de América* (1945), or the penetrating biographical sketches of *América mágica* (1959), these three elements—Americanism, the passion for history, and *Don Nadie*—are seldom absent. In Arciniegas' America even the greatest political and literary figures, a Juan Montalvo or a Simón Bolívar, assume very believable, human proportions. This is accomplished by a literary method which tends toward the anecdotal and by Arciniegas' complete freedom from the pretentiousness often found among successful men of letters. A trivial personal confession perhaps best reveals the forthright humanity of the man: on a certain occasion his colleague at Columbia University, Federico de Onís, asked Arciniegas to deliver a talk on a rather difficult topic. To complicate matters, the situation was such that Arciniegas would have very little time to prepare his address. He nonetheless observes: "How could I refuse? I'm incapable of refusing any request. If I had been a woman, I would have stained the family honor, because I always say yes to everything."[151]

Arciniegas' Americanist attitudes may be summarized readily. "The American essence," he tells us, can be equated with mankind's yearnings for "emancipation and . . . a free life."[152] Though he cannot be accused of indulging in the artificial glorification of the continent's autochthonous past, Arciniegas does feel that the inhabitant of the New World is substantially different from the European. This difference is not attributable to race; along with many other essayists who have pursued this theme, Arciniegas stresses the role of environmental forces in producing a distinctly American personality: "Regardless of how much we think we are Spaniards or Frenchmen, we are Americans. This continent has marked us with a manner, an accent, a luster, a color. . . ."[153] Or expressing the same idea in more typically Arciniegan terms, "it is clear that there is a funda-

150. Germán Arciniegas, "La academia, la taberna, y la universidad," *Revista de las Indias*, No. 58 (Oct., 1943), pp. 5-15.
151. Cited by Joaquín Maurín, "Arciniegas o la conciencia de América," *Cuadernos*, No. 1 (July/Aug., 1953), p. 102.
152. Germán Arciniegas, *Este pueblo de América* (México, 1945), p. 75.
153. *Ibid.*, p. 61.

mental difference between the Spaniard who remained on the Peninsula seasoning his *paella* with olives and shellfish, and the Spaniard who came here to eat potatoes, *yuccas* and Indian corn."[154] But what defines the American, and the American spirit even more than these physical determinants, is his thirst for liberty, justice, and democracy. Arciniegas is not afraid to state what he believes to be obvious truths, though they may appear to be commonplace and are things "neither the kings of Spain . . . nor even Ortega y Gasset could see."[155]

The search for an adequate definition of Americanism, for a clearer understanding of cultural realtionships between the Old World and the New, takes many forms in contemporary Spanish America. With few exceptions the essayists whom we have been discussing all belong to what may be termed the liberal persuasion. For better or for worse, the connotation of "liberal" in the Hispanic context has a strongly religious flavor: economics and political philosophy of course enter into the definition, but traditionally the term suggests if not an anticlerical attitude, at least a marked disinclination to view mankind, society, and history in terms of Catholic thought.

In recent years, however, a number of very provocative essays have appeared by writers who are sympathetic to the established church. Important literary journals have attempted, and with considerable success, to dispel the feeling among the intelligentsia that the Catholic viewpoint was unsophisticated and anachronistic. In a few cases—that of José Vasconcelos is perhaps the most striking—an essayist has "returned" to the Catholic position late in his career. Others have made their mark as writers and thinkers from within a consistently Catholic frame of reference. These essayists have felt that the facile equation of certain positions—indigenism, humanism, idealism, and economic equalitarianism—with the liberal viewpoint has done the church a great injustice. The defenders of what might be called the "Catholic Americanist" movement hold, for example, that racial prejudices and the inequalities arising therefrom are products of the northern European, Protestant tradition. Many would agree with the conservative Mexican writer Alfonso Junco, who succinctly titled an article "El hispanismo auténtico es el mejor indigenismo" ("True Hispanism is the Best Indigenism").[156] His-

154. *Ibid.*, pp. 54-55.
155. *Ibid.*, p. 174.
156. Alfonso Junco, "El hispanismo auténtico es el mejor indigenismo " *Mercurio Peruano*, No. 196 (July, 1943), pp. 279-82.

torical support for this view is often gained by citing the work of the celebrated "defender of the Indies," Father Bartolomé de las Casas, or by pointing out the benevolent paternalism of the Jesuit missions in Paraguay.

In addition to re-interpreting the church's role in New World history, this group has been very receptive to certain recent trends in European thought, notably that of Catholic humanists such as Jacques Maritain, and that of religious Existentialists like Nicholas Berdyaev and Gabriel Marcel. Spanish America's Catholic intellectuals can be conveniently grouped in relation to the journals which have provided them a means of expression. In Mexico the *Abside* writers include the director, Alfredo Junco, the philosophers Oswaldo Robles and José Sánchez Villaseñor, as well as important foreign contributors such as the Chilean, Clarence Finlayson. In Perú, the influential *Mercurio Peruano*, while publishing material of considerable ideological breadth, has served as a sounding board for several Catholic essayists, such as the journal's editor, Víctor Andrés Belaúnde and the philosophical essayist Alberto Wagner de Reyna. Of the Argentine Catholic reviews, *Criterio* is well known, though its adherence to fascism and its intellectual narrowness have restricted its appeal substantially. In Colombia, *Bolívar*, a journal which flourished during the Rightest regime of the early 1950's, best represents Catholic thought in that region; its writers included Finlayson, Wagner de Reyna, and the very interesting historical essayist Víctor Frankl (1905——). Although the Austrian-born Frankl could hardly be considered a major Spanish American literary figure, his essays, collected in the volume *Espíritu y camino de Hispanoamérica* (1953), present some provocative interpretations of a number of the problems we have been examining.

Frankl takes as his point of departure a fundamentally cyclical-historicist view of culture; in his own terms he refers to this as "the organic interpretation . . . of cultures."[157] Acknowledging his obvious debt to such well-known historicists as Spengler and Toynbee, he holds that civilizations have a youth, a middle age, a decline, and a death. Spanish America, he maintains, has followed or has unsuccessfully tried to follow an "alien" cycle, i.e., that of Europe. The Old World now finds itself in "a senile epoch" imbued with a ". . . profane, empirical, relativistic tendency characterized by an individualistic social structure; or, in short, by . . . 'modernity.' "[158] In reality, how-

157. Víctor E. Frankl, *Espíritu y camino de Hispanoamérica* (Bogotá, 1953), p. 11.
158. *Ibid.*

ever, Spanish America's own "organic age" is youthful, and the unfortunate attempt to make her culture conform to Europe's decadent "modernity" has resulted in an acute crisis, characterized by a sense of "inauthenticity." Frankl feels that the Spanish American is, or should think of himself as, living in a kind of "New Medieval" period, an era in which a sense of solidarity and community has not yet been "mutilated" by the modern world's unbridled individualism and pernicious intellectualism.[159] The European source of these ideas is of course Berdyaev, whose very radical though profoundly religious views have had considerable appeal in contemporary Spanish America, even among writers who are not primarily defenders of the church.[160] Certain historical periods and specific ideological movements are singled out by Frankl as exemplifying the neomedieval spirit: the age of St. Augustine, the Middle Ages themselves, the first few decades of German romanticism, and in Spanish America, the period of spiritual ferment following the Mexican Revolution. In Frankl's rather tortuous logic, Herder, Fichte, and Hegel are viewed as renovators of the medieval spirit of community and solidarity in that they opposed the modern notions of "liberalism, positivism, and individualism." Parenthetically one may well question whether Frankl is confusing the Hegelian concept of the "State" with the early Christian concept of "community." Frankl feels that Vasconcelos and Caso exemplify the kind of "romantic organicism" which the Spanish American continent needs; he cites their revolt against scientism in the name of idealism and spirituality as one of the great recent movements toward authentic Americanism.[161] In addition to the Mexicans, at least two other Spanish American thinkers are lauded for having utilized this "organic" viewpoint of culture. Curiously, these two are the fana-

159. *Ibid.*, pp. 45-46.
160. Nicholas Alexandrovich Berdyaev (1874-1948) was born in Russia and enjoyed a chair in Philosophy at the University of Moscow shortly after the Revolution. He was subsequently expelled by the government (1922) and spent most of his remaining years in France. He was deeply radical, deeply religious, and very critical of modern society, both capitalistic and communistic. Spanish American writers come into contact with his work through France, where in the last few years of his life he became associated with the Existentialists. Some of his better known works are *The Bourgeois Mind, The Origin of Russian Communism, The Russian Revolution, The End of Our Time, The Meaning of the Creative Act,* etc. Perhaps the idea in Berdyaev which appealed most to Spanish American intellectuals is his view of genuine Christianity as the perfect expression of the propertyless, "communistic" society. See Leopoldo Zea, *América en la conciencia de Europa* (Mexico, 1955), pp. 173-76, for further discussion of the "humanitarian" and "communal" nature of primitive Christianity. In Zea's work, as in Waldo Frank's, there is remarkable parallel of Berdyaev's critique of modern Christianity, particularly in its Protestant, "materialistic" expression.
161. Frankl, *Espíritu y camino* p. 449.

tical dictator of nineteenth-century Paraguay, Dr. Francia, and the more recent Paraguayan essayist and statesman, Juan Natalicio González.[162] Frankl, in his very complimentary discussion of González' works, points out another important aspect of his own Americanist position: namely, the great role he assigns to the land. Frankl agrees with González' inversion of Sarmiento's well-known position on "civilization and barbarity." He believes that "the servants of autochthonous culture" are the true civilizers and that the "Europeanizers" are the "barbarians."[163] The genuine Americanist must always conceive of the New World's culture as something in constant contact with the land, though this "telluric fatalism" should not be confused with the determinism of a Taine or a Spencer. Rather, Frankl feels, it is to be thought of as "man's mystical surrender to the creative energy of the land."[164] Frankl's Americanist views are thus compounded of several diverse elements: a passionate telluricism (the roots of which he traces to the German Romanticists and especially to the romanticized geography of Karl Ritter); the notion that liberalism, intellectualism, and especially individualism, have destroyed that sense of community embodied in the church and which must be considered esssential to the human condition; and lastly, the acceptance of a kind of cyclical historicism best expressed in his phrase, "the contemporariness of the non-coetaneus." It would be difficult to say just how representative Frankl's views of the Catholic Americanist position are without a thorough investigation of many other Catholic essayists; however, the pages of writers such as Vasconcelos, Derisi, or Finlayson reveal many ideological similarities.

The discussion of the rediscovery of America has served to point out a number of themes which were shared and developed by many writers of different national backgrounds and of different ideological formation. Most conspicuous among these is the constant reference to what may be termed the "nativism-versus-universalism" polarity. Significantly, most of the essayists are aware that this polarity must in some way be transcended before Spanish America can realize her full potential. Of equal significance is the commonly shared sense of the American destiny: implicitly or explicitly these writers are cogni-

162. The two works of Juan Natalicio González which Frankl cites at considerable length are *Proceso y formación de la cultura paraguaya* (Asunción, 1938), and *El Paraguay y la lucha por su expresión* (Asunción, 1945).
163. Juan Natalicio González, *El Paraguay eterno* ,as cited by Frankl, *Espíritu y camino*, p. 446.
164. Frankl, *Espíritu y camino*, p. 476.

zant that their task of rediscovering the New World is as crucially important to the future of humanity as it is to that of Spanish America herself. As the editors of the journal *Cuadernos Americanos* succinctly stated in the *avant-propos* of their fine review, "América es el porvenir del mundo. Tú estás llamada a salvar el mundo." ("America is the future of the world. You have been summoned to save the world.").

The process of defining what Reyes at times has called "The Position of America" and at other times "The Meaning of America" continues to the present, and yet many of the questions suggested in the opening paragraphs of this chapter remain unanswered or are only partially answered. Evidently the broad focus which many of our essayists have attempted to maintain has had serious limitations. We have already witnessed the tendency toward a narrowing of this focus; toward the application of a specific viewpoint, such as that of the "Catholic Americanist" writers. There has also been a strong trend toward restricting this search for definition to a clearly national frame of reference. In later chapters this quest for national essence —be it *argentinidad, mexicanidad,* or *peruanidad*—will be discussed in some detail. At this point in our survey, however, our attention will be directed toward those writers who have attempted to define the Americanist position in terms of some of the most vigorous and persuasive ideology shaping present-day Spanish America: that of the radical Left.

V / THE NEW HUMANISM

AND THE LEFT

NORTH AMERICANS HAVE BEEN HARD PUT IN RECENT
years to account for the obvious vigor of the Spanish American
Left. The explanations most frequently heard are based on the
view that the sociological, the political, and most of all the economic
conditions "which breed Communism" have provided a fertile field for
the agents of Moscow. Students of the Latin American Left have
maintained, moreover, that the Spanish American Communist is
essentially no different from any other supporter of international
communism,[1] and that a sharp line may readily be drawn dividing
the "democratic nativist" movements of the Left from those that
are obviously Moscow—or Peking—dominated. Although these
views undeniably have some basis in political realities, they are
inadequate and deceptively simplistic. They fail to account for the
appearance of radical Leftist movements when the material conditions hardly warrant their existence,[2] and they fail to consider the

1. A responsible and well-informed student of Spanish American radicalism'
Robert J. Alexander, has stated on page 32 of his *Communism in Latin America* (New
Brunswick, 1957) that "There could be no greater mistake than to believe that the
Communists of Latin America are somehow 'different,' that because they are Latin
American, they do not share the characteristics of Communists in other parts of the
world." This statement, written incidentally before the Sino-Soviet split had appeared,
has only limited validity. The fact that Communists in Latin America "share the
characteristics of Communists in other parts of the world" does not, for example,
preclude the possibility that they may have *additional* distinctive characteristics of their
own. It must also be remembered that in our study we are discussing a generalized
radicalism rather than the specific question of Communist political activity.
2. The recent Cuban revolution is of course the most striking case. Responsible
commentators—Theodore Draper, for example—have frequently pointed out that
Cuba was not by Latin American standards a poor country before Castro's rise: the
middle class was rather well developed and the economy, despite the substantial
profits reaped by North American interests, was functioning reasonably well. It
is true that some 25 per cent of the laboring force were very poor cane-workers who

cultural distinctiveness of national groups. Most important, such views are predicated upon the belief that Marxism can appeal only to man's stomach, never to his head, and even less likely to his heart. It is not proposed here that "the material conditions which breed Communism" have had no causal relationship to Latin America's revolutionary movements, nor that Communist governments outside the Western Hemisphere have not attempted to take full advantage of these. What I do propose is simply that a numerous, articulate, and—on occasion—influential group of Spanish American writers have embraced the ideology and program of the extreme Left for reasons which are often ignored by writers who are not well grounded in Spanish America's past and present and who are insensitive to Marxism's intellectual and spiritual attraction.

Although there were important essayists writing from a Leftist viewpoint toward the close of the nineteenth century, it was in the 1920's that a distinctive Spanish American radicalism began to emerge. The century, we have seen, opened with a broad-fronted attack upon scientism and related movements. Voluntarism, intuitionism, and a revived emphasis upon idealism and spirituality characterize the times. The essayists of the period—Rodó, Vasconcelos, Caso, Henríquez Ureña, Tamayo, and others—sought to liberate the Spanish American from the adoration of materialism and of technical advance for its own sake. Yet most of these writers were very much aware of Spanish America's material needs.

In short, they did not propose idealism, spirituality, or *desinterés* as a substitute for bread and land. The indigenist writers, a group which took an active part in defining the century's new Americanism, were likewise deeply concerned with the obvious material inadequacies of life for the continent's masses. But this material preoccupation has not, in the best of these essayists, been considered an end in itself; rather it is viewed as a means by which man may realize his full potential free of the trammels imposed by the physical struggle for life. Confidence in the capabilities of the native American, a deep sense of the utopian destiny of the New World, and the belief that the ethnic richness of America demands that the continent play

---

suffered long seasons of unemployment, but their poverty clearly was not the prime force behind Castro's rise and his succeeding shifts to the Left. A host of other "non-materialistic" reasons such as feelings of national pride, a romantic, utopian, vision of the ideal state, a deep probing for a new humanism, an existential commitment to a "project," etc., lie behind recent events in Cuba. An interesting (but partisan) view of these aspects of Castro's regime is presented in Jean Paul Sartre's impressions of contemporary Cuba, *Sartre on Cuba* (New York, 1961).

a profoundly ecumenical role in humanity's present crisis have encouraged Spanish American intellectuals to hope that what they
term *un nuevo humanismo*—a new humanism—might emerge in the
hemisphere. That the instruments by which material problems
might be solved and the stage set for this flowering of the human
spirit would not be those of laissez faire capitalism may be appreciated
readily. The rejection of everything which the nineteenth century
stood for—the cult of material progress, the dog-eat-dog world of
biological survival—made *homo economicus*, be he financier, in-
dustrialist, or *petit bourgeois*, an object of scorn and derision. These
attitudes were, of course, heavily underscored by Spanish America's
political and economic experience during the early decades of this
century. Simply stated, the underlying feeling of Latin Americans
was that the great industrial capitalist nations were the exploiters,
and they were the exploited. Whether this view is factually defensible
is not under discussion here; but the fact of its existence and persistence must be reckoned with.

Though it may come as a surprise to few, North America, the
most obvious representative of contemporary industrial-capitalist
society, has traditionally been singled out as the foremost example
of such a society's shortcomings. Yet the writers of nineteenth-
century Spanish America professed sincere admiration for the United
States. The pages of Domingo Faustino Sarmiento (1811-88), the
greatest Spanish American essayist of his day, are full of appreciation of North American grass-roots democracy, of our respect
for the individual, and of the United States' material progress.
Sarmiento was perhaps more outspoken in this regard than were
most of his contemporaries, yet there are good indications that his
attitude was typical. Toward the end of the century, the United
States continued to be respected, but with something less than the
blind devotion of earlier years: the great Cuban essayist and patriot,
José Martí, in his penetrating observations of the North America of
the 1880's and early 1890's, expressed a more realistic view of the
United States as a nation undergoing substantial changes in character
and values.[3] The economic development following the Civil War,
the emergence of the nation as a world power, the search for
foreign markets and for lucrative foreign investment, led to new
economic and political relationships between the United States and

3. A good source, in English translation, of Martí's writings on the United States
is Manuel Pedro González, *Jose Martí, Epic Chronicler of the United States in the
Eighties* (Chapel Hill, 1953).

Spanish America. The "holy kiss of fraternal amity"[4] of which the early nineteenth-century Spanish Americans sang was giving way under pressure of Manifest Destiny and the Big Stick. It was soon replaced in Latin America by such catch-phrases as "Yankee imperialism" and "the Colossus of the North."

The turn of the century witnessed a veritable flowering of anti-Yankee sentiment among the essayists. Rodó, always polite, always somewhat "cold and haughty,"[5] set forth in his *Ariel* the now famous symbolism of the spiritual, ethereal representative of Latin civilization (Ariel) contrasted with the materialistic, self-centered Caliban. Rodó's critique of North American culture is neither hateful nor completely one-sided; he simply pointed out that the spirit of Caliban dominated in the United States, and that Spanish America should be on her guard to preserve the best of her traditional Latin humanism. Rodó's followers, the *arielista* writers, continued this line of criticism. Carlos Arturo Torres warned Spanish America against imitating the "degenerated" empiricism and exaggerated utilitarianism of the United States,[6] and Manuel Díaz Rodríguez, concerned specifically with the position of the creative artist in Spanish America, decried the prostitution of art for material gain—or "Universal Yankee-izing" as he put it.[7] These essayists, it should be borne in mind, were far from the Left: if anything, they were either apolitical or tacit supporters of the Right.

Writers of a more political bent, however, did not limit their critique of North America to a generalized attack on her materialistic values. Venezuela's Rufino Blanco Fombona (1874-1944), in his highly volatile journalistic style, wrote a series of impassioned essays attacking North America's policies and propaganda in the Caribbean area.[8] During this same period, the second decade of the century, the Argentine critic and essayist, Manuel Ugarte (1878-1951), produced one of Spanish America's most realistic analyses of North American economic imperialism. His work is significant in that Ugarte, a Socialist, was one of the first Spanish Americans to discuss

4. The phrase is from the Ecuadorean poet José Joaquín Olmedo's patriotic ode "To the Victory of Junín," written in 1825.
5. Fernando Díez de Medina, *Sariri: Una réplica al Ariel de Rodó* (La Paz, 1954), p. 12. For this *indigenista's* attitudes toward Rodó, see above Chapter IV, p. 91.
6. Carlos Arturo Torres, *Estudios de crítica moderna* (Madrid, 1917), pp. 104-8.
7. Manuel Díaz Rodríguez, *Camino de perfección* (Caracas, 1942), p. 24. The original edition of the book is 1908.
8. See especially his sketch "Noticias Yanquis" probably written during 1917 or 1918 and included in E. H. Hespelt *et al.* (eds.) *An Anthology of Spanish American Literature* (New York, 1946), pp. 621-22.

the Yankee menace in Marxist terms. However, like many of the moderate Socialists of the period, he lacked the passion of the zealot and the philosophical intensity of the genuine radical. In a frequently quoted speech, delivered in New York at Columbia Univeristy in the year 1912, we see Ugarte admiring North American culture on the one hand, while maintaining a sharply critical view of her high-handed policies in Spanish America on the other. He speaks of "the good sense and basic honesty of this admirable country,"[9] and yet maintains the attitude of the political realist. In one of his best known essays, *El destino de un Continente* (1923), he tells his readers that "To invoke ethics in international affairs is almost always a confession of defeat."[10] Neither an appeal to ethics nor an emotional response to Yankee imperialism is called for; rather Spanish America must dispassionately analyze the nature of the menace and organize itself to meet it. Ugarte achieved considerable notoriety as a defender of Latin America against the imperialists, but by the mid-twenties he had faded into obscurity. Recent critics have noted a certain superficiality in Ugarte's writing.[11] Rather than superficiality, his greatest shortcoming was his insensitivity to a fundamental problem which concerned the *arielistas* as well as many of Ugarte's Marxist brethren: that of achieving material goals without sacrificing human values. In short, Ugarte seems to view Spanish America's economic well-being and political independence as an ultimate objective rather than as a prelude to a radically new era characterized by a Utopian vision of human liberation and creativity.

Like the *arielistas* and the political essayists, the *indigenista* writers have played an important part in the development of a distinctive Spanish American radicalism. While the nineteenth century brought substantial material gain to the continent's small middle and upper classes, the continued existence of a huge agrarian population, barely subsisting within a virtually feudal economic order provided reformers and radicals with abundant material for their polemics. Since the bulk of the lowest economic class was composed of Indians, mestizos, and Negroes, those who have sought a more equitable economic order have, of necessity, been vitally concerned with the indigenist movement. Thus, in the Andean region

9. Cited by Robert G. Mead, *Breve historia del ensayo americano* (Mexico, 1956), p. 85.

10. J. Fred Rippey (ed.), *The Destiny of a Continent*, trans. C. A. Phillips (New York, 1925), p. 125.

11. See Alberto Zum Felde, *Indice crítico de la literatura hispanoamericana: El ensayo y la crítica* (Mexico, 1954), pp. 316-17; and Mead, *Breve historia*, p. 86.

indigenism and radicalism have together formed the background for the work of one of the most significant groups of contemporary Spanish American essayists: Manuel González Prada (1848-1918), J. Carlos Mariátegui (1895-1930), Antenor Orrego (1892————), and Víctor Raúl Haya de la Torre (1895————). While proclaiming the racial equality and cultural achievements of the native American, these writers also sought fundamental changes in the continent's political and economic order. Some of these writers—notably Mariátegui—in their desire to bring about an "inner revolution" in man's nature have added another dimension to the Spanish American Leftist movement—that of "personal radicalism." During the 1920's and early 1930's the crucial period in the shaping of the contemporary Spanish American Left, the Peruvian group wrote extensively; their important literary-political journal, *Amauta*, became a focal point of continental radical interest, and several of their members played major roles in organizing the powerful APRA party.[12]

As in the Andean region, the indigenist movement in other areas was closely connected with radicalism. The unique history of twentieth-century Mexico, however, has tended to make her radicals appear rather respectable. In view of the fact that the majority in Mexico has, since the Revolution of 1910-17, been committed to "revolutionary institutions," a good deal of Mexican radicalism has borne the government stamp of approval. For example the radical indigenism of Vasconcelos (at least the Vasconcelos of the second and third decades of the century) might well have been considered "'dangerous" in a different political atmosphere. Likewise, the radical humanism of a Samuel Ramos in a more conservative environment than that of Mexico of the 1930's would quite probably have been suspect. Of course Mexico has produced, and continues to produce, writers and artists of radical leanings who operate outside the confines of the PRI.[13] In the late 1920's and early 1930's an interesting group, including such ardent *indigenistas* as the painters Atl and Rivera, gathered about the journal *Crisol*. While some of

12. A valuable study of the APRA—The Alianza Popular Revolucionaria Americana —is Harry Kantor's "The Ideology and Program of the Peruvian Aprista Movement," *University of California Publications in Political Science*, IV, No. 1 (1953), pp. 1-164. See also Eugenio Chang-Rodríguez, *La literatura política de González Prada, Mariátegui y Haya de la Torre* (Mexico, 1957).
13. Perhaps the best known of these radicals is the pro-Communist labor leader and organizer Vicente Lombardo Toledano. Since Lombardo is fundamentally not a man of letters he has been excluded from this study. An analysis of his precise relationship to the majority party of Mexico, the PRI (Partido Revolucionario Institucional), is presented by Alexander, *Communism in Latin America*, pp. 342-49.

the contributors to this review appear to be orthodox Communists (Carlos Gutiérrez Cruz, for example), others, such as the young poet and prose writer-to-be Octavio Paz, represented a more heterodox position—and often an essentially more radical one.

Mexican and Peruvian radicals are not alone in their *indigenista* orientation: all genuine Spanish American radicals have, regardless of the racial composition of their own nation, felt more or less committed to a sympathetic view of indigenism. The problems of the Negro and mulatto proletariat of the Caribbean have consistently concerned the Cuban Leftists, and even in "white" Buenos Aires, radicals have shown interest in indigenism and related matters.[14]

Anti-Yankee sentiments and indigenist sympathies, though typical attitudes of the Latin radical, do not lie at the very root of his world view. Nor does his adherence to a specific economic or political praxis, such as that of Russian communism, define his position satisfactorily. Stated simply, these writers—like Rimbaud and the French Surrealists of the 1920's—seek to "changer la vie" rather than simply to "transformer le monde" along the lines of say a strict Marxist pattern. Nietzsche's cry for a thoroughgoing reform of human values, Caso's interpretation of distinctively human acts as those motivated by disinterest, and Waldo Frank's infectious personalist mystique are all part of this movement. If one accepts the proposition that a fundamental change in the material, technical ordering of society—government, economic institutions, etc.—is inconceivable without a corresponding fundamental change in man's inner self, the "radical humanism" of Spanish America becomes much more comprehensible.

The writings of the Peruvian Leftists—Prada, Mariátegui, Antenor Orrego, and Haya de la Torre—form a body of material which yields valuable insights into the development of what I have called a distinctive Spanish American radicalism. Moreover, the general lines of the continent's intellectual history, sketched out earlier in this study are well illustrated in the group's thinking. It is noteworthy, too, that the political impact of these Peruvians has been substantial: in the 1962 elections, Haya and his *Apristas* were suc-

14. The Cuban leftists of the late twenties and early thirties—Juan Marinello, Alejo Carpentier, Jorge Mañach, Francisco Ichaso, and others—grouped themselves about the review *Avance*. Parenthetically, Marinello and Carpentier at present hold important educational posts in the Castro regime.

The Buenos Aires Leftists of the same period were associated with the review *Claridad*, which ran into the late thirties. Some of the leading contributors were Alvaro Yunge, Ramón Doll, Antonio Zamora, and many non-Argentineans: the *Apristas*, Raúl Róa, etc.

cessful in winning a plurality, though succeeding events have prevented this victory from being consummated.[15]

The "father of Peruvian radicalism," it is generally acknowledged, was Manuel González Prada. Significantly, the critics usually refer to him as a "liberal" and, if we keep in mind the basically anticlerical connotation of the term in Hispanic America, they are quite right. Reared in an extremely Catholic environment, as a youth he reacted sharply against all forms of religious ritual and practice.[16] As a young man he undoubtedly was exposed to the eclectic positivism of Guyau and the religious skepticism of Renan.[17] The disastrous defeat of Peru by Chile in the War of the Pacific (1874-83) served as the catalyst for his career. In his attempt to discover the weakness which might account for his country's collapse, he isolated several factors: the unwillingness of the Indian to fight for an oppressive, vaguely comprehended national state; the backwardness of the nation's intellectuals; and the cynical self-interest of Peru's political leaders. Lying behind all these flaws, Prada felt, was the debilitating cultural heritage of Spain—her religion, her pretentious aristocracy, her fanaticism, and her legacy of administrative inefficiency.[18] In a series of forthright essays—*Páginas libres* (1894), *Horas de lucha* (1908), and many others published separately and then collected in posthumous volumes—Prada boldly criticized all that was traditional not only in Peruvian society but, by extension, throughout Hispanic America.

It is quite difficult to categorize González Prada's fundamental positions, for his diagnosis of his country's ills is much more extensive than his specific remedies. It is clear that he had a deep positivistic faith in science and technology as the great deliverers of humanity: in one of his best-known early speeches he proclaims that "Positivistic Science . . . in only one century of application to industry has produced more good for Humanity than have thousands of years of Theology and Metaphysics. . . ."[19] It is equally apparent that he desired the complete separation of church and state,[20] the redemption

15. Though the situation was very different from 1962, the *Apristas* claimed that the national elections of 1931 were won by the third party. See Kantor, "Ideology of Peruvian Aprista Movement," *University of California Publications in Political Science,* p. 13.
16. Chang-Rodríguez, *La literatura política,* pp. 77-78.
17. *Ibid.,* pp. 79-83.
18. For a clear expression of these ideas see Manuel González Prada's "Discurso en el Politeama" in his *Páginas libres* (Lima, 1946), pp. 63-71. The original date of the piece is 1888.
19. González Prada, *Páginas libres,* p. 67.
20. Chang-Rodríguez, *La literatura política,* p. 83.

of the exploited Indian, and a more equitable distribution of the national wealth. Although he recognized the relationship of the Indian problem to those of land tenure and attacked the idea that property was sacred, he proposed no clear program of radical agrarian reform.[21] Prada's radicalism was personal, eclectic, and, in his later writings, tinged with a vaguely conceived anarchism. He distrusted governments—even those established in the name of the Revolution. He had a wonderful understanding of human failings and of the way in which revolutionary ideals age, become rigid and, eventually, conservative. His writings will indicate at one point a fatalistic acceptance of this process ("... every triumphant revolutionary degenerates into a conservative"), and then, just a few pages later, he will proclaim the future success of a sweeping humanitarian revolution.[22] Critics who have sought consistency in Prada's thought —particularly when his earlier and later works are viewed as a single body—are usually frustrated in their attempts. The marked nationalism of his work of the 1880's contrasted with the broad internationalism of many of the essays written in the closing decades of his life is a case in point. The scientism, and great respect for a technologically ordered world seen in his early essays can hardly be accommodated to the social thought of the nineteenth century's foremost anarchist, Bakunin, whose ideas supposedly influenced Prada substantially.[23] Whether he was a Positivist or an anarchist, a materialist or romantic idealist, a Bakuninite or Marxist, would be difficult to say; for Prada was a bit of all these. But most of all he was an agitator, an awakener of men's minds and spirits, an *apóstol* to use a favorite epithet of Spanish Americans. And despite the vagueness and inconsistency of his intellectual equipment, he was capable of understanding the revolution in terms which clearly approach the humanistic radicalism of more recent writers:

> ... Humanity has stopped agitating for secondary things and is asking for radical changes. No one now expects that the happiness of the downtrodden will come about through parliaments. ... governmental machinery does not operate in favor of the populace but in favor of the dominant clique.
> Recognizing the insufficiency of politics in achieving the greatest good for the individual ... the proletariat will resolve the ultimate question by the only efficient means: revolution.

21. *Ibid.*, p. 114.
22. González Prada, "Discurso de Mayo 1," *Horas de lucha* (Buenos Aires, 1956), p. 55. Originally delivered to workers' meeting, May 1, 1905.
23. Zum Felde, *Indice crítico*, p. 372.

Not those local revolutions that overthrow presidents or czars and convert a republic into a monarchy or an autocracy into a representative government, but the world revolution; the revolution that erases borders, that abolishes nationality, and that summons all Humanity to take possession and to cultivate the land.[24]

One wonders what Prada's precise conception of this great revolution was, and to what extent might it involve fundamental transformations in man's values and in his very nature.

Despite the fact that Prada offered few answers to these questions, he remains unique in the Spanish America of the turn of the century. Not until the period following the First World War did writers emerge who could challenge him in the degree of their radicalism, in the boldness of their critique of existing institutions, and in the profundity of their indigenism. The date of Prada's death, 1918, is significant, for it marks the end of the World War, the culmination of the Russian Revolution, and, if we go back a few months to 1917, the termination of the military phase of the Mexican Revolution. In Peru, Prada's writings were eagerly absorbed by the generation approaching maturity during this tumultuous period. In his waning years, from his desk as director of the National Library and in his Lima residence, Prada exerted a direct personal influence upon a number of these young radicals: Mariátegui, Haya de la Torre, César Vallejo, and Federico More, to name only a few.[25]

Of this group, José Carlos Mariátegui, despite the brevity of his life (or perhaps by virtue of his untimely death), has achieved the status of a legend among Spanish American radicals. A list of writers and intellectuals who paid him homage during his life and after his passing includes some of the most illustrious names in Spanish America.[26] His short but brilliant career is noteworthy for many reasons: in few men has the tension between nativism and Europeanism been so great; in few thinkers has the inner struggle between spirituality and materialism been so acute; and few political leaders have been so forced by circumstance to walk the razor's edge between expedient compromise and personal integrity. Mariátegui began his literary career as a rather typical dilettante: a writer of sketches, poems, and plays—works which were, even in the opinion of their author, characterized by "end-of-the-century

24. González Prada, "Discurso de Mayo 1," *Horas de lucha*, pp. 52-53.
25. Chang-Rodríguez, *La literatura política*, pp. 71-72.
26. See below, pp. 117-18.

decadentism and ornamentation."[27] The internal factors which led Mariátegui to abandon the ornate, decadent style of his earliest writings are not readily apparent; however, the external factors— chiefly the hardships suffered by the lower classes as a result of the inflation of the Peruvian economy during World War I—have been pointed out as a logical cause for his increasing concern for sociological, political, and economic matters.[28] In 1918 Mariátegui joined forces with several young radicals in the establishment of a decidedly Leftist newspaper, *La Razón*. The following year he emerged as an outspoken defender of a general strike initiated by Peruvian workers in protest against the high cost of living. During this same period he founded, with César Falcón, the *Comité de Propaganda Socialista*, a group which shortly afterward became the Socialist party of Peru. Mariátegui's radicalism, however, was as yet in the formative stage. Toward the close of 1919, he was faced with a crucial decision. Peru's new strong man, Augusto B. Leguía, recognizing the threat posed by Mariátegui and several others, offered these dangerous young intellectuals government scholarships for foreign study. Mariátegui, poor and for the most part self-educated, accepted. He was, of course, roundly criticized for his decision, though recent writers have justified his position by pointing out that this contact with Europe was essential in his development as a radical leader.[29] From the end of 1919 until 1923 he traveled in Europe, observing at close range what he later called "the great movements of renovation." In Paris he met Henri Barbusse, a leading French radical of the day; in Italy he witnessed the rising tide of Mussolini's fascism; and in Germany he hopefully watched the attempts of the Communists to establish a radical Marxist state. He constantly read those writers whom he considered "renovators" (*renovadores*)—principally the Marxists, but also many others. The essays which grew out of these European experiences are sprinkled with references to a wide range of authors including Romain Rolland, Ortega, Sorel, Croce, Papini, Spengler, Freud, and Lenin. By the mid-twenties, after returning to Peru, Mariátegui's distinctive radicalism had taken shape. As was the case with so many Americans of the period—Americans of the North as well as of the South—the New World was "rediscovered" following the *wanderjahre* in the Old. Thus Mariátegui's major writings—the essays collected under

27. Chang-Rodríguez, *La literatura política*, p. 131.
28. *Ibid.*, p. 134.
29. *Ibid.*, p. 137.

the titles of *La escena contemporánea* (1925), *Defensa del Marxismo* (1934), *El alma matinal* (1950), and perhaps most important, the *Siete ensayos de interpretación de la realidad peruana* (1928), are characterized by a preoccupation with contemporary European thought and by the application of this thought to the American scene.

Mariátegui's critics have suggested that certain "errors" in his understanding of Spanish American reality are results of this "Europeanism." Professor Chang-Rodríguez, for example, explains the racist terms which Mariátegui uses in writing of the Negro and Oriental on this basis.[30] Mariategui believed that the Indians and workers who were to achieve Spanish America's revolution required a new mythology to replace traditional beliefs. This too may be viewed as a bookish application of a European idea to the American reality. Mariátegui, incidentally, admitted readily that his faith in the revolutionary *mythos* stemmed from his reading of Sorel.[31] Further examples could easily be given; the fact remains that his frequent assertions to the contrary, Mariátegui's Americanism and indigenism were strongly colored by his contacts with Europeans and by his familiarity with European thought of the period.

What fascinates the present-day reader of Mariátegui most, and what may account for his great appeal among Spanish American Leftists of the 1920's and 1930's is the remarkable heterodoxy of his radicalism. Despite the fact that he led a small group of doctrinaire Marxists who formed a radically "Socialist" party in the late 1920's,[32] one wonders how long Mariátegui would have remained a follower of the Third International had he lived to witness the Moscow trials of the 1930's, the assassination of Trotsky, or the Hitler-Stalin pact. There is abundant evidence that Mariátegui differed with "official" communism even during his lifetime. On specific matters of historical interpretation, and on the broad subject of the organization of the future society of Peru, he clearly deviated from the Third International's position.[33] At the First Latin American Communist Conference (Buenos Aires, June, 1929) the Communists themselves had substantial doubts regarding the program he submitted for the political organization of the Peruvian Left.[34] However, the essence

30. *Ibid.*, p. 182.
31. José Carlos Mariátegui, *Siete ensayos de interpretación de la realidad peruana* (Lima, 1959), p. 167.
32. Alexander, *Communism in Latin America*, pp. 222-23.
33. *Ibid.*, p. 223. Note especially Alexander's footnote regarding the varying opinions held by Mariátegui's fellow radicals concerning his precise position. See also Chang-Rodríguez, pp. 197-98.
34. Chang-Rodríguez, *La literatura política*, pp. 197, 164-65.

of Mariátegui's heterodoxy lies deeper than matters of "practical" or tactical differences with the Communist leadership.

Mariátegui, unlike many radicals, held to a profoundly non-materialistic world-view. He never expresses a forthright denial of the religious, the mystical, or the spiritual nature of man. Very much a part of the Spanish American intellectual movement against scientism, rationalism, and the cult of material progress, Mariátegui's revolutionary exhortation bears little resemblance to the rather earthbound appeals of many "practical" Communists. His ringing essay "La emoción de nuestro tiempo" (1925) brings this attitude out with great force. The skepticism and nihilism of the post-World War period, he tells his readers, has brought about a terrible human crisis. But, he adds, "from the crisis of this skepticism and nihilism, life is born anew (and) the powerful, urgent necessity of a faith and a myth capable of moving men to live dangerously."[35] Like so many of his Spanish American contemporaries he points out the hollowness of the nineteenth century's materialistic values; the pointlessness of attempting to live *avec douceur*, and the absurdity of the "super-stitious respect for the idea of progress."[36] Although Mariátegui devotes many pages to specific social, economic, and political problems, and to a decidedly revolutionary resolution of these, his deepest commitment is to the inner revolt, to an essentially human rather than to a political radicalism. To effect this transformation a new mythology is called for: "Neither reason nor science can satisfy completely the need for the infinite that exists in man . . . only myth has the rare power of filling the depths of his being."[37]

The heterodoxy of Mariátegui's radicalism may be better understood by considering certain details of his early life. His biographers point out that he was reared in a profoundly Catholic environment;[38] one of his first literary pieces is a sonnet steeped in the spirit of Spanish religious mysticism, "Elogio a la celda ascética" (1916). At about the same time he won a prize for his religious chronicle, "La procesión del Señor de los milagros." Even during his European travels, when his radicalism was in its formative stage, he made certain that his first-born received baptism. And in Peru shortly afterward he refused to join Haya de la Torre in the latter's campaign for a strict separation of church and state.[39] In several articles

35. J. C. Mariátegui, *El alma matinal* (Lima, 1959), p. 18.
36. *Ibid.*, pp. 13-14.
37. *Ibid.*, p. 18.
38. Chang-Rodríguez, *La literatura política*, p. 152.
39. *Ibid.*, p. 153.

on the question of lay education versus religious education he expresses a position which, for a Leftist, is surprisingly neutral.[40] He doubted that what he termed the "demo-liberal-bourgeois" secular school would contribute to the revolution; it is only through the revolution (and after it) that true "liberty of education" will be achieved.[41] Writing in 1925, he finds that in such countries as Mexico and Russia "the revolution has given ... the schools their myth, their emotion, their mystique, and their religiosity."[42] One would conclude that education without these qualities holds little, if any, appeal for Mariátegui. In the rather academic chapter devoted to "the religious factor" in his *Siete ensayos*, he begins by stating "the days of anti-clerical a priori reasoning have been completely surpassed—that period when 'freethinking' criticism contented itself with a sterile and cursory dismissal of all dogmas and churches, in favor of the orthodoxly atheistic, secular and rationalistic dogma of 'free thought.' The religious concept has grown in breadth and in depth.... And religious institutions and feelings are now recognized as being very different from what was naïvely assumed by those who used to identify religiosity with obscurantism."[43] He follows these remarks by reference to Waldo Frank's favorable estimate of the role of religious belief in the Western World, and by an analysis of the role of catholicism in Spanish America. Carefully avoiding a frontal assault on the church, he concludes that socialism rightfully considers diverse "ecclesiastical forms and religious doctrines" as peculiar and inherent to the political and economic regimes which produce them: it is the Marxist's primary objective to change these regimes rather than to attempt to change the religious institutions which are purely derivative.[44] What Mariátegui is obviously saying is that religious belief—faith, an irrational mythos of some sort—is an undeniable concomitant of the human condition: this view is substantiated—on a slightly different level—when he parenthetically warns his readers not to confuse historical materialism with philosophical materialism.[45] It is clear that as a Marxist he accepted the former, but as a religious humanist he rejected the latter.

40. *Ibid.*, pp. 154-55.
41. *Ibid.*, p. 156.
42. J. C. Mariátegui, "Introducción a un estudio sobre el problema de la educación pública," *Repertorio Americano*, XI (Sept. 7, 1925), 13, as cited by Chang-Rodríguez, *La literatura política*, pp. 155-56.
43. Mariátegui, *Siete ensayos*, p. 140.
44. *Ibid.*, p. 167.
45. *Ibid.*, p. 166.

A section of Professor Chang-Rodríguez' valuable analysis of Mariátegui's political writings bears the appropriate title "Religion is not the opiate of the people." The same critic also notes that Mariátegui's radicalism "altered his religious ideas very little, on the other hand, his religious concepts did alter his political ideas."[46] This point is well taken; less defensible is his statement that "[Mariátegui] never succeeded in freeing himself completely from the religious training that he received during his childhood and youth."[47] For one thing, it is quite clear that Mariátegui was philosophically a relativist. Although he recognizes that religious beliefs, "blind" faith, or a completely irrational devotion to a particular cause, have undeniable reality for human beings, Mariátegui clearly rejects the idea that absolute truth is embodied in any one religious belief. A specific dogma has, he feels, merely an instrumental value: "Dogma is useful as is a navigator's chart or a map: it is the only guarantee of not repeating again, under the illusion of advancing, the same course. . . . Dogma is not an itinerary but rather a compass for the journey. To think freely, the first condition to be met is that we give up our concern over absolute freedom."[48] What is important, and what gives men as well as societies their strength, is a willingness to live dangerously, to believe in something, to live "agonically" as Unamuno might have put it. All this and much more, Mariátegui holds, can be incorporated into a Marxist world-view. "Vitalism, activism, Pragmatism, relativism—none of these philosophical currents, to the extent that they have been able to contribute to the Revolution, have remained on the sidelines of the Marxist intellectual movement."[49] He consistently attempts to present Marxism as a position based upon "science, not scientism"; he points out that the deterministic element in Marxism has been overemphasized by the movement's enemies; rather, he feels, it is creative and voluntaristic.[50] He could even state that ". . . Only because of a convention of language can Marxism be opposed to or distinguished from idealism."[51] Finally, he was disturbed that a philosopher of Unamuno's sensibilities could oppose the movement, and he felt certain that if the great Spanish thinker would study "the spirit—not the letter—of Marxism" he would modify his criticism.[52]

46. Chang-Rodríguez, *La literatura política*, p. 160.
47. *Ibid.*, p. 159.
48. J. C. Mariátegui, *Defensa del Marxismo* (Lima, 1959), p. 105.
49. *Ibid.*, p. 39.
50. *Ibid.*, pp. 55-58.
51. *Ibid.*, p. 52.
52. Mariátegui, *El alma matinal*, p. 157.

Mariátegui was intensely interested in the concrete problems of his native Peru. But just as his Marxism was modified by a profound humanism, one might even say by an existentialist view of man, his nationalism was inseparable from a broad Americanism. One of the most striking aspects of this position is seen in his attitude toward North America. Unlike many Spanish American radicals he rejects wholesale, simplistic anti-Yankeeism. He finds certain North Americans, such as the essayist Waldo Frank and the writers of the New Republic, following a philosophical trajectory similar to his own. When he speaks of the "magnificent idealistic forces which have been at work in Yankee history" he singles out several groups which have played a significant role as the leavening in this nation's life—the Puritans, the Jews, and the American Transcendentalists. These ideas clearly parallel those of Frank, whose books—especially the *Re-discovery of America*—are warmly praised.[53] Mariátegui understandably felt attracted to other Spanish Americans who shared this Americanist fervor. He was particularly sympathetic toward the ideas of José Vasconcelos, whose indigenist sympathies, radical idealism, and religious views coincided closely with his own.[54] A good indication of Mariátegui's stature as an Americanist and of his impact upon other Spanish American writers can be seen in the many fervent tributes dedicated to him by his contemporaries. Many of these articles appeared as special *homenajes* published on the occasion of his death in leading literary journals of the continent; a substantial selection of these essays was reprinted in the widely circulated review *El Repertorio Americano*.[55] His admirers include doctrinaire Communists (the Cuban Marinello, for example); less orthodox Marxist sympathizers (Cuba's Mañach, Argentina's Alberto Gerchúnoff, and North America's Waldo Frank); and a host of others—Chile's Gabriela Mistral, Uruguay's Horacio Quiroga, Colombia's Sanín Cano, and many of the Peruvian *Apristas*. Even a conservative like Víctor Andrés Belaúnde, editor of the pro-Catholic

53. *Ibid.*, p. 153.
54. *Ibid.*, pp. 28, 121. Had Mariátegui lived longer his attitude toward Vasconcelos might well have changed, since the Mexican essayist turned sharply to the Right during the mid-thirties: Vasconcelos became a vociferous defender of the church and an impassioned anti-Communist. Of course, given Mariátegui's deep-seated religiosity it is not inconceivable that had he not died in 1930, his own ideological trajectory might have been similar to that of Vasconcelos.
55. See especially "Del homenaje peruano a J. C. Mariátegui," *Repertorio Americano*, XX (1930), 308-10, "Del homenaje argentino a J. C. Mariátegui," *Repertorio Americano*, XX (1930), 344-47; and "Del tributo cubano a José Carlos Mariátegui," *Repertorio Americano*, XXI (1930), 121-23, 142-44.

Mercurio peruano, could find much to praise in Mariátegui's most famous work, the *Siete ensayos de interpretación de la realidad peruana*.[56]

While the Communists questioned Mariátegui's heterodox tendencies,[57] the most powerful native Leftist movement of the time, the APRA, doubted his devotion to genuinely indigenous radicalism. It has been suggested that the superficial rift between Haya de la Torre, the *Aprista's* leader, and Mariátegui, was in effect widened by the deliberate efforts of Moscow.[58] It is certainly clear that a great deal of Mariátegui's ideology was substantially the same as that of the *Apristas*, though differences did exist. One of these lay in the fact that Mariátegui conceived of the Peruvian—and the Spanish American—class struggle as part of a broad international movement. Another lay in religious attitudes: the *Apristas* were outspoken anti-Catholics while Mariátegui was not. Further differences are apparent in the general view of history, wherein Mariátegui, in contrast to Haya, repeatedly underscores the priority of economic factors in determining the course of events. Aside from these specific matters, there is, in Mariátegui's writing—even when he discusses his native Peru—the ring of European inspired Marxist orthodoxy. Finally, it is ironic that the *Aprista* movement, with its emphasis upon education, the moral code, and an almost religious devotion to a political cause, should have offered Spanish America's masses precisely what Mariátegui consistently called for—the "revolutionary myth." It must be remembered that José Carlos Mariátegui died early in life, after a considerable period of chronic illness, and before many basic inconsistencies in his thinking could be resolved. But despite these inadequacies, his life, his works, and his mystical humanism brought forth an impressive chorus of sincere admiration: for Leopoldo Lugones—hardly a political bedfellow—he was "the best of all the leftists"; for Juan Marinello he was "a far advanced defender of our destiny"; and for the French radical Henri Barbusse, "a new specimen of American man."[59]

Among the *Aprista* essayists who continued the Peruvian radical tradition initiated by Prada and further developed by Mariátegui, two merit special attention: Antenor Orrego and Victor Raúl Haya de la Torre, the movement's political leader. Orrego, whose works are somewhat less known than those of Haya, first wrote in the review

56. Víctor Andrés Belaúnde, "En torno al último libro de Mariátegui," *Mercurio Peruano*, XX, No. 139/140 (Mar.-April, 1930), 132-36.
57. See above, note 34.
58. Chang-Rodríguez, *La literatura política*, p. 196.
59. Cited in *ibid.*, pp. 202-3.

Amauta and later amplified and organized his ideas in the volume *El pueblo continente* (1939). Orrego builds his essays around several key themes: Americanism viewed as a mission or destiny; Marxism accepted as a socio-economic instrument; indigenism seen as an almost mystical force emanating from the land; and a neohumanism held as the defining characteristic of the creative, suprarational society which was to emerge in the New World.

Orrego's earliest essays in *Amauta* deal with fundamental philosophical positions, rather than with specific analyses of political or cultural problems. He states in 1926 that " . . . the major error of systematic philosophy has been that it availed itself of reason to constrict concepts, when reason is the instrument for arousing and transmitting intuition. . . ."[60] In an essay written shortly afterward, "Racionalismo y revolución" he continues this same line of attack while adding an Orteguian tone to his discussion of reason. He praises the thinker who doesn't merely manipulate pure categories, but who "ascends" from "the *circunstancia* or realm of daily events towards the speculative domain."[61] An even greater debt to the Spanish writer is evident in Orrego's later work when he adopts the distinction between "history" and "pre-history" as developed by Ortega in his essay "Hegel y América."[62] Orrego's discussion of freedom and determinism is likewise set forth in Orteguian terms. Thus, when the Peruvian thinker speaks of "a vital modality . . . a style" for a given people as "the resultant of an equation of biological, psychic, telluric, and historical factors which are brought together and organized in a definite structure,"[63] Ortega's *circunstancia* is immediately suggested. Orrego does not, however, slight the other side of Ortega's equation, "I am myself and my circumstance." He thinks of individual human endeavor as working with and "from" the *circunstancia*: "Personality is subject to the determinism which has been created by man as a collectivity . . . as group consciousness. . . We are not, then, creators, nor are (external) events creators, except in the sense that we are the faithful translators or vehicles of expression of these dynamic forces which are the ever flowing essence of history."[64]

60. Antenor Orrego, "Apuntes para una filosofía o interpretación del pensamiento," *Amauta*, I (Dec., 1926), 17.
61. Antenor Orrego, "Racionalismo y revolución," *Amauta*, I (Feb., 1927), 1.
62. Antenor Orrego, *El pueblo continente: Ensayos para una interpretación de la América Latina* (Santiago de Chile, 1939), p. 52.
63. *Ibid.*, p. 49.
64. *Ibid.*, p. 111.

As we saw earlier, the Orteguian interest in the *circunstancia* leads inevitably to a pressing desire for self-knowledge, for a deeper understanding of what Orrego would call the "style" or "group spirit." For it is only through this process of autognosis that the individual—or nation—can achieve a degree of creative freedom. This position is clearly formulated by Orrego in one of his later *Amauta* essays: "We Americans are convinced that America will emerge from its own limitations only in proportion to the effort and courage we demonstrate for self-discovery."[65] The same idea is amplified and incorporated into his concept of Americanism in the *Pueblo continente*: "A people or race does not succeed in becoming a vehicle of historical expression unless it penetrates deeply the hidden intimacy of its own being."[66]

Closely related to Orrego's analysis of freedom, its limitations, and the *circunstancia* is his philosophy of revolution. Any "idea" that is to be effective—that is to exert an "historic belligerency"— must be developed as an expression of certain economic, social, and spiritual conditions, i.e., the *circunstancia*. Yet to have historical efficacy, ideas must also "participate in a personal venture; they must be incarnated in the dramatic and even tragic twists of fortune of a single life or group of lives. . . ."[67] Without this personal direction, without "a group of human beings who are willing to live tragically or "dangerously," as Mariátegui would have put it, the "revolutionary idea" will come to naught. Most important, Orrego maintains that the basic conditions required for this "revolutionary idea" to become more than an ineffectual utopian notion, are fulfilled in the *Aprista* movement. He bases this view on the fact that *Aprismo* is "an historical movement, conditioned by economic, social, and moral determinism . . . a profoundly vital movement which in turn engenders its own instruments of fulfillment. . . ."[68] The specific human instrument, the "political agglutinator, the point of convergence where one generation polarizes the vital content of the past with humanity's future trajectory" is the APRA leadership, especially Haya de la Torre himself.[69] Orrego's critique of the Third International is correspondingly predicated on the belief that it is not rooted in an American *circunstancia*. Therefore, Spanish Ameri-

65. Antenor Orrego, "¿Qué es una filosofía?," *Amauta*, III (Nov.-Dec., 1929), 3.
66. Orrego, *El pueblo continente*, p. 59.
67. *Ibid.*, p. 113.
68. *Ibid.*, p. 116.
69. *Ibid.*

cans who attempt to view their revolution in terms of the International's orthodoxy see only a distorted image of Europe.[70]

Orrego, like other supporters of *Aprismo*, did not regard the political and economic structures which the revolution was to achieve as ends in themselves but rather as the necessary conditions by which man will eventually create a more distinctively human world. Thus, in his *Amauta* essays he concerns himself with such basic problems as the continent's general cultural trajectory and the relationship between literary nationalism and Americanism. Orrego's discussion of these themes parallels the thinking of Waldo Frank to a remarkable degree. Like his North American contemporary (a portion of whose *Re-discovery of America* had appeared in *Amauta* in 1927) he struggled to clarify the precise cultural relationship of the New World to the Old. Orrego's version of this relationship takes the form of a biological metaphor: he states in an early essay that European culture, when transported to America, "decomposes and rots." And from this humus, from this "compost heap," a new vigorous plant will come forth.[71] The metaphor is further developed in the *Pueblo continente* when Orrego explains that decomposition necessarily occurs when a fully developed "cultural organism" matures, becomes brittle, and is hence incapable of further evolution.[72] This was precisely the fate of European culture when it came into contact with the New World. The process of "decomposition" was aided, moreover, by the fact that some American societies, the Incan, for example, had already attained a "maturity" equal to—or even more advanced than—that of Europe. Orrego views the clash of the two cultures as a return to "the primordial chaos, to the formless slime, to the original and primitive humus."[73] This disintegration, he warns, must not be thought of in absolute terms, for although given forms of cultures perish, what might be called the genes of a potential new culture persist, albeit disunited. These seeds await only an organizing principle to initiate a recomposition, an integration which will lead to new and original expressions. Orrego gives us only a hazy idea of just how this process will be started. At times he states that the spiritual force, the revolutionary mystique embodied in the *Aprista* movement, will provide the catalytic action;[74]

70. *Ibid.*, pp. 101-7.
71. Antenor Orrego, "¿Cuál es la cultura que creará América?," *Amauta*, II (April, 1928), 3.
72. Orrego, *El pueblo continente*, p. 29.
73. *Ibid.*, p. 39.
74. *Ibid.*, pp. 123-24.

while on other occasions he looks for the "terrestrial vital fluids"—the intimate contact with telluric forces—to provide the needed initial spark. This view of telluric forces is not completely consistent with Orrego's more deterministic notion of the *circunstancia*. Can the land restrict man's freedom on one hand and liberate his creative potential on the other? Although Orrego may not resolve this inconsistency completely, his outlook is fundamentally optimistic: "Nowhere as in South America does the lower, abysmal world exercise so powerful an influence upon man; but, in no other place in the world does man have any greater possibility to express the non-material potentialities of his spirit, since he has, by virtue of his having translated the telluric essence into human expression, appropriated to himself a substance of great density and hence of great richness."[75]

Orrego's debt to Waldo Frank is, we have seen, not inconsiderable. Orrego's extensive use of "organic" metaphors in the *Pueblo continente*, was clearly foreshadowed in Frank's *Re-discovery of America*. The very first sentence of the North American's book reads "Take Europe as an alive organic body."[76] This statement is followed closely by such statements as ". . . organic death does not mean inanition. Look at any corpse advanced in its decay, and see how live it is. Europe swarms in death."[77] It is not mere coincidence that Orrego's *Amauta* articles of 1928, in which he speaks of the rot and decomposition of European culture as "fertilizing the new plant" of American culture, should appear only a few months after the same journal published portions of the then incomplete *Rediscovery of America*.[78] In several other details Orrego follows Frank's thinking closely. He frequently attacks the modern tendency toward the worship of the machine, toward specialization, and toward the loss of "the panoramic vision of things. . . ."[79] These views parallel Frank's recurring theme of "Wholeness" as the "value which alone can make valid the America we discover." As the term "Wholeness" underlies Frank's idea of the American destiny, so the phrase "an integral culture" (*una cultura integral*) constantly

75. *Ibid.*, pp. 154-55. Orrego is also interested in the telluric theme as expressed in indigenous mythology. He has, for example, suggested a serious reinterpretation of the symbolic deity Pacha-Mama. This interest parallels that of G. Francovich. Cf. above, Chapter IV, pp. 88-89.
76. Waldo Frank, *The Re-discovery of America* (New York, 1929), p. 11.
77. *Ibid.*, p. 15.
78. See *Amauta*, II (July, 1927).
79. Antenor Orrego, "¿Cuál es la cultura que creará América?," *Amauta*, II (Sept., 1928), 14.

reappears in Orrego's essays. This "integration" will come about through the adoption of new social structures and—even more important—the acceptance of new intellectual positions such as Ortega's "vitalization of reason—the restoration of reason's intermediate role in thought."[80] Orrego would also have a kind of mysticism recognized as a valid form of human experience, especially since he holds that the native American possesses an "inchoate orientalism," an ability to appreciate life "in its subjective totality . . . in its fusion or submersion in God."[81] Finally, Marxism, freely interpreted and reformed to suit the needs of the New World, would also contribute to the ideological synthesis.[82]

Orrego considers all the existing human elements of the continent as a fertile, potentially great, but as yet unformed mass: "For four centuries all races have been melting in the American bonfire. Yesteryear required a disjunctive process; the future demands one of integration and reconstitution!"[83] How does Orrego believe that this American melting-pot will eventually produce the desired integration? A possible way may be found through the unifying role of the APRA. Yet, to accord such importance to a mere political ideology would do Orrego an injustice. For at the root of his concept of the "Pueblo continente" is a deep and mystical faith in the American destiny: the fortuitous mixing of races and cultures— albeit with some guidance by farseeing leaders—will necessarily, and almost spontaneously, lead to the desired integration. The Indian, retaining his "oriental," suprarational, intuitive, tellurically sensitive nature, will unite with the technically and politically skilled European;[84] while the Negro will contribute aesthetic richness, the fruit of his profound eroticism.[85] Again echoing Waldo Frank, Orrego indicates that the new culture and the new human product will not be simply a combination or a mere composite, but that it will be a new and unique entity.[86] Frank's "orchestral" metaphor describing the relationship of the parts to the whole, figures significantly in the *Pueblo continente.* Typical examples of its use are seen in Orrego's statement that each group must "discover its own melody in the vast

80. Orrego, "¿Cuál es la cultura que creará América?," *Amauta*, II (April, 1928), 4.
81. Orrego, *El pueblo continente*, p. 55.
82. *Ibid.*, p. 125.
83. *Ibid.*, p. 53.
84. *Ibid.*, pp. 55-56.
85. *Ibid.*, pp. 165-68.
86. *Ibid.*, p. 47.

harmony of Humanity," and that ". . . the tonic notes of America are different from the tonic notes of Europe. . . ."[87]

Although Victor Raúl Haya de la Torre (1895——) is primarily a political leader, any discussion of Spanish American radicalism must include a consideration of his contributions. As the actual founder of the APRA and as the movement's leader since its beginnings in 1924, Haya's literary production has served as an intellectual foundation for his political position. As writer and thinker he is similar to Orrego in several respects. Both men were born in the provincial city of Trujillo; and both attended the university there—the first institution of higher learning in Peru to feel the impact of Spanish America's widespread university reform movement. Both took an active interest in Leftist politics in their native city: Orrego as the founder of a radical newspaper, and Haya as a student leader. As we have seen, Haya's importance as a political leader was frequently underscored by Orrego; likewise, Haya recognizes his intellectual debt to Orrego. Though the writings of the *Aprista* leader are voluminous, they are, with some notable exceptions, primarily political in intent. As such these articles, speeches, letters, manifestos, pamphlets, clarifications of the APRA position, etc., can only be included in an extremely broad definition of the essay.

One work of Haya which does stand out as an important expression of several themes which we have been pursuing is *Espacio-Tiempo histórico* (1948). Actually this work is a series of more or less independent essays, the first of which was written as early as 1935. The close connection with Orrego's thought is immediately seen in the *Espacio-Tiempo histórico* in the repeated use of the term "Pueblo-continente" ("that fortunate phrase created by Antenor Orrego"[88]) to designate the distinctive cultural units upon which the essay is framed. Haya follows Orrego quite closely in that he shares an Hegelian-Marxist sensitivity to historical development, and an Orteguian appreciation of the uniqueness of each specific *circunstancia*. But while Orrego considers Ortega's concept of "vital reason" crucial, Haya's thought has been shaped more by the Spanish philosopher's essay, *El tema de nuestro tiempo*—i.e., on the implications of Einsteinian relativity. Although Haya might well have studied Einstein as early as 1918 or 1919, as Chang-Rodríguez suggests,[89] it seems logical that Ortega's provocative essay of 1923

87. *Ibid.*, p. 68.
88. Victor Raúl Haya de la Torre, *Espacio-tiempo histórico* (Lima, 1948), p. 24.
89. Chang-Rodríguez, *La literatura política*, p. 306.

had a greater impact upon the young Peruvian than did the very technical writings of Einstein himself. The fact that in May of 1923 Haya published an article in *El Tiempo* of Lima on some philosophical implications of relativity corroborates this view,[90] and is, moreover, another indication of Ortega's catalytic effect on Spanish American intellectual activity.[91]

The chief features of Haya's position as expressed in the *Espacio-Tiempo histórico* may be sketched out readily. Marxism, within which he places his own philosophy of history and society, must be viewed as a genuine product of its Hegelian roots, and hence subject to the "law of the negation of negation."[92] Although conceived before the advent of the theory of relativity, Marxism must be interpreted according to twentieth-century science—Einsteinian physics, non-Euclidean geometry, the field concept, etc.: "The application of Relativity to historical determinism presents an exact case of negation and dialectical continuity in the philosophy of Marx. Moreover, the foundations of the *Aprista* philosophic standard are based precisely on the relativity of time and space, applied to the Marxist interpretation of history. This is the dialectical line which divides and unites orthodox Marxism and *Aprismo*."[93]

This specific "application" of the theory of relativity involves the development of a philosophy of history based upon an inseparable "Space-Time continuum." Haya apparently feels that this is a reality and not merely an analogy or construct. He speaks at length of a "subjective time" (not unlike the Hegelian *Ich Zeit*) which is conceived with relation to a given "geographic scenario." Thus, a distinctive notion of time, resulting from what might be called the indigenous rhythm of life, will be characteristic of a particular set of environmental conditions. For example, the Andean Indian compared with a European will think of time as "slow"; his days will be "long" and the pulse beat of his life will be sluggish, at least as viewed by the European. This conjunction of a specific geographic setting, a unique sense of time, and a corresponding individual pace of historical development, characterize each "Pueblo-continente."[94] Again borrowing from contemporary scientific thought, Haya notes that

90. Cited in *ibid.*, pp. 306-7. Haya's article appeared on May 11, 1923.
91. In addition to Einstein, several other thinkers have helped shape Haya's political and historical theories. An analysis of his debt to A. S. Eddington, J. S. Haldane, and of course to Arnold Toynbee, could prove very valuable.
92. Haya de la Torre, *Espacio-tiempo*, p. 5.
93. *Ibid.*, p. 7.
94. *Ibid.*, pp. 8-9.

absolute notions of historical development are untenable; that just as the mathematical concept of parallel lines has been reinterpreted, "we must recognize that the parallelism in the development of peoples—a principle already sketched out by Marx—is also relative in the vastness of history."[95] He goes on to point out that this application of relativity implies that "the history of the world, viewed from Indo-American 'historical space-time,' will never be what the philosopher observes from the vantage point of European 'historical space-time.' Likewise we hold that what is 'last' in Europe, may perhaps be 'first' in Indo-America."[96] This view is applied to specifics: Haya will maintain, for example, that imperialism, though looked upon by orthodox Marxists as the ultimate or supreme stage of capitalism, from the "Indoamerican" historical space-time must be considered the first stage.[97]

Haya clarifies and refines his concepts in the essays which follow this 1935 statement of *Espacio-Tiempo histórico*. In these later writings he takes particular pains to point out fundamental differences between his position and that of other thinkers whose ideas bear a superficial resemblance to his own. Thus he denies that his own view of history partakes of Spengler's fatalism,[98] or of the facile, opportunistic theorizing of Mackinder and the geopoliticians.[99] At least one important new element is incorporated into his earlier exposition of historic space-time. In the *Cuadernos Americanos* restatement of the theory, written in 1945, he notes that for a given historic space-time to become effective "it must exist . . . as a vital function of its social consciousness. . . ." This "social consciousness" is in turn dependent upon the development of "the psychological capacity of a social group to be aware of its history and to interpret it from the vantage point of its own reality."[100] Although this point is not expanded to any extent, it indicates a definite sensitivity to a theme that has frequently been noted in many of Haya's contemporaries; the urgent need for self-knowledge as a condition for understanding the potentialities of the emerging New World. And here again the debt to Ortega and the *circunstancia* concept must be recognized.

95. *Ibid.*, p. 13.
96. *Ibid.*
97. *Ibid.*
98. *Ibid.*, p. 20.
99. *Ibid.*, p. 30.
100. *Ibid.*, p. 35.

Haya de la Torre has suggested an interesting resolution of the problems centered about the relationship of the Old World to the New. In doing so, he has provided a point of view from which Spanish American radicals could appreciate, on the one hand, their connections with orthodox Marxism and, on the other, the possibility of creating an independent political philosophy grounded on American realities. Haya, however, has directed his attention more toward concrete political matters and the study of history than he has toward what I have called the "interior revolution." Although he would not consider the material revolution more important than this other revolt—his admiration for a figure such as Romain Rolland bears this out—he has not shown that almost mystical passion for a profound radical humanism which one finds in Mariátegui or even in the less politically oriented Alfonso Caso. His relativism notwithstanding, the great emphasis he places upon environmental forces and his utilization of constructs drawn from the least human of disciplines—physics and mathematics—indicate that man's creativity and freedom are in fact substantially limited. In short, Haya suggests that although cultures differ in form and in rate of development they nevertheless have a determined "unfolding"; what the individual human being can do to shape this development seems to be limited to a minor cooperative role predicated on his awareness of the process. This position differs from the well-known historicist views of Vico, Spengler, and others chiefly in its denial of cycles and in its denial of a single universal pattern. That these differences are sufficient to place Haya's thought in the mainstream of Spanish America's reaction against scientism and determinism is clearly open to question.

In few areas of Spanish America have political radicalism and intellectual radicalism existed in as intimate a relationship as they have in Peru. But even without a vehicle of concrete expression, such as that provided by the *Aprista* movement, radical essayists in other countries have substantially influenced thought, literature, and even mass attitudes. The kind of writers I have in mind— Mexico's Samuel Ramos (1897-1957), Argentina's Francisco Romero (1891-1963), or Ezequiel Martínez Estrada (1895-1964)—have distinguished themselves as men of letters rather than as politicians; yet in that they attack the very roots of contemporary society— what they view as the materialistic, technologically dominated world of the Western bourgeoisie—they are profoundly radical. These essayists are not Marxists in the usual sense of the term: they conceive of the founder of socialism not simply as a political or economic theorist, but as a man of passion, fervently committed to the creation of a world dominated by distinctively human values. In a work such as Ramos' *Hacia un nuevo humanismo: Programa de una antropología filosófica* (1940)[101] this view of Marx the humanist is set forth particularly well. Again it must be made clear that Ramos is not a politician; indeed he strongly resembles the typical *intellectuel pur.*

A leader of the generation of young thinkers and writers who may be considered "the children of the *Ateneo*," Ramos made his intellectual debut by attacking what he then thought of as the "neo-romantic," "anti-intellectual," and "critically weak" philosophic position of Antonio Caso.[102] Shortly afterward he turned toward the analysis of Mexican personality; the fruit of this interest and perhaps his most famous work, *El perfil del hombre y la cultura en México* (1934), will be examined later in the context of the very crucial theme of the search for national essence. The Ramos work which concerns us here grew out of certain long-standing philosophic preoccupations. One of the most important of these—the possibility or impossibility of grounding moral theory on an irrational view of man—formed the subject of a 1936 article,[103] while an essay dealing with the broader question of the predicament of modern humanism,[104] gives an early indication of some of the ideas to be developed in his major work of 1940.

The radical ring of the *Nuevo humanismo* is apparent in the very early pages of the work. In support of the position that "infrahumanity engendered by bourgeois capitalism and materialism" threatens to "petrify" values, "dehumanize" art and society, etc.,[105] Ramos cites a number of widely diverse thinkers. A striking example of this diversity may be seen in that he quotes the North American Sydney Hook (on the point that Marx attacked capitalism not as a utilitarian, but rather because it made men "inhuman") on the same page with a citation from the mystical national socialist Werner

101. A testimonial to the continued timeliness of Ramos' ideas is seen in the fact that his *Nuevo humanismo* recently (1962) appeared in a second edition.
102. Samuel Ramos, "Antonio Caso," *Ulises*, I (June, 1927), 12-20. Many years later, Ramos' attitude toward Caso became considerably less critical. See his "Antonio Caso, filósofo romántico," *Filosofía y letras*, XI (April-June, 1946), 179-96.
103. Samuel Ramos, "Sociología de la obligación moral" *Universidad de México*, 2ª época, I (May, 1936), 26-30.
104. Samuel Ramos, "La crisis del humanismo" *Universidad de México*, 2ª época, IV (Aug., 1937), 1-10.
105. Samuel Ramos, *Hacia un nuevo humanismo: Programa de una antropología filosófica* (México, 1940), pp. 24-25; hereinafter cited as *Nuevo humanismo*.

Sombart (on the contemporary bourgeois spirit as showing "a complete indifference toward the destiny of man"[106]). Ramos' stated intent in this book is to "plan an itinerary" for the understanding of man "in accord with the present state of philosophical anthropology."[107] The specific reference to "philosophical anthropology" clearly reflects the thought of the German philosopher Max Scheler (1874-1928) who, by the late thirties, had gained a very substantial intellectual beach-head in Spanish America.[108]

Considering his impact upon such major figures as Ramos, Romero, and others a brief examination of Scheler's thought is in order. Although he was not a political radical, Scheler's attempt to develop a unique axiology and his quest for "man's place in nature" bespeak a decidedly radical personality. Scheler uses the term "spirit" to describe a distinctively human awareness of the self as an object. His term "psyche," by contrast, stands for consciousness, and the ability for intelligent organization of the environment. All of the "higher" animals, Scheler maintains, possess a "psyche"; but only man has "spirit," defined as the ability to "objectify" one's own self—to see one's own psyche *and* the surrounding environment from an external vantage point. On the basis of this framework Scheler constructs a philosophy of values: the individual, to the extent that his "spirit" is sufficiently developed, will be able to see the outcome of his actions in the objective world. The person in a sense becomes a god, though nothing mystical or other-worldly is implied by this term. Scheler in fact insists that man be ever mindful of the concrete effects of his acts in the real world. He further holds that the "pure values" which guide the individual are derived from experience; that they are only seen in their purity by virtue of the "spirit"; and that they may not be completely realized in the objective world. In short, Scheler's philosophy represents an impressive attempt to establish a morality without reference to external arbiters of traditional religion or utilitarian social theories. Scheler was not a true radical, but rather an "outsider"; a passionate, often prejudiced, and frequently inconsistent commentator on political matters.[109] Yet his very radical concept of man's moral commit-

106. *Ibid.*, p. 26.
107. *Ibid.*, p. 28.
108. See above, Chapter IV, note 110.
109. A good explanation and critique of these ideas is available to English readers in Hans Meyerhoff's "Translator's Introduction" to Scheler's *Man's Place in Nature* (New York, 1961). For a very different and very critical analysis of Scheler see also Alfred Stern, "Max Scheler, filósofo de la guerra total y del estado totalitario," *Minerva: Revista continental de filosofía*, I (Jan.-April, 1945).

ments implied a clear rejection of the role of established institutions of moral suasion: church, state, etc. Thus, when Ramos says that "genuine morality can only be evaluated by knowing what goes on within each man, in order to find out how aware he is of the end result of his activity,"[110] his debt to the German philosopher is apparent.

Although Ramos appreciated the "humanness" in Marx, he objected to historical materialism as a world view: ". . . historical materialism . . . must take into consideration that economics is also merely a branch and that the trunk of the tree is man himself. . . ."[111] This position is, and was, a virtual commonplace; however, I suspect that what was decisive in this rejection was the Schelerian relegation of historical materialism to the category of "naturalistic" theories that fail to grasp the crucial relationship between "spirit" and "life."[112] It is clear that Ramos' view of man as an arbiter of his own morality—not by means of mystically achieved insights, not by reference to traditional religious codes, and certainly not by perpetuating the materialistic ethic of the bourgeoisie—is distinctly radical. Here again the debt to Scheler is obvious. Both men were attempting to walk the narrow path between what Scheler calls the "naturalistic" philosophies and those of the "classical" Greek and Judeo-Christian traditions, which stressed "untenable" notions of the self-generative power of Ideas, the Godhead, etc.[113] Both writers strive to establish "pure," unchanging, values such as justice, heroism, and charity. These would not be subject to individual whims, and yet they would not be "derived" theologically or in any other manner except by the process of human self-awareness (i.e., by the Schelerian

110. Ramos, *Nuevo humanismo*, p. 103. Several other thinkers, whose work is closely related to Scheler's, also figure prominently in the *Nuevo humanismo*. Ludwig Klages' philosophy of personalism, Nicolai Hartmann's work on the problem of liberty, as well as more familiar thought of Bergson and Ortega, all contribute to Ramos' synthesis. A detailed critique of the manner in which the Mexican thinker utilizes these varied sources would be beyond the scope of this study; a few points, however, may be made. Ramos views the Bergsonian "intuition" as a method of getting into "direct contact with real things." As such he feels that it parallels the "primitive naivete" which the phenomenologists stress as *the* approach to reality. He thus links Bergson with at least one expression of the emerging Existentialist movement. As so often happens in Spanish American thought of this period, the Orteguian concepts of the "circumstance" and of "perspectivism" are, in general, accepted. If we were to plunge more deeply into Ramos' thought, certain antitheses may be seen: for example, the question might be raised as to the possibility of his accepting on the one hand Ortega's fundamental vitalism and, on the other, Scheler's unique concept of "Spirit."
111. Ramos, *Nuevo humanismo*, p. 148.
112. Scheler, *Man's Place in Nature*, pp. 81-83.
113. See Scheler's chapter on "Philosophical Anthropology and Religion," *ibid.*, pp. 88-95.

"spirit"). Lastly, a word regarding Ramos' application of some of these ideas to his own Mexico: he warns his countrymen that a rigorously objective order of values is possible and that to justify the modern Mexican's skepticism and *desconfianza* (distrust, suspicious fear) as "natural characteristics" may not be warranted.[114] To pursue this point, however, will lead directly to an important aspect of Ramos' work which will concern us later; namely, his impressive anaylsis of Mexican character.

Argentine intellectuals, like their Mexican counterparts, have been quick to assimilate new and provocative philosophical positions. Their introduction to Scheler's thought was, as in the Mexicans' case, through a series of translations in Ortega's *Revista de Occidente* and through the Spanish translation of *Die Stellung des Menschen im Kosmos* (*Man's Place in Nature*, 1928). Scheler's ideas soon appeared in the works of several important Argentine essayists and philosophers: Carlos Astrada, Carlos Alberto Erro, and most notably in the writings of Francisco Romero (1891-1962). A distinguished disciple of Alejandro Korn, the dean of contemporary Argentine philosophers, Romero parallels Samuel Ramos to a considerable degree. Much of his *Filosofía de la persona* (1938) is simply a sympathetic exposition of the basic Schelerian position, which is viewed as a valuable check on the extremely voluntaristic, irrational philosophy of the Nietzschean tradition. The same desire for "objective," "pure" values—yet ones which would be derived by man "to the extent that he is a spiritual being"—is evident in both Romero and Ramos. And like his Mexican contemporary, Romero sees an analogy in Ortega's concept of the *circunstancia* and Scheler's unique view of the world which "spirit" provides. Other thinkers of Schelerian orientation—Nicolai Hartmann and especially Ludwig Klages—fascinated Romero as they did Ramos. Klages' distinction between "individual" and "person," based upon an intriguing etymological study of the latter term,[115] was especially appealing to the Argentine thinker. However Romero, perhaps even more than Ramos, is a philosophical rather than a literary essayist. While he shared with many of the writers discussed a desire to assert radically

114. Ramos, *Nuevo humanismo*, p. 88.
115. 'Persona' is analyzed in its Latin derivation from *per sonare*, i.e., 'to sound through,' as a god's voice coming through a classic mask. Thus, 'the person' in one sense is thought of as a mask through which a universal 'spirit'—the absolute Ground of Being, Scheler might say—expresses itself. Opposed to man *qua* person is man *qua* "individual" with all his volitions, individual desires, material wants, etc.

humanistic values, his place in the present study must be considered peripheral.

By contrast, Romero's compatriot and contemporary, Ezequiel Martínez Estrada, was a literary essayist of major proportions. Though he was not a philosopher, his writing reflects a strong philosophical bent. His essays are written with passion and poetry; if Martínez Estrada was a philosopher in any sense, he belonged with the *pensadores agónicos* of the modern world, with Kierkegaard or with Unamuno, though one writer has suggested G. B. Shaw as a fitting soul-mate. Martínez Estrada's radicalism is of great interest. Much of the idealistic, irrational, anarchic, profoundly human, and profoundly humane thought of the essayists we have been studying is summed up in his writings. Though no respecter of political doctrine, Martínez Estrada has nonetheless frequently espoused the extreme Left, and his critique of everything implied by the word "bourgeois" has been unceasingly vitriolic: yet he can be quite sensitive to the spiritual and aesthetic inadequacies of the Marxist world as it actually exists.[116] An early admirer of the Castro government, he was awarded a literary prize by the Cuban *Casa de las Américas* in 1960.[117] At approximately the same time he was being roundly attacked by many of Argentina's young Communists for his "anarchistic leanings," and for his denunciation of all dictatorial regimes without taking into consideration "the social content of dictatorships and . . . their future rather than just their present form. . . ."[118]

The usual presentation of Martínez Estrada's career begins by noting that he made his literary debut as a poet in the 1920's, and that his own feelings of frustration and dissatisfaction with his verse made him turn to the essay as a vehicle of expression in the early 1930's.[119] A slightly different version of his development stresses the fact that the political and economic debacle of 1930 jarred him—as well as other Argentine writers—into an attitude of critical circumspection. One writer carries this view to the point of saying that the Martínez Estrada of the early thirties was simply "an Argentine intellectual, of the middle class, terrorized by the

116. See Martínez Estrada's account of his experiences at the University of Moscow in his "Lo real y el realismo," *Cuadernos Americanos*, XVII (July-Oct., 1958), 258-64.
117. A portion of Martínez Estrada's prize-winning essay "Análisis funcional de la cutura" appeared in the Cuban periodical *Lunes de Revolución*, No. 47 (Feb. 15, 1960), pp. 3-5. I have not been able to ascertain whether the complete essay was actually published.
118. J. J. Sebreli *Martínez Estrada una rebelión inútil* (Buenos Aires, 1960), pp. 77.
119. Hector A. Murena, *El pecado original de América* (Buenos Aires, 1958), p. 122.

economic crisis, disillusioned and skeptical. . . ."[120] His prose from then on, so this theory holds, continues to reflect this terror and this disillusionment. It is true that Martínez Estrada's major essays, *Radiografía de la Pampa* (1933), *Cabeza de Goliat* (1940), *Muerte y transfiguración de Martín Fierro* (1948), *Exhortaciones* (1957), and others, reflect a sense of futility, of disenchantment, and often of extreme pessimism. It is quite understandable that Argentina's political and economic crisis of the early thirties lies behind the gloomy tonality of Martínez Estrada's essays: it is also conceivable that his feelings of insufficiency as a poet contributed to the overriding pessimism of his prose. However, Martínez Estrada's commentators have not given due attention to what must be thought of as the man's "raw," unmodified personality. This bedrock of Martínez Estrada's character is best seen in his very first works, a series of articles appearing in the well-known review *Nosotros*, and written before their author gained recognition as a poet. Neither Murena nor Sebreli, nor any other interpreter of Estrada, mentions these revealing early essays, though they go far toward providing the key to his entire career as an essayist.

The first of these pieces, "Hidden Treasures," dates from October of 1917. In it, the twenty-two-year-old Estrada takes a Pascalian, sentimental tack in criticizing rationalism, and the systematizing of life. He speaks in very general terms: "Are not our errors the results of having wished, by means of reason, to turn aside the course of events?"[121] Shortly afterward, he simply asks "And just what purpose does systematizing serve?"[122] He then discusses various forms of antirationalism: he writes of Schopenhauer, of Maeterlinck, and especially of love in almost mystic terms. Eros—broadly conceived—redeems and enlightens. Woman is thought of virtually in a redemptive role; and poetic creation, always viewed as an erotic process, yields very special insights: "I believe the poets are right. They live closer to facts, to things. . . ."[123] These attitudes are not particularly unique for the second decade of the twentieth century; indeed Martínez Estrada was apparently responding in a predictable manner to typical ideas of the times. In terms of his own literary trajectory, however, the essay is quite significant, for the seeds of his

120. Sebreli, *Martínez Estrada*, p. 21.
121. Ezequiel Martínez Estrada, "Tesoros velados," *Nosotros*, XI (Oct., 1917), 193.
122. *Ibid.*, p. 194.
123. *Ibid.*

future anguish are clearly observed virtually at the moment of their germination.

The second of the *Nosotros* articles, "The Stimulus to go on Living" (December, 1917) is unquestionably the most crucial of the series. He introduces his theme by citing Pascal on the relatively greater pleasures of anticipation as compared with those of realization. He then relates, in a simple and yet poetic style, an old folk tale. A child strays into the forest seeking delicious fruit and finally discovers that the anticipated morsel has turned to stone. The lad then hears reports of fantastically beautiful birds in the forest; he eagerly hunts them and when he is about to capture his prey, the birds are miraculously changed into a handful of unattractive feathers. The young writer then meditates on the role of anticipation and hope in our lives:

> And above all these minor, simple, daily hopes, let us very deliberately hold fast to a much greater one, and let this hope be above and beyond all others . . . like an impossible dragon in a remote and unknown land. And may the only path which might guide us to it be discovered only when the clock of our life is about to strike the final hour. . . .[124]

Much of what Martínez Estrada will say in the future flows logically from this attitude. The seed which we saw germinate earlier has now sprouted and taken root; it will only be a matter of time until the bitter fruit of his pessimism will ripen. For a person of Estrada's psychological make-up, it is the striving, the seeking—not the achievement—which is all important. I think that it is precisely this attitude which defines Martínez Estrada's concept of that which is characteristically human: man is the being that strives. Carrying this view somewhat further, we can appreciate why Martínez Estrada will often react sharply against success—successful people, successful movements, successful cities, successful nations, etc. Whether this attitude is justified in specific cases need not concern us here; the fact remains that it defines the man's relationship to the world and even more important, to himself. How well even the very title of Sebreli's critical essay, *Martínez Estrada, A Useless Revolt (Martínez Estrada, Una rebelión inútil)*, is thus refuted! What matters is that he has rebelled; his success or failure is, at least in terms of his own values and psychological make-up, quite beside the point.

124. Ezequiel Martínez Estrada, "El estímulo de vivir," *Nosotros*, XI (Dec., 1917), 466.

Estrada's heroes are, in a word, underdogs. Whether he is describing the long-vanished figure of the nineteenth-century gaucho,
as in the *Radiografía* and the *Muerte y transfiguración*, or the pathetic,
tortured soul of a Simone Weil, as in *Exhortaciones*, this commitment
to the martyr, the scapegoat, the defeated is everywhere in evidence.
Further corroboration of this fundamental attitude may be seen in
his sympathy for the French idealist Charles Péguy, killed in World
War I; for Waldo Frank, virtually an outcast in his own country;
and for whatever group may be occupying the base of the social
pyramid—the pariahs, the North American Negro, the "Chandala
class," etc.[125] Martínez Estrada's love of the underdog is underscored in his feelings toward children and animals. These sentiments
have no doubt been strengthened by two facts. The first of these is
that for a portion of his life he worked as a postal employee, occupying a routine position on the lower levels of a typically stultifying
bureaucracy. The second is the simple fact that, though married,
Martínez Estrada was childless. When one reads his defense of birds
(he kept many as house pets), his glowing evocations of Argentine
wild life, and his fervent condemnation of prisons and penal practice,[126] the picture of the postal worker "imprisoned" behind his
barred window is immediately suggested. The discussion of children
in *Exhortaciones* and elsewhere reveals another aspect of Martínez
Estrada's cult of nature. In a sentimental tone suggestive of a
Rousseau, he decries our callousness in not heeding the "message"
of children. Martínez Estrada believes that in our desire to in-
doctrinate, we deform and corrupt our children, and most important,
we miss the opportunity to receive the mystic communication of
nature which they bear.[127] The burden of Martínez Estrada's
message and the crux of his radicalism lie precisely in this polarity of
nature and civilization. His underdogs are with few exceptions
"naturally good" beings destroyed or corrupted by what he considers to be the unnatural institutions of modern civilization. Re-
duced to this bare scheme, his position is remarkably simple. It is,
of course, quite unoriginal; its antecedents may be traced back
through Rousseau, Las Casas, and earlier. Among more recent
writers, there is a good deal of this kind of primitivism in the North

125. Martínez Estrada's ideas on what he terms "closed" societies and on the
pyramid-like form of such societies are well expressed in his article, "El complejo
Chandala," *Cuadernos Americanos*, IX (Jan.-Feb., 1950), 116-29.
126. These themes are treated extensively and poetically throughout Martínez
Estrada's *Cabeza de Goliat* (Buenos Aires, 1940).
127. Ezequiel Martínez Estrada, *Exhortaciones* (Buenos Aires, 1957), p. 36.

American Waldo Frank and in Henry David Thoreau—two writers for whom Martínez Estrada expresses high regard.[128] But simple ideas in the hands of talented writers acquire unusual impact.

H. A. Murena (1924———), one of the most brilliant young essayists writing in Argentina today, gives us some idea of this impact in the case of Martínez Estrada. In his provocative essay, *El pecado original de América* (1958), Murena describes the cultural ethos of the Argentina of the 1940's in dramatic terms: "The air we were breathing was stale and dead, and when we thought that this might be the definitive atmosphere, a paralyzing anguish would attack us."[129] Those familiar with Argentine writing of the period will appreciate the accuracy of Murena's characterization: not only is this feeling of inertia and disorientation seen in Martínez Estrada himself but in a number of other important authors—Eduardo Mallea being perhaps the most notable example. Murena claims that his "discovery" of Estrada gave him, and many of his generation, nothing less than a "spiritual rebirth": "He utilized the virus, the very pus, to vaccinate, to cure. . . . This fact explains why there is an abyss between the works of Martínez Estrada and those that came before. . . . Sarmiento . . . Alberdi . . . Martí . . . Echeverría . . . Ingenieros . . . were men who would hit upon a truth once a week, a bit by chance, whereas Martínez Estrada holds fast to truth every moment, unceasingly. . . ."[130] But what exactly is this great truth, or more precisely, this "virus" which Martínez Estrada isolates and then utilizes in his therapy? The essence of Martínez Estrada's message, Murena feels, is that the people of the New World are in a very real sense, another "pariah," or "outcast" group; "we are the most wretched of the wretched, we are the dispossessed. . . ."[131] Moreover, a careful analysis of American life reveals many subterfuges which the inhabitant of the New World has employed to avoid facing this unpleasant truth. Some typical examples of these masks would be the cult of gross materialism and of false erudition. Martínez Estrada implies that if men would accept the utter wretchedness of their essential nature, they would be much the better for it. But

128. On Frank, see Martínez Estrada, see *Cabeza de Goliat*, pp. 174-75. Regarding Thoreau and other nature writers see *Cabeza de Goliat*, pp. 55-56.

129. H. A. Murena, *El pecado original de América* (Buenos Aires, 1958), p. 113. Another good discussion of Martínez Estrada's relationship to the younger generation of Argentine writers appears in E. Rodríguez Monegal's *El juicio de los parricidas* (Buenos Aires, 1956), pp. 15-28.

130. Murena, *El pecado original*, p. 123.

131. *Ibid.*, p. 115.

hey refused to do so, and hence their misery is compounded by the resulting estrangement from reality.

Terms such as anguish, solitude, dispossession, and alienation—typical of those who write on the periphery of existential thought —are often used by Martínez Estrada to characterize the human condition in general and the Spanish American condition in particular. However, when he describes the Gaucho, and by extension the entire continent's poor, rural, mestizo class, he prefers to write of a deep-seated feeling of *orfandad* (orphanage) which he places at the root of this group's psychology. His brilliant analysis of the *hijo humillado* (humiliated child) complex in the *Radiografía de la Pampa* rests upon the idea that the Gaucho is the illegitimate son of the European conqueror and the violated Indian woman.[132] The forces that constantly take advantage of the Gaucho—the archetypal *hijo humillado* of the New World—are those of the city, of the central authority. In a sense they are the projection of the European conqueror's appetites; viewed psychoanalytically, they of course represent the father image. Buenos Aires, the swollen encephalitic "Head of Goliath" which Martínez Estrada so poetically berates in his essay of the same name, stands for all that is corrupting, hateful, and authoritarian; as such, it too is metaphorically a father figure. The city with its rationality, its law and order, its administrative machinery, etc., further aggravates man's "dispossession"—his isolation from the natural realm, the source of his goodness and his vitality. The city not only corrupts the country, towards which it extends its lines of communication "like the tentacles of an octopus,"[133] but it also keeps its own population virtually imprisoned: ". . . we are prisoners, though our keeper has disappeared years or centuries ago. He locked us all up and then went away or died. . . ."[134]

Martínez Estrada's attitude toward the city can legitimately be taken to represent his over-all view of modern civilization. As such, it reveals a great deal about his radicalism. On the first page of the *Cabeza de Goliat* he cites a letter of Rainer Maria Rilke in which the poet, writing from Paris, describes a large city as "a thing against nature"; while in the early pages of his 1957 essay, *Exhortaciones*, he speaks of his countrymen as not having "roots in the land."[135] A

132. Ezequiel Martínez Estrada, *Radiografía de la Pampa* (Buenos Aires, 1933), p. 88. The same concept of the *hijo humillado* figures prominently in his later work, the *Muerte y transfiguración de Martín Fierro* (Mexico, 1948).
133. Martínez Estrada, *Cabeza de Goliat*, pp. 37-38.
134. *Ibid.*, p. 50.
135. Martínez Estrada, *Exhortaciones*, p. 28.

mystique of the land—not unlike that found in several of his Spanish
American contemporaries—complements his critique of modern
society and of the city. The folk, those who live in intimate contact
with the land, have great reserves of "force" (*fuerza*); while the
"rulers"—read Buenos Aires and its provincial "tentacles"—have
only "power" (*poder*), equated with that which is imposed and that
which is "unnatural."[136] Aside from the telluric basis of the people's
"force," Martínez Estrada holds to a belief in the "natural solidarity" of humanity which, he feels, further strengthens uncorrupted
man.[137] There is, however, in a number of Martínez Estrada's
works, the idea that the land exercises a malevolent influence upon
man as well as a beneficent one. At times the land, the realm of
nature, is a "paradise lost"; at times it is a fearful and destructive
adversary.[138] This polarity may be explained in several ways. We
may say that this apparent malevolence arises from the fact that
"civilized" man is so alienated from nature that he is incapable of
appreciating his relationship to it, and hence he fears it. We may
also look upon this polarity as an example of Martínez Estrada's
dialectical method: the land, as the place where life germinates *and*
the place to which we return as dust, represents both life and death.
Like the mother image (with which the land is inextricably linked)
the natural realm gives rise to rich ambivalences: attraction, re-
pulsion, love-hate, and most of all, life-death. The highest reality,
accepting for the while the validity of the dialectical approach,
results from the interaction of these apparent opposites rather than
from the choice of one over the other. It is in this manner, that
Martínez Estrada's telluricism is best appreciated.

Given Martínez Estrada's belief in human solidarity as a "natural"
phenomenon and in what he calls "innate qualities of sociability,"[139]
his attitude towards existing political institutions makes a good deal
of sense. Political parties, he states, are inherently bad for the
establishment of true democracy.[140] In the specific context of
Argentina, he notes that the *institution* of the party, with its natural
tendency to work for the self-interest of restricted groups represents
a greater evil than that posed by any one particular party, even the

136. *Ibid.*, pp. 8ff.
137. *Ibid.*, p. 27.
138. In the *Radiografía de la Pampa* he states simply, "la tierra es la muerte," p. 16.
Compare Sebreli's treatment of the nature ambivalence in his *Martínez Estrada*,
pp. 61-71.
139. Martínez Estrada, *Exhortaciones*, p. 27.
140. *Ibid.*, pp. 15ff.

hated *Peronistas*.[141] He finds support for this view in Marx and in Simone Weil, both of whom he cites to the effect that "where political parties exist, democracy has died."[142] Politics, written constitutions, the structure of the modern state itself, are all immoral, unnatural, and inhuman: "He who loves politics hates morality" is his essential view. "A written constitution, even if it were technically perfect, is not what is needed today with as much urgency as the moral re-constitution of the people. . . ."[143] Sebreli, citing a passage from the essay *Cuadrante del pampero* ("Every state, therefore, still assumes, as originally, the characteristics of a government of occupation"), argues that Estrada views any state as an "alien body" in "natural" society.[144] Sebreli's observation, incidentally, helps explain many of Martínez Estrada's specific political attitudes, such as the coolness he maintained even to the post-Peron governments of Argentina. In a word, the epithet of "anarchist" with which his critics have attacked him is not completely inapplicable. That this "anarchism" is grounded upon a very sympathetic humanism and is not of the bomb-throwing sort, however, must be made clear. Martínez Estrada's radicalism does not aim at inciting mobs to riot; rather it aims at encouraging the individual to cleanse himself of civilization's corruption, to permit that innate goodness—in which Estrada so des-perately believes—to come to the fore. As his disciple, H. A. Murena eloquently states, "Martínez Estrada signifies the resurgence of the American conscience."[145] Martínez Estrada is a revolutionary who can say of the masses (it should be pointed out that he is speaking of Argentina here): "They do not want bread, because they already have what is necessary and they are fed up. They are hungry, but not for bread. They are hungry for honor, for love, for cordial treatment, for human consideration. . . ."[146] Martínez Estrada, like so many other contemporary radicals of Spanish America, is repelled by any society, capitalist or Marxist, wherein the ordering of life for material ends relegates man to the position of a cog in a rationally conceived machine. An apparently insignificant episode which occurred during his visit to the Soviet Union bears this out clearly. Speaking before students at Moscow University on the theme of the absurd in contemporary literature, Estrada went to considerable

141. *Ibid.*, pp. 16-18.
142. *Ibid.*, pp. 20-21.
143. *Ibid.*, p. 76.
144. Sebreli, *Martínez Estrada*, pp. 73-74.
145. Murena, *El pecado original*, p. 123.
146. Martínez Estrada, *Exhortaciones*, p. 7.

length in pointing out the profound humanism of one of his very
favorite authors, the novelist Kafka. Not only were the Soviet
students unable to understand what he termed the "World of
Kafka," but also the very fact that "unrealistic," "disinterested"
artistic creation could be considered a legitimate human activity
was utterly incomprehensible to them.[147] Estrada does not use this
incident as a point of departure for an overt attack upon the Soviet
state, but his obvious disappointment with her youth and with her
values is readily apparent.

It is easier to discuss Martínez Estrada's critique of society than
it is to describe the kind of a world which he might wish to see
established. Certainly neither the present Soviet state, nor North
America,[148] nor Argentina, represent to any degree the type of society
that he envisions. On rare occasions he gives us an inkling of the
socio-economic order to which he might subscribe. In *Exhortaciones*
he speaks fondly of "cooperatives," of *gremios* (a kind of Medieval
craft-guild), and of "syndicates."[149] A picture of decentralized,
independent, self-governing communities—not unlike those proposed
by Bakunin or perhaps even by William Morris—is immediately
brought to mind. Certainly the "shape" of modern society—the
hated "pyramid" with its huge "outcast" groups at the base—would
have to be changed. Human relationships would be characterized
by altruism, "the giving of oneself" and a deep mutual understanding. The proper relationship of man to the products of land and
factory would be restored. Man would once again be considered the
usufructuary, the beneficiary of his material bounty. He would
not be the "obligatory consumer" of modern North America, where
"the demands of the market can determine that at one moment a
Buick must be put into use, and at another moment that the atomic
bomb be put into use—and all this with the same ignorance of the
true objectives of this forced consumption."[150] Above all, the
Estradian Utopia—for it would be just that—would contain no
minorities, no underdogs, no pariahs. These words would in effect
lose all meaning. Creatures of nature—domestic animals, birds,
and children—would go about unharmed, loved, and respected.

147. See note 116 above.
148. See his interesting but bitter reply to Mary McCarthy's eulogy of the United
States, "America the Beautiful," which appeared originally in *Commentary* and was
reprinted in translation in the Argentine journal *Sur* (Nov.-Dec., 1950), pp. 146-55.
Martínez Estrada's essay, "Norteamérica la hacendosa," appears in the same issue,
pp. 156-59.
149. Martínez Estrada, *Exhortaciones*, p. 29.
150. Martínez Estrada, "Norteamérica la hacendosa," p. 159.

In such a society, political activity as we know it, national states, militarism, and war would simply become curious and primitive institutions of an earlier and less human epoch.

Practical men of widely divergent political beliefs will see all this as a fantastic pipe-dream. Martínez Estrada has been called many things—a self-appointed prophet,[151] a pessimistic determinist,[152] and an impractical "petty bourgeois anarchist."[153] One must agree that his politics are fuzzy, his economics anachronistic, and his view of human nature sentimental. But one must also recognize the fact that he is neither a politician nor an economist nor even a philosopher. He is simply a human being, caught in the web of contemporary technological society, who has felt it necessary to proclaim that something is radically wrong with the modern world. His message is negative and "impractical" in that it warns us not to continue in our present ways. It is in this context that we must consider Murena's view of Martínez Estrada as the embodiment of the "American conscience." Estrada's critics would do well to ponder this point, for we are on dangerous ground when we demand too much practicality of our conscience.[154]

The writers under discussion share many similar viewpoints. What is perhaps their most striking common denominator is their rejection of political orthodoxy, be it of the "bourgeois" or Marxist camp. Underlying this rejection is the conviction that human existence requires redefinition and that such redefinition must not take as its point of departure the realm of the political. A corollary of this view is that a mere change in the form of economic and governmental organization will not achieve this objective. It follows that much of the revolutionary ideology of these essayists is grounded upon an emotive, a nonmaterialistic, and often an antimaterialistic appeal. Thus Mariátegui's thought will be strongly colored by the "mystique of the Revolution"; Ramos will seek in philosophical anthropology a new method of determining "man's place in nature" and his moral obligations; and Martínez Estrada will once again state the case for modern man's return to the natural realm of benign innocence. The foreign writers who have done most to shape the

151. See the critique by Jorge Luis Borges, "Una efusión de E. Martínez Estrada," *Sur* (Sept.-Oct., 1956), pp. 52-53. The article is in answer to Estrada's criticisms of Borges' lack of real anti-Perón sentiments.
152. Sebreli, *Martínez Estrada*, pp. 37-47.
153. *Ibid.*, p. 80.
154. Martínez Estrada continued to see in the Castro regime the possibility of a genuine Utopia. See his curious historical essay, "El nuevo mundo, la isla de Utopía y la isla de Cuba," *Cuadernos Americanos* (March-April, 1963), pp. 89-122.

radicalism of the group are clearly those who have either deviated from the orthodoxy of the Third International, or who represent quite individual approaches to radicalism: thinkers such as Romain Rolland, Nicolas Berdyaev, Max Scheler, Waldo Frank, and Simone Weil. When Marx himself appeals to these writers it is as the romantic humanitarian of the 1840's rather than as the older, more cynical author of *Das Kapital*. The *leitmotif* running through the works of virtually all these essayists is the idea that man's transformation must be brought about by a profound liberation. He must be liberated from an animal-like existence stemming from the constant pressure to satisfy his material needs. He must be liberated from considering himself a mere pawn in a great game of gods or heroes; and he must be likewise liberated from considering himself and his fellows as "things"—as objects subject to the "rational" laws of a mechanistic universe. It is with these terms, rather than with those of the existing political vocabulary, that Spanish America's radical humanism must be described.

There are, of course, many orthodox Communists in Spanish America; and some of these, though not included in the present study, have some stature as writers. However, the heterodox radicalism which we have been analyzing is, I think, dominant. This is so for two reasons. The qualities of *dignidad* (dignity, self-respect), of individualism, even of anarchism which characterize the works of these essayists are rooted deep in the bedrock of Hispanic tradition. And secondly, the awareness of a unique American destiny—inherent in virtually all the writers discussed above—makes it incumbent upon them to seek a more flexible, more adaptable ideological framework upon which to build their own theories and practical programs. Thus Spanish American radicals have shown an ever-increasing desire to find a "third way" and to reject the "either-or" posed by the Cold War. An interesting statement of this attitude was formulated for Hispanic America by Waldo Frank in a speech at the University of Havana in the Spring of 1950. Speaking at a meeting of the Leftist *Conferencia interamericana "Prodemocracia y libertad,"* he attacked both the United States and the Soviets for their "dehumanizing" tendencies, for their deliberate "manipulation" of human beings. Professing little faith in existing political groups, Frank proclaimed that only a movement "more radical than Communism" could bring about the true revolution. Of particular significance, he restated his belief that Spanish America was the ideal place for the genesis of such a movement.[155] One cannot help wondering whether the youthful Fidel Castro, then completing his law studies at the University, was among those present.

The current dilemma of the Spanish American radical has been stated with great force and eloquence by Estrada's disciple, H.A. Murena, in a well-wrought essay, "El estridor del conformismo," which appeared not long ago in the review, *Cuadernos*. I shall not attempt to summarize all that Murena says in this tightly packed piece; a few substantial citations will give the spirit of the essay. Murena first describes what might be called the "soldier of humanity" forced to "take sides" in the contemporary ideological struggle. Noting the wide gap which exists between propagandistic claims and actual fact, he feels obliged to choose between the two warring camps, to venture into no man's land. He therefore investigates the claims made by both sides and, more important, the nature of propaganda itself:

> Within this imagined "no man's land" of the person who has not been convinced by either of the two vociferous ideologies which have been saturating the world's atmosphere, one notices that after all, both sides are propagandistic. And propaganda —and by now this must be said openly—is essentially negative. For propaganda consists of a malignant exploitation—be this done consciously or unconsciously—of man's "openness" to the world, of that capacity for love which makes communication possible. It is evil since it opposes communication, and to this extent, it is contrary to the Revolution, to all revolution. The Revolution which, under many different names has inspired . . . wishes to free man from the myths that oppress him, in order that he may exist in his fullness. The Revolution wishes man to become once again completely his own master, while propaganda seeks to take full control of him. Propaganda proposes to change man, to alienate him from himself. Though it claims to be promoting the Revolution or defending liberty, its real effect is to paralyze man, to possess him, and enslave him.[156]

Murena next presents a very striking analysis of religious essence (*lo religioso*) in contrast with historical manifestations of religion: "Life is movement. It is history, which must flow continually. . . . Full participation in this movement is the unchanging essence of religion—which should not be confused with specific, ephemeral religious organizations that eventually take hold of this essence,

155. Waldo Frank, "Necesitamos crear un mundo nuevo," *Cuadernos Americanos*, IX (July-Aug., 1950), 40-47.
156. H. A. Murena, "El estridor del conformismo," *Cuadernos*, No. 69 (May, 1960), p. 20.

codify it, embody it truthfully for a brief moment, and then become empty, leaving as the only sign of the religious essence having passed through their body, a certain stiffness of the joints. . . ."[157] Murena consistently equates the fullness of life, authentic human existence, with movement and "flow." By contrast our concern for material goods—for the possession of worldly things—impedes this flow and is, in Murena's terms, essentially antireligious. His discussion of Marxism in this context is extremely interesting:

> Compared with capitalism, Marxism is—in an ideal sense—a religious movement, since in that it has come to fight against the retention of material goods, it works towards movement in life. This is the basis for our affirming that in the new society which will come forth from the "cold war" . . . Marxist characteristics will predominate. Nevertheless, there is another characteristic of Marxism that permits us to affirm that it cannot be the victor. For though it is religious to the extent that it proposes the non-retention of property, it uses violence to impede this possession. And in using violence, Marxism retains coercive power. This means that it goes against life, and is thus anti-religious to a greater extent than is capitalism.[158]

Working toward the conclusion of his thesis Murena restates the problem faced by "the soldier of humanity" in the present crisis: "He who would fight for the sake of Revolution in this day knows that the ground on which he must stand is as narrow as the razor's edge. It is the no man's land in which the combatant, labeled by both sides as defeatest and traitor, is condemned to death."[159] But Murena does not feel that his symbolic soldier is completely abandoned: "Surely, if his ear is attuned, he will eventually hear a voice that will soothe his soul and encourage him to bear up under a situation which doubtlessly is beyond his own strength and capacities. It is a voice which comes to him from a far-off age, and which, as a proof of its validity, has made the journey without aid of Churches, National states, political parties, or sects."[160] This voice, Murena feels, arises from one of the greatest sources of all uncompromising humanism: it is the voice of the condemned Socrates, the corrupter of youth. Paraphrasing the philosopher's advice to the young people of ancient Athens, Murena writes: "leaving aside those things which the majority holds most dear—money, a home,

157. *Ibid.*, p. 22.
158. *Ibid.*
159. *Ibid.*, p. 23.
160. *Ibid.*, pp. 23-24.

political power and leadership—I shall try to convince each one of you to be concerned with yourself rather than with your material interests, in order that you may become better and wiser."[161]

The shallowness of many of the terms currently employed to characterize radicalism in Spanish America should now become evident. A negative label—such as the "non-Communist Left" really does not define a great deal; it leads one to assume, moreover, that those who are "non-Communists" necessarily favor our own political and economic institutions. At least with regard to the intellectuals—and the substantial force that Spanish American intellectuals exert among the continent's directive classes must again be underscored—this assumption is often invalid. Our inability to find a satisfactory term to define the Castro movement,—at least as it existed during its first year, is a further illustration of the inadequacy of contemporary political vocabulary. Interestingly enough, during the early years the Cubans themselves were hard put to find the right word to describe their embryonic new order. In the light of the foregoing analysis Castro's repeated use of the term *humanismo* to designate his regime's admittedly ill-defined philosophic position acquires considerable significance. Our examination of radical humanism was undertaken in an attempt to focus upon one aspect of what in an earlier chapter was called the rediscovery of America. The men whose work has just been discussed are all passionately concerned with discovering the New World's mission, her destiny, her reason for being. The instruments with which they have attacked these matters have led them from the realm of economic and political institutions toward a consideration of man himself. At about the same time other writers were also changing their intellectual focus. The broadly conceived, rather generalized Americanism of the early decades of the century gradually gives way to an interest in national character which in turn leads to an intense analysis of the individual and his immediate *circunstancia*. New viewpoints, existentialism in particular, come forth to provide fresh answers to old problems. The Spanish American essay of most recent years shows a growing preoccupation with basic questions of human definitions, with what Murena might term the Socratic concern for the self, and with what we shall call the "Search for Essence."

161. *Ibid.*, p. 24.

VI / ARGENTINA'S
QUEST FOR IDENTITY

THE REDISCOVERY OF AMERICA, THE DESIRE TO CLARIFY
the position of New World culture with respect to the Old, and the
attempt to probe the relationship of the individual to his environment are aspects of the ever-increasing passion for self-definition
characteristic of the contemporary essay of Spanish America. In
recent decades a gradual refinement in the techniques by which
writers approach the problem of self-definition has become dramatically evident. Many writers shift their interest from broadly
Americanist considerations to a more restricted analysis of the
national ethos: hence the essays dealing with *"argentinidad," "mexicanidad," "peruanidad,"* etc.[1] Narrowing their focus even more,
some writers look to the microcosm of the individual in their search
for essence. Armed with the potent weapons of psychoanalysis and
existentialism they have placed the traditional Spanish American
polarity of universalism versus nativism in fresh perspective. Significantly, the work of the most advanced of these writers suggests
that the very positing of this polarity is pointless. Finally, the essay
itself responds to the changing character of its content and to the
aesthetics of its cultivators. As a result, the genre in the hands of
writers such as Ezequiel Martínez Estrada or Octavio Paz may well
be considered to have undergone a fundamental transformation.

We have already touched upon some attempts to define the
national character or essence: for example, the indigenism of Díez de

---

1. The suffix *"dad"* in Spanish is equivalent to English "ty" or "ness." Hence
argentinidad would be equivalent to "Argentinity" or "Argentineness." Similarly
americanidad suggests "Americanity" or "Americaness." Note that the *"dad"* ending
is free of the political and doctrinary connotations of *"ismo"* as in *argentinismo, americanismo,* etc.

Medina or Antenor Orrego was closely linked with the desire to discover the essential nature of Bolivians and Peruvians. In Argentina, this interest may be traced back to Sarmiento or even earlier, though it is particularly evident in the work of the "Generation of the Centenary," an important group of writers who appear during the first decade of the present century. Ricardo Rojas, though certainly vulnerable to much criticism, is for our purposes the most significant essayist of this generation. A prolific writer, his works were widely read and unquestionably influential. Admittedly he was wordy, intellectually diffuse, often jingoistic, and particularly prone toward selecting the least satisfactory terminology to express his ideas.[2] The fact remains that Rojas popularized the term *argentinidad*—chronologically the first of many similar words which were to appear in other Spanish American countries—and that the Argentine essayists who began to write in the twenties and thirties took him as a fixed point upon which to orient their own work. However more often than not, these essayists—Carlos Alberto Erro (1899——), Eduardo Mallea (1903——), Jorge Luis Borges (1899——), Bernardo Canal Feijóo (1897——), and others—reject a good deal of what Rojas set forth in such works as *La restauración nacionalista* (1909), *Blasón de plata* (1912), *La argentinidad* (1916), and *Eurindia* (1924).

In virtually all of these essays Rojas develops an unsophisticated dualism of *exotismo* ("exoticism") versus *indianismo* ("Indianism"). The same opposing terms are employed in organizing the material for his well-known *Historia de la literatura argentina* (1921). One must agree with the critic Zum Felde that Rojas' contribution to the analysis of Argentine culture has been limited. When he relegates all that has emanated from Europe to the "exotic," Rojas dodges some very basic questions: obviously Argentina's language, literary traditions, and customs are European by origin; but to what extent have they been transformed, reinterpreted, and modified by the American ethos? Rojas will answer simply that European culture has indeed undergone a process of "nationalization" in Argentina, but just how and to what extent he leaves unresolved. However, a possible answer is implied by his telluricism: the land itself, through the mystical *genius loci*, has wrought this transformation.[3] This notion of the force of the land, though hazily and sentimentally conceived, may have been Rojas' major contribution to the future

2. See Alberto Zum Felde, *Indice crítico de la literatura hispanoamericana: El ensayo y la crítica* (Mexico, 1954), p. 452.
3. See above, Chapter IV, pp. 61-63.

course of *argentinidad*. Rojas in effect presented his generation with a provocative inversion of Sarmiento's celebrated formula of "civilization versus barbarism." Sarmiento, it may be recalled equated "civilization" with that which was European, urban, cultural, and coastal; "barbarism" was associated with all that was rural, indigenous, and of the interior. Granted that this formula was as simplistic as the one employed by Rojas, the fact remains that several generations of Argentine intellectuals had considerable difficulty in transcending it. The creative literature of the seventies and eighties, for example, is decidedly "Europeanized" and cosmopolitan. And it is virtually a commonplace that the *porteño* (inhabitant of Buenos Aires) of the late nineteenth century took inordinate pride in the belief that he was the foremost representative of European civilization and racial purity in all Spanish America.[4] It was, conceivably, an historical necessity that a heavy-handed writer, one who expressed himself in a "prophetic tone" and with "puffed-up eloquence"[5] should be instrumental in redirecting the intellectual path of the nation.

Rojas' approach to *argentinidad* has been controversial from the outset. José Ingenieros, speaking as a typical social-democratic liberal of "European" Buenos Aires, sharply criticized the *Blasón de plata* in an open letter published in the influential *Revista de América*.[6] Briefly, Ingenieros considers the exaltation of the land, the provinces, and the interior as "reactionary": he feels that the hope for a great Argentina of the future lies with those people who have achieved an "ethnic modification" of the fundamentally barbaric and feudal "hispanic-indigenist oligarchies." His critique finally takes a personal turn when he points out the fact that Rojas was of a distinguished provincial family, whereas he, Ingenieros, was merely the son of an Italian immigrant.[7] Nevertheless in terms of the themes we have been analyzing, Ingenieros' narrow Europeanism and equally narrow scientism place him, rather than Rojas, squarely among the reactionaries. This does not mean that Rojas was by contrast a radical; indeed, neither his aesthetics nor his politics could be so characterized. Contemporary writers, such as the critic Luis E. Soto, have pointed out specifically that he was cool to the

4. Two of the most outspoken Spanish American racists, it will be recalled, were the Argentinians Bunge and Ingenieros. See above, Chapter II, pp. 16-19, 29-31.
5. These descriptive terms are Zum Felde's. See his *Indice crítico*, p. 453.
6. José Ingenieros, "Nacionalismo e indianismo: Carta a Ricadro Rojas," *Revista de América*, II (May-Aug., 1913), 185-94.
7. *Ibid.*, p. 194.

Mexican Revolution, to the university reform movement, and to the efforts of men like José Vasconcelos to rally support against North American imperialism.[8] His sentimental mystique of the land was perhaps as untenable as the Positivists' barren scientism; Soto describes Rojas' Indianism as "a gesture of ardent indigenist idealism but without roots in the historical reality of the present-day Indian."[9] He also considers the celebrated essay *Eurindia* quite inferior to the writings of Pedro Henríquez Ureña on the same theme.[10] Bernardo Canal Feijóo, a contemporary essayist deeply involved in the analysis of *argentinidad*, feels that Rojas' indigenism and telluricism may be thought of as interesting aesthetic motifs, but not as valid insights into historical reality.[11] On the other side of the ledger, a number of critics have accorded Rojas substantial praise. Alfredo Coviello has called him the "Prince of Argentine letters"; and one of the nation's leading philosophers, Coriolano Alberini considers his role in Argentinian national life parallel to that of Herder in the development of a German national consciousness.[12] More significant than these rather grandiose appraisals of Rojas' importance is the fact that many of his severest critics will either explicitly or implicitly acknowledge their debt to him.

The relationship of Rojas to the generation of Argentine essayists which follows him—men born at the close of the nineteenth century or in the early decades of the twentieth—is seen particularly well in the writings of Carlos Alberto Erro. Erro began his career in various literary magazines during the mid-twenties; and for a brief period he directed the ephemeral but important Buenos Aires *Revista de América*. His first major work, *Medida del criollismo* (1929), contains a number of pieces which had appeared earlier in magazines as well as some newer material. This book, however, cannot be appreciated fully without considering the milieu of which it was a part.

A remarkable amount of literary activity is in evidence in the Buenos Aires of the 1920's. An entire generation of writers—many of whom were close friends of Erro—was testing its literary wings in the colorful, often highly volatile atmosphere of the city. Many

8. Luis E. Soto, "Ricardo Rojas y la americanidad," *Revista Iberoamericana*, XXIII (July-Dec., 1958), 323.
9. *Ibid.*, p. 322.
10. *Ibid.*, p. 331.
11. Bernardo Canal Feijóo, "Sobre el americanismo de Ricardo Rojas," *Revista Iberoamericana*, XXIII (July-Dec., 1958), 221-26.
12. Cited by Soto, "Ricardo Rojas y la americanidad," *Revista Iberoamericana*, p. 333.

would soon become the leading writers of the nation: Jorge Luis Borges as a poet, essayist, and short story writer; Eduardo Mallea as Argentina's most celebrated contemporary novelist; and Ezequiel Martínez Estrada as one of her most penetrating essayists. Some members of the group edited and others collaborated on a host of literary reviews: Erro's *Revista de América*, Borge's *Proa* and *Martin Fierro*, the philosophically oriented *Valoraciones* of Alejandro Korn and Francisco Romero, the left-of-center *Vida Literaria* of Samuel Glusberg, the Rightest, anti-Semitic *Inicial*, the Americanist *Síntesis*, and toward the close of the decade, the radical *Claridad*. These reviews reflect the rich intellectual life of the period: the literary polemics, the visits of distinguished intellectuals, and the impact of new ideological currents from Europe. In their pages nativist argued with universalist, radical with conservative, vanguardist with traditionalist, Trotskyite with Stalinist. The philosophically oriented writers of the day—men like Miguel Angel Virasoro and Carlos Astrada—introduced Scheler, Heidegger, Husserl, Dilthey, and early existentialist thought to an intelligentsia reared on Spencer and Ingenieros. In 1924 *Martin Fierro* published the futurist manifesto of Marinetti and, in the very same year, an important statement of political aims by the indigenist-oriented APRA.[13] But underlying all this ferment, this "fervor of Buenos Aires," to appropriate the provocative title of Borges' poetry of the period, was the question of *argentinidad*—what Rojas, in his unsophisticated manner, thought of as "the pristine spirit of nationality."[14]

"If I had to state my objective concretely in a few words, I would say that I am looking for the universal *criollo*."[15] With these well-chosen words, Carlos Alberto Erro sets his task in the *Medida del criollismo* (1929). His debt to Rojas is made quite clear only a few pages later: he states that he had agreed with many of Rojas' ideas in the early and mid-twenties, but that he gradually felt obliged to reject the older writer's view of Argentine "individuality." Erro is very specific in his admission that it was Rojas' work which initiated his own concern for the problem of "what we are and what we are to be." Yet he finds it very difficult to point out exactly

13. For an interesting summary of the activities of the *Martin Fierro* group see Vera Beck, "La revista *Martin Fierro*," *Revista Hispanica Moderna*, XVI (Jan.-Dec., 1950), 133-41.

14. Ricardo Rojas, *La argentinidad*, (2ª ed.; Buenos Aires, 1922), p. 369.

15. Carlos Alberto Erro, *Medida del criollismo* (Buenos Aires, 1929), p. 10. I choose to leave *criollo* untranslated, since its English equivalent "creole" would lead to confusion. At first *criollo* meant the American-born children of Peninsular stock. Today it is virtually synonymous with "native American."

wherein his disagreement with Rojas lies. His critique of the earlier writer's work merits attention: "The knowledge that America is not Europe nor the Indies, but rather a distinct entity resulting from the union of the two—the only precise statement in four thousand pages of text—does not clarify in the least my consciousness of what I am. . . ."[16] He further criticizes Rojas for confusing the traditional Argentinian political dispute of federalism and unitarianism with the analysis of the psychological make-up of the Europeanized *porteño* as opposed to that of the rural *criollo*.

Erro touches upon a number of other writers, contemporary and historical, who have attempted a national characterology. He apparently accepts Borges' picture of the *criollo* as hardheaded, undeceived, intolerant of verbiage, and, most of all, fatalistic—the man who will, like the Gaucho hero Santos Vega, die "with fine mockery on his lips."[17] Yet Erro is acutely aware of the fact that *criollismo* has become, rightly or wrongly, associated with an ineffectual cultivation of the past. Thus, in Güiraldes' widely read Gauchesque novel *Don Segundo Sombra* (1926), Erro finds a picturesqueness, an evocation of vanished memories rather than any real penetration into *criollo* character.[18] He realizes, moreover, that any contemporary author who discusses flaws in the *criollo's* character is immediately placed in the camp of the most unilateral Europeanists.[19] What Erro seeks is some valid means of resolving this either-or of *criollismo* and universalism: "There is a genuinely native mode of putting into practice enthusiasm, boldness, and faith. The task faced by our generation consists in discovering the native rhythm of these great sources of action."[20]

Erro's search for the meaning of *criollismo* is closely linked with his views on time and on history. In his attempt to show that the *criollo* spirit does not simply belong to the past, he discusses a number of contemporary theories of historicism. Although he respects Spengler and Ortega to the extent that they recognize a degree of historical continuity ("molecules of the past always survive"), he apparently sides with Russell and the relativists in that past and future are *relative* to the observer; that the discerning student of history must "avoid all differences in attitude regarding the past and the future, and [must] embrace in a single vision the integral

16. *Ibid.*, pp. 12-13.
17. *Ibid.*, pp. 14-16.
18. *Ibid.*, p. 20.
19. *Ibid.*, p. 18.
20. *Ibid.*, p. 20.

development of time."[21] For Erro the authentic *criollo* spirit is something which is "forever emerging." If any temporal absolute is to be accepted in the New World it is that America is young—in his more ecstatic moments Erro implies that this youth is virtually perennial—and that America's future "is constantly being realized." Throughout the *Medida del criollismo* he stresses that Argentina—and by extension the New World—must not feel that the weight of history restricts her growth and development, that Argentinians must study their own "situation in the world," their own manner of being.[22] He rebukes his countrymen for "laughing dionysically" with Nietzsche, and for being pessimists with Spengler; in a word, for slavishly following European intellectual fads.[23]

Erro's views on literature have a direct bearing on his concepts of *criollismo* and of the Argentine essence. His fundamental aesthetic position is set forth in the statement that great art "is the eternalization of that which is momentary."[24] He develops this idea further by noting that "in the realm of the eternal, time does not move on, or more accurately, it moves on, but it is as if it did not; time only exists, time only has meaning in the finite, in the realm of the fleeting, ephemeral moment."[25] It follows that much of the so-called *criollo* literature of Argentina—that of the Gaucho—cannot be considered great art. The limitation of *criollismo* "to the Gaucho, to that which is legendary and traditional," he feels, is "as absurd as judging the character of a man by his conduct at twenty years of age."[26] He apparently would have Argentine writers seek historical constants—unchanging motifs—which might appear in any historical period. He implies, moreover, that the genuine *criollo* spirit may be found in both city and country. Erro considers the cultivation of an obviously rural Gauchesque literary style to have little or nothing to do with the creation of authentic *criollismo*: in his favorable critique of Borges' poetry of the twenties, he makes it quite clear that despite his compatriot's stylistic vagaries and despite his focus upon urban life, he nevertheless succeeded in capturing the essence of *criollismo*. Speaking directly to Borges, he writes: "You feel the foreign, un-*criollo*, cosmopolitan city with the emotion of an old *criollo*."[27] By contrast Güiraldes' protagonist in *Don Segundo Sombra*

21. *Ibid.*, pp. 51-52.
22. *Ibid.*, p. 91.
23. *Ibid.*, p. 61.
24. *Ibid.*, p. 100.
25. *Ibid.*, p. 101.
26. *Ibid.*, p. 75.
27. *Ibid.*, p. 107.

is simply a memory, a picturesque hero drawn from a vanished past. As such, Erro feels, he represents a typical example of the justification of *criollo* authenticity merely by virtue of rural setting and anachronistic flavor.[28] In the chapter on "El simbolismo y la poesía de nuestras cosas" the *modernista* poets, specifically the imitators of Rubén Darío, are viewed as even more "un-*criollo*." The butt of Erro's attack here is Leopoldo Lugones, in his youth Argentina's leading *modernista* and in his later period a cultivator of popular, "Gauchesque" poetry of questionable authenticity. In short Erro approves of the less obvious, but more profound *criollismo* of Borges and of Silva Valdés. The secret of the effective *criollista*, he maintains, "consists in viewing the details of local life as transcending the frontiers of the nation, in fraternal communion with all that is American."[29] We see here a good indication of how the search for essence, be it *argentinidad, mexicanidad* or *cubanidad*, tends to be intimately related to a broader quest. What Erro calls the continental "communion" (and conceivably the attainment of universality) represents the terminus of this search rather than the starting point. Thus, the more sophisticated writers look even closer at their own immediate surroundings: they no longer begin the process of self-discovery by speaking of a vaguely defined continental destiny and of a general American character from which the nation or the individual "deduces" its own role.

Erro's interest in *argentinidad* and in the resolution of the *criollo* versus universal polarity is further developed in his essay of 1936, *Tiempo lacerado*. This work deals with these problems in the context of a changing political and economic atmosphere. In the section of the essay titled "El sentido del momento actual en la Argentina," Erro notes that the severe depression of the early thirties had jarred the nation into a mood of disenchantment, of facing up to a new reality.[30] The generation of writers who were struggling to find themselves a decade earlier were now piercing beneath the surface of national character: Martínez Estrada, cited by Erro as an important new interpreter of *criollismo*, had just written his merciless *Radiografía de la Pampa* (1933); and Eduardo Mallea, after abandoning the studied cosmopolitanism of his earliest prose, was seeking out the "invisible Argentine" in such works as the *Historia de una pasión argentina* (1937). It is very probable that the political and

28. *Ibid.*, p. 20.
29. *Ibid.*, p. 123.
30. Carlos Alberto Erro, *Tiempo lacerado* (Buenos Aires, 1936), p. 204.

economic crisis of the period intensified the search for deeper values in Argentine life: in a speech delivered shortly after the publication of *Tiempo lacerado*, Erro explores this point at some length. In terms which certainly suggest the existentialist spirit, he notes that "passion and anguish" are prime requisites for self-discovery, for the discovery of the individual or the group essence.[31] He holds that what Argentina had lacked—at least until the depression of the early thirties—were the difficulties and adversities which lead to anguish and passionate self-appraisal. Hence the superficiality of the bulk of Argentine writing before this period, and conversely the "authenticity" of the *argentinidad* of recent decades.[32] The title of the essay, *Tiempo lacerado* (*The Unhappy Time*), is not completely descriptive of Erro's estimate of Argentina of the mid-thirties. Though these were troubled, painful times they were also dramatic and creative. Just as there are individuals who live dramatic, tortured lives, there are epochs in history wherein nations suffer, strive for self-knowledge, and so eventually progress. By contrast, there are individuals and historical periods which never face up to life in its full dramatic intensity. Erro holds that the late Roman Empire—materialistic, overorganized, and dominated by its Stoic and Epicurean philosophers—exemplifies this kind of period. Early Christianity, the epoch of St. Augustine, however, represents a deeply dramatic one. Similarly, the twentieth century with its vitalism, irrationalism, and (in the mid-thirties) its embryonic existentialism is a time of passion and ideological ferment.[33] That this century has also been witness to catastrophic events—wars, revolutions, and dictatorships—is further corroboration that these are times in which a "dramatic concept of life" holds sway.

The association of the "dramatic" historical periods with youth and "antidramatic" periods with old age is, of course, obvious. The application of Erro's historicism to Argentina and to Spanish America is seen in his contention that the New World of the twentieth century is profoundly youthful. Although Europe has dominated for centuries, the cultural independence of recent decades has presented the continent a future rich in possibilities. The youthfulness of the New World has, nonetheless, been modified substantially by the fact that its cultural independence has taken place only after a long

31. Carlos Alberto Erro, *Posibilidad y realidad de la vida argentina*, Conferencia del Instituto Cultural Joaquín V. González (Buenos Aires, 1937), pp. 44-47.
32. *Ibid.*, p. 49.
33. Erro, *Tiempo lacerado*, p. 9.

period of domination by an older, somewhat decadent parent civilization.[34] Thus Erro compares the emergence of an authentic Argentine—and by extension of an authentic Spanish American culture—to the rebirth of a child "already 10 years old."[35] That Spanish America was colonized by men who wished to prolong the trajectory of Europe in the New World explains this late flowering of a genuinely independent Americanism and the only very recent attempt at authentic self-knowledge: "He who has within easy reach pre-arranged solutions, formulas and guide-lines for every necessity, is confronted with a tremendous handicap to successful self-discovery. . . ."[36]

Although there is a good deal of freshness in Erro's thoughts on Americanism and *argentinidad*, the influence of certain non-Hispanic thinkers is clearly reflected in his work. His relationship with Waldo Frank, for example, was one of mutual interest and respect. Both writers were familiar with each others' work in the late twenties and early thirties.[37] In the *Tiempo lacerado* Erro quotes Frank's *Rediscovery of America* at length on the decay of Europe in relation to the birth of the New World.[38] If we recall the opening statement of Frank's chapter on "The Grave of Europe,"—America, the New World, "was a world born old"—we may immediately appreciate the similarity in viewpoint of the two writers. In his speech of 1937, *Posibilidad y realidad de la vida argentina*, Erro again admits his debt to Frank. In this instance what appeals to the Argentine writer is the North American's analysis of Europe's discovery—not of America, but, as Frank puts it, of " . . . the Ocean . . . the antithesis of these Latin seas . . . uncharted . . . boundless . . . ."[39] Both writers accept this boundlessness of the ocean as symbolic of America's unformed destiny and unlimited possibilities. Thus Erro will state simply ". . . Argentina is a part of America and America is the continent of possibility."[40] Aside from the attractiveness of his ideas, Frank's decidedly dramatic personality certainly could not fail to appeal to Erro. Erro shows a similarly sympathetic attitude toward the ideas and person of Nicolas Berdyaev. In the *Tiempo lacerado* Erro states that he prefers a "fiercely atheistic" Bolshevik

34. *Ibid.*, pp. 197-221.
35. Erro, *Posibilidad y realidad*, p. 14.
36. *Ibid.*, p. 37.
37. See Waldo Frank's appreciation of Erro in *America Hispana* (New York, 1931), p. 337, note 1.
38. Erro, *Tiempo lacerado*, pp. 153-54.
39. Waldo Frank, *The Re-discovery of America* (New York, 1929), p. 18.
40. Erro, *Posibilidad y realidad*, p. 4.

to a "luke-warm" liberal; significantly, he goes on to say that "extremes come together."[41] The implication is, of course, that men of dedication and passion are united in a great fraternity which transcends doctrinal divisions. Berdyaev clearly was a member of this fraternity: profoundly radical, he could appreciate the spiritual aspect of Marxism and could hate the dehumanizing, technologically oriented world of bourgeois capitalism. By the same token he could not accept the massive machine-like state which the Bolshevik revolution had spawned. Somewhat like Waldo Frank, Berdyaev envisioned an "integrated" world of heterogeneous individuals: he considered racism, most forms of nationalism, fascism, and communism to be divisive and to lead to the establishment of suprahuman political structures capable of destroying the "person." Berdyaev viewed "individualism," upon which these divisive "isms" feed, as bad; he saw "personalism," however, as the proper term to describe the Christian philosophy of man as an expression of God. Another facet of Berdyaev's thought which appealed strongly to Erro was his attempt to establish an historical parallel between the early Christian period and the twentieth century. The freshness, vigor, and intrinsic humaneness of the church of Augustine, Berdyaev felt, must be born again in the sterile, mechanized, dying world of today. Erro's characterization of the early Christian period as "dramatic" and his emphasis on the youthfulness of contemporary Spanish America are clearly echoes of these ideas.

Erro's literary soul-mates are men of intense commitment and of fervent spirituality: Berdyaev, Unamuno, Kierkegaard, and especially Charles Péguy, whose dramatic life, religious convictions, and tragic death obviously moved Erro deeply. Citing the French writer in *Tiempo lacerado*, he states that the great emphasis placed on political revolution is pointless without a corresponding inner revolution: "No revolution is genuine unless it is a moral revolution."[42] This movement—this change in modern man—Erro feels, must be accomplished "in the realm of practical life," by means of clear principles established by Christ himself. In the spirit of both Péguy and Berdyaev he calls for "injecting new energy, new dynamism into Christian principles" which, in our contemporary materialistic world, have remained in a state of "languid inertia."[43] Erro concludes this

41. Erro, *Tiempo lacerado*, p. 82. Regarding Berdyaev, see above, note 160 to Chapter IV.
42. Erro, *Tiempo lacerado*, p. 191.
43. *Ibid.*, p. 193.

point by calling for "great leaders, or saints, or apostles" to champion, by their example, a revitalized Christian humanism.

Erro has not written a great deal about specific national characteristics in his study of *argentinidad,* and only occasionally has he set forth concrete programs for future development of the country.[44] Rather he has attempted to analyze the historical and moral situation of contemporary Argentina and to *prescribe* an attitude which the nation's intellectual leaders might adopt. The implication throughout his work is that only through a profound comprehension of the national reality will the tremendous possibilities open to Argentina be realized: "The great problem of the Argentinian is that of his authenticity; or better stated, the Argentinian is a man whose genuine being is not a certainty, but rather a living problem."[45]

Though Erro was one of the first Spanish American writers to come under the sway of early existential thought, he retains a basic optimism with respect to human endeavor. While some essayists and novelists on the periphery of this movement have been sensitive only to existentialism's gloom, preoccupation with death, and anguish, Erro views this philosophic revolution as one which may have a profoundly liberating effect upon human thought and action. He suggests that Argentina's poets, intellectuals, and scholars should undertake a joyful, "architectual" molding of the future,[46] based upon an existential appreciation of reality. In his *Diálogo existencial* (1937) Erro sheds a bit more light (but only a bit) upon how the new philosophy will serve as an instrument for the apprehension of this reality. Before any conclusions may be drawn regarding Erro's understanding of the relationship between existentialism and *argentinidad* (or *americanidad,* by extension), his concept of existential philosophy itself requires clarification. In the *Diálogo existencial* Erro apparently looks upon the development of existential thought as the necessary culmination of the revolt against scientism and rationalism. These older philosophic positions had to give way because of "a profound divorce between the ideals of an entire century and the present state of things."[47] He goes on to note that reality is too "rebellious and unmanageable" to be apprehended in terms of the past century's philosophic framework. This situation, he feels, has resulted in the widespread acceptance of irrationalism.

44. Erro does make a few specific recommendations regarding land-reform and de-urbanization in *Posibilidad y realidad,* pp. 26-28.
45. *Ibid.,* pp. 49-50.
46. *Ibid.,* pp. 20ff.
47. Erro, *Tiempo lacerado,* p. 96.

However, Erro fails to develop these introductory remarks adequately, despite the fact that he enjoyed a first hand acquaintance with Heidegger and that this essay was for the most part a version of an actual dialogue with the German philosopher in the summer of 1936. Erro merely limits himself to brief mention of some of the important exponents of this new philosophic trend—Chestov, Husserl, Dilthey, Hoffding, among others—and to a superficial description of various aspects of existential thought. He points out, for example, that there is a definite religious wing to the movement (Barth, Berdyaev, and Chestov) opposed to a nonreligious group of existentialists; or he praises his compatriot, the philosophical essayists Carlos Astrada, as one of the few good interpreters of Heidegger.[48] In one of the few instances where he actually comes to grips with the basic tenets of existential thought he seems to accept the Heideggerian definition of being as "a continuous presence" rather than as "substance."[49] The absence of further definitions may itself be indicative of Erro's understanding of the existential viewpoint: if existence indeed precedes essence—to use the classic statement of the existential position—then the process of defining, clarifying essential positions becomes rather secondary. The intent of Heidegger's great work *Sein und Zeit*, Erro claims, is "to make visible the existence of man as temporality."[50] The emphasis here is upon a "doing," an action or process rather than upon a libresque definition. This same intent characterizes Erro's "application" of this philosophy to Argentina and to the continent. Although we must accept Zum Felde's observation that Erro never clarifies the precise relationship of existentialism to *argentinidad*,[51] the presence of Heideggerian attitudes in Erro's essays is undeniable. A good example of this presence is seen in Erro's ideas of commitment and participation.

Heidegger's exegetes have pointed out that one of the main differences in the German philosopher's position and that of Kierkegaard is that Heidegger stresses an "essential participation . . . with the world" whereas the Dane—and others like him—are radically individualistic.[52] In Heidegger's view we are always "open to the world" or in "direct relation with the world." The celebrated existential theme of "isolation," at least in the Heideggerian view, refers more to the individual's fundamental separation (his "alien-

48. *Ibid.*, p. 61.
49. *Ibid.*, p. 122.
50. *Ibid.*, p. 114.
51. Zum Felde, *Indice crítico*, p. 470.
52. Jean A. Wahl, *A Short History of Existentialism* (New York, 1949), p. 15.

ness," his being "outside") from his own being, than to any isolation from other individuals. In fact, Heidegger even affirms a natural, or perhaps metaphysical, communion of individuals. The idea of relationship with the world is characterized, on the one hand, by recognition of future possibilities and, on the other, by an awareness of the limitations stemming from conditions imposed by the past. The present, or the "third ecstasy of Time," to use the Heideggerian phrase, implies a ceaseless searching for a trajectory, an orientation in terms of these limitations and possibilities. As Jean Wahl observes, this is the starting point of the Heideggerian ethic: "the 'Resolute Decision' by which we take upon ourselves our past, our future and our present and affirm our destiny." Erro's concern for his country and his continent led him toward a similar position in which social commitment and participation were heavily emphasized. The implication is that the process of creating *argentinidad* is not unlike the Heideggerian "resolute Decision," the act by which one's destiny is constantly "affirmed" in the historical and circumstantial context. Since the understanding of this context involves a thorough analysis of past experience and future possibility, the proper activity of the nation's intellectual leaders is clearly marked out. Erro, like many of his fellow essayists in Spanish America, is really searching for a method, a set of guidelines by which concrete observations or suggestions regarding the national life may be made. Rather than sketch out the national character or propose specific programs, he simply calls attention to the need for analysis, self-knowledge, and, most important, the need for intellectuals and statesmen to affirm *argentinidad*: "Let us assume our direction . . . by the most certain route . . . that of the study of our own place in the world."[53]

Erro believes that one of the greatest dangers in the present world is the preoccupation with immediate problems rather than with basic long-term questions. He underscores this view by criticizing Ortega's notion that the constant relegation of the present to the future is in effect "the sickness of our time."[54] In the light of his later essays and excursions into existentialism, his characterization in 1929 of *criollismo* as "something that is arriving" contains the kernel of his message and the essence of his contribution to the pursuit of *argentinidad*.

Among Erro's very closest literary acquaintances of the mid-twenties was the youthful Eduardo Mallea of provincial Bahía

53. Erro, *Medida del criollismo*, p. 91.
54. *Ibid.*, p. 53.

Blanca—essayist, short story writer, and novelist-to-be. A great deal of common ground unites these two writers: both shared the same general outlook, the same tonality, the same love for dramatic, tortured personalities. The same *tertulias* (literary and social gatherings) in the cafes of Buenos Aires and the same mutual friends are fondly recalled by both.[55] Mallea, however, is better known as a writer of prose fiction than as an essayist, though the fine line which divides his fiction from his essays is often barely discernible. For example, in the novelettes which comprise his *Ciudad junto al río inmóvil* (1935), the personalities portrayed are in effect the same anonymous Argentinians who are the subjects of his most important essays: "Millions and millions of American men who are searching for themselves . . . their conscience enduring the dark, subterranean task of gestation. . . . Men of America, men of Argentina as yet unborn unto themselves . . . unborn unto knowledge of themselves."[56]

Apparently the early thirties were as crucial in determining the trajectory of Mallea's work as they were in shaping the literary future of many of his compatriots.[57] In his earliest book, the *Cuentos para una inglesa desesperada* (1926), Mallea is deeply, almost neurotically, preoccupied with "finding himself": in his later works the search for self-knowledge comes to be viewed as a process necessarily operating within a social framework. In his essay of 1935, *Conocimiento y expresión de la Argentina*, this point is central to his thesis. Knowledge, and here self-knowledge is clearly indicated, is only one half of man's "supreme unity." The other half is "expression"—hence the title of the essay. Both processes are difficult and are only achieved through anguish: both require that the individual be in intimate contact with other individuals. The initial steps in achieving this "supreme unity" of self-knowledge and expression demand that the individual be intensely, radically alone. In the *Conocimiento y expresión* Mallea speaks of the need to "negate" oneself, to suppress all that is "contaminated by a visible wilderness of passions, desires. . . ."[58] One must be, in a sense, "outside oneself" to really know oneself. It is no mere coincidence that many of Mallea's most fertile ideas were developed while he traveled either abroad or in

55. See especially Mallea's *Historia de una pasión argentina* (Buenos Aires, 1939), pp. 45ff., for a description of this circle of writers.

56. Eduardo Mallea, *La ciudad junto al río inmóvil* (Buenos Aires, 1935), p. 15.

57. Recall the "mood" of Argentine intellectuals during the early 1930's as described by Murena. See above, Chapter V, p. 136.

58. Eduardo Mallea, *Conocimiento y expresión de la argentina* (Buenos Aires, 1935), p. 51.

remote regions of his native country: the *Conocimiento y expresión*, which contains the germ of many of the ideas to be developed in later essays, was composed entirely in France. Although residence abroad undoubtedly sharpened Mallea's appreciation of the positive nature of solitude, he notes that aloneness is a general condition of contemporary man and that it does not necessarily result from unusual circumstances. It is to be found, for example, as a characteristic of virtually all of the younger generation of America. It is particularly acute among the many Argentinians who have flocked to the city— Buenos Aires—in search of contact with others similarly afflicted by "restlessness, loneliness, desolation," and perhaps by their desire to find Argentine authenticity: "they have been frightened by their solitude, and . . . have left in anguish to seek this contact in the city. . . ."[59] The experience of these men, young artists and writers very much like Mallea himself, was in a sense a radical exile, albeit within the confines of their own country. The nature of this experience forms the matrix of Mallea's most impressive essay, *Historia de una pasión argentina*.

This work may be approached best by first examining its concluding chapter. The tone, as in most of the book, is intensely personal; the style, poetic prose at its best. After an extended period of travel Mallea returns to his old residence on the upper floor of a Buenos Aires building. It is daylight, and gazing out over the broad flat plains upon which the bustling modern metropolis now rises, he muses: "I was almost crying to myself . . . I was a mass of sorrow and reflection . . . and as I looked out over this nation which stretched out so close to me, and yet so far off. . . I could not contain in the depths of my being a great sadness towards the land in which we have suffered and in which we have left a bit of ourselves."[60] Mallea then describes how in his meditation he loses all awareness of time and external reality: "I felt myself to be free of all bonds, to be isolated in a universe of my own. . . . I was far from everything, but I sensed a vibration, as if my skin were in contact with unknown but numerous human presences . . . the more I would isolate myself from everything, the more I would unite myself with everything."[61] For a brief moment of poetic lucidity, the particular and the universal fuse. The consuming study of his country, the ambivalent vision of the great city—powerful and proud yet somehow empty—the distant

59. *Ibid.*, p. 54.
60. Mallea, *Historia de una pasión*, p. 190.
61. *Ibid.*, p. 191.

glimpse of river merging with the horizon, and the memories of foreign places recently visited, all seem to vanish while a sudden awareness of human communion takes hold of the writer:

> Through the interior fatherland one progresses to the others, to those that are external, to the nation and to the universal fatherland, since the genuine and profound fatherland is not created independently, but within each man. . . .
>
> You can't go anywhere without exiling yourself. The path to creation is the path of exile; and there is a time to reject this exile and there is a time to accept it; there is a time to decide between remaining bound to the fiction that surrounds us or going into exile.[62]

This "beautiful and unfortunate exile," Mallea seems to say, has many of the characteristics of a religious, if not a mystical, experience. The individual suffers "incomparable pain" and "intense pleasure"; when he "returns" from this state he is "cleansed," and "made better from head to toe." The return itself implies that the exile is now ready "to give himself," to offer something of value to his fellow man.[63]

Mallea believes that all things have a dual existence: the physically apparent (the "external shape") as opposed to the "spiritual realm." A crucial point in Mallea's work is that this duality very definitely applies to the land itself: ". . . nations, like all things, have two realms: their physical appearance, their external shape, and their inner territory; their spiritual territory." Nationalism or patriotism in its purest form results when "a man has created within himself his spiritual territory and has wedded it to the spiritual territory of his country. . . ."[64]

A mystique of the land itself, then, is as important in Mallea's thinking as is his concept of the dual nature of human existence. His attitude toward the land suggests a number of writers, both Argentine and foreign. A recent study of Mallea's work points to the Spanish essayist of the turn of the century, Angel Ganivet, as its chief source.[65] There may well be some parallelism here, but Ganivet's interests in deriving national or group characteristics from the very shape of the land mass (the "insular personality," etc.) seems to imply an acceptance of geographic determinism quite absent in

62. *Ibid.*
63. *Ibid.*, p. 192.
64. *Ibid.*
65. John H. R. Polt, *The writings of Eduardo Mallea* ("University of California Publications in Modern Philology," Vol. 54 [Berkeley, 1959]), p. 20.

Mallea. One could probably make as good a case for tracing Mallea's passion for the land to his compatriot Ricardo Rojas, who, as we saw earlier, urged Argentinians to seek out the *genius loci*, the mystical telluric forces appreciated by the Indian, but ignored by the cosmopolite. Another important influence upon Mallea's telluricism was Pascal: the Argentine appreciates the French thinker's feelings of terror and anguish when confronted by "the eternal silence of infinite spaces." Mallea, however, believes that emotions of human insignificance amidst the immensity of nature provide a stimulus, a challenge for human endeavor. The conviction that men in general and Argentinians in particular are capable of meeting this challenge distinguishes Mallea's telluricism from that of more pessimistic, deterministic writers. His concept of the "man versus land" relationship suggests even a classical attitude.[66] This view is further corroborated by his reaction to the ideas of Keyserling, whose book, *South American Meditations*, written after his visit to the New World, was widely discussed by Spanish American writers. Mallea takes issue with the German thinker when the latter notes that man must "free himself of the land." Rather than "free himself" (*librarse*) of the land man should "rise up" (*levantarse*) from the land, while maintaining contact with this powerful vital source. Mallea further rejects Keyserling's notion that the land inspires "terror" in man—a terror which must be overcome: what man must do, claims Mallea, "is live on the land without being terrified."[67] In short, Mallea views the land in decidedly positive terms; it is the constant nutrient, the source of life for man's spiritual being and of his possible regeneration:

> Every great fertilization of life and humanity comes from a deep feeling for the land ... color, vital fluids, substance all come in different ways from land; the powerful sense of life, the spiritual anguish, and the feeling of cosmic sorrow of a Tolstoy or of a Dostoyevsky came from the land.
> And everything that exists on the surface of the land is in a state of regeneration. In a state of growth and ceaseless multiplication.[68]

These three points—the solitude-communion polarity, the duality of the physically apparent versus the spiritually real, and the mystique of the land—form the basis of Mallea's concept of *argentinidad* and

66. Note the similarity of this view of nature to Reyes' "classical" attitude toward the land. See above, Chapter IV, pp. 82-84.
67. Mallea, *Historia de una pasión*, p. 131.
68. *Ibid.*, p. 132.

his crucial distinction between the "visible" Argentine and the "invisible" Argentine. The "visible" Argentinians are the ambitious, self-centered, hollow men of everyday affairs who suffer from a very simple malady: "The lifeless way in which they live."[69] The life of the "visible" Argentinian lacks drama, conviction, passion. Moreover, he is inarticulate, isolated, and given to the exaltation of "mere individuality."[70] His isolation and egocentrism must not, moreover, be confused with the profound introspective solitude which, we have seen, may lead directly toward a broadly humanitarian communion.

Although the "visible" Argentinian seems to be more in evidence in the city, and his opposite, the "invisible" Argentinian, more frequently encountered in the country, Mallea is careful to point out that it is not his intention to establish a simplistic equation of this kind.[71] Nonetheless, the city, in Mallea's earliest work as well as in his later novels, is often pictured as a chaotic, disorienting force. It "de-naturalizes" man; it leads toward a desperate sort of individualism, to the pursuit of artificial, materialistic goals rather than toward a sense of communion. But the implication is present that the inhabitants of the city may, in their own way, achieve an "authentic" existence and attain that "severe exaltation" of life which Mallea considers essential to the "invisible" Argentine. Mallea does not make clear exactly how this is to come about, for it is precisely the intimate relationship with nature and the land which defines the authentic "invisible" Argentinian, who exists "in relation to stars, plants, rocks and the general form of everything that is." The "invisible" Argentinian, moreover, has the strength and courage of a man "faced with the primeval and unchained challenge of nature."[72] Since Mallea believes that the history of America is the history of man versus the "rebelliousness" of nature, the "invisible" Argentinian is equated with the authentic man of the New World. But why the adjective "invisible?" For one thing, Mallea, like so many of his contemporaries, envisions a flowering of genuine American culture in the future. Of the American he states simply: "The reality which faces him is unwritten."[73] The spirit of American authenticity thus remains, at the present time, more or less unseen. Yet Mallea has glimpsed this spirit in the *argentino invisible*. These glimpses afford

69. *Ibid.*, p. 51.
70. *Ibid.*, p. 58.
71. *Ibid.*, p. 84.
72. *Ibid.*, p. 88.
73. *Ibid.*

us a good idea of the kind of continent and nation that Mallea hopes
to see emerge: the character of "invisible" Argentinian and, by
extension, of the authentic American is one of intense dedication,
of a "severe exaltation" of life born of solitude, introspection, and an
ultimate recognition of what is termed "the unity of the human
bond."[74] The ideal Argentine—and certainly the ideal man, regardless of nationality—will do his duty, exercise his profession honestly,
work confidently in the faith that what he is doing as an individual
is necessary to his fellows and to humanity as a whole. In some of
the most dramatic pages of the *Historia de una pasión argentina*,
Mallea recalls seeing just such men in action:

> I have seen men with only an extra kerchief around their
> necks go out to their fields in winter. . . . I have heard of doctors
> struggling in the back country for want of a proper instrument
> to save a dying patient and I have known how my skilled
> father in the midst of the wilderness once opened a patient's
> stomach with a sterilized jack-knife. . . . I have seen men who
> wished to teach honestly go hungry, ill-paid, and persecuted by
> higher officialdom. . . . I have anxiously and frequently waited,
> listening for the almost imperceptible rising up . . . of all those
> people who carry in their eyes the universal image of a new
> Argentina.[75]

What distinguishes Mallea from a writer such as Ezequiel Martínez Estrada is the conviction that despite the egoism, insincerity,
and mediocrity of the "visible" Argentinians, the desired authentic
characteristics of the "invisible" Argentinians will emerge eventually.
When it is clearly recognized that the false goals of the Positivists—
"well-being" and "progress"—are means rather than genuine ends,
this process will be realized. Mallea appeals to his countrymen's
spirituality, to their "creative dream," to their disinterest. Stated
in its most elemental terms, if Argentinians are to achieve national
authenticity (*argentinidad*), and thus genuine universality, it is
imperative that they "give themselves": "The gesture of giving is
the first manifestation of faith, and since faith is the purest expression of the soul, it is . . . the essential form of man."[76] Mallea finds
it inherent in Argentine life that the men controlling the destiny of
the nation have forced this spirit of giving oneself (*el ánimo de
donación*) into the subterranean realm of the "invisible." There is,
however, a peculiar irony in this situation, for Mallea believes that

74. *Ibid.*, p. 87.
75. *Ibid.*, pp. 88-89.
76. *Ibid.*, p. 153.

nature herself provides a lesson in generosity: "In this land humanity gives of itself, plants give of themselves, animals give of themselves; even the rocks give of themselves in a general panorama of offering."[77] Argentinians, like others in the New World, must not be less generous than the land itself. Thus the utopian dream—the idea of America as a land of promise, a continent whose abundant natural wealth provides an example of benign generosity upon which men must pattern themselves—also underlies Mallea's *argentinidad*. This attitude places Mallea clearly within the Americanist tradition of the present century: the Mexican, Alfonso Reyes, while his frame of reference is distinctly classical, reflects a similar viewpoint; and Martínez Estrada, though he adheres to a more romantic and more pessimistic position, parallels Mallea quite closely. Further evidence of this exaltation of America's natural gifts may be seen in many other writers already discussed: Germán Arciniegas, M. Picón Salas, and, very clearly, in Waldo Frank.

Mallea's relation to the latter was unique. In a crucial chapter of the *Historia de una pasión argentina*, "América," he describes in detail his acquaintance with the North American writer. At this point in his life, Mallea describes himself as in a state of utter despair. Vaguely aware of what his mission as a formulator of *argentinidad* might be, he finds, nevertheless, that he is unable to organize any coherent statement of this mission: "A new country had taken possession of me. . . . It was imperative that these destinies should form a single body. . . . But since I did not have a leader's power to weld these destinies together, I already had the taste of failure on my lips. I was unable to remedy the situation in any way. My impotence and my sorrow because of this impotence were tremendous."[78]

At precisely this critical moment Waldo Frank, some of whose work the Argentine essayist had already read, appeared in Buenos Aires, bearing his "difficult" but important message. Mallea describes how the two met, how he had earlier found much to admire in the pages of Frank's *Our America*, and finally, how Frank invited him to his Buenos Aires residence to discuss the basic lines of his Americanist philosophy. In recalling this conversation, Mallea writes that the most significant feature of Frank's thought was that it was "a completed whole," and "in spirit . . . was ecumenical."[79] He

77. *Ibid.*
78. *Ibid.*, pp. 110-11.
79. *Ibid.*, p. 113.

recalls that that very morning he resolved to collaborate with Frank in the translation of the lectures which the North American was to deliver in Buenos Aires. Mallea goes on to describe Frank in glowing terms; he speaks of his "solid purity," of his "understanding of universality," and of his "tragic and constructive sense of things." Dozens of similar expressions in the *Historia de una pasión argentina* attest Mallea's respect and admiration for Frank.

The question remains, however, what exactly did Mallea find so appealing in Frank's ideas? The view that the New World was, very literally, *new* is perhaps the most important of these. Although the simple fact of newness did not resolve all the problems inherent in defining *argentinidad* and the American destiny, it unquestionably helped clarify Mallea's thinking on these fundamental questions:

> We are diametrically different from a Frenchman, a Finn, or a Roumanian. Why? In all these works and speeches that I was translating the answer was given: because we are a new world; but that didn't strike me as a sufficient explanation.
> Something else had to be known: what part was ours in this new world. And that is what I wanted to tell this North American. . . . I wished to tell him about the natural forces that formed the basis of our possible role in the new human order.[80]

The chapter on Frank in the *Historia de una pasión argentina* ends on a very Mallean note. The interchange of ideas between the two men has proved to be quite fruitful; the warm personal relationship suggests the tremendous possibilities which might come from a real comprehension between North America and Latin America. The real "problem of America," Mallea feels, is the same throughout the hemisphere: the "act of comprehension" which has taken place between himself and Frank must occur between many others; such acts of genuine communication will ultimately reveal "the pure ore" of humanity which now lies hidden below the surface.[81] This flowering of the human spirit can only be achieved through a process of radical solitude, followed by a reaching out towards others, which in turn leads to a sense of communion—what Mallea terms "the accommodation of one's being to that of others in our midst."[82] Borrowing from Frank's terminology he speaks of the "integral" nature of any nation, culture, or community—a harmony of differing

80. *Ibid.*, p. 122.
81. *Ibid.*, p. 125.
82. *Ibid.*

parts in which each individual unit is ever aware of his relationship to the whole. Mallea concludes this crucial chapter of his essay by again stressing the value of "giving" (*donación*): the meeting with Frank has been fruitful because each man "gave something to the other." Mallea further remarks that men of spirit exist throughout the continent only awaiting the spark which writers such as Frank could provide.[83] Mallea's closing statement—that he was certain that his collaboration with Frank produced much more than the mere translation of a few speeches—is abundantly true. Indeed, the North American did much to enrich Mallea's "Argentine passion" with a universal passion.

Our introduction to Mallea's work linked him closely with Carlos Alberto Erro, an essayist whose writings frequently touched upon existentialism. Though references to men associated with this philosophical movement are common in the essays of both Erro and Mallea, writers like Kierkegaard, Unamuno, and Berdyaev can hardly be considered orthodox exponents of the existential position. Rather, they are men whose passionate and often tormented writings reflect a wide range of attitudes which have come to be thought of as "existential." Mallea, unlike Erro, has made no attempt to organize and explicate his ideas on the subject. Yet what we now call existential themes—anguish, solitude, the yearning for genuine communication, "commitment," etc.—are frequently found in his work. The fact that Mallea seldom discusses the technicalities of existentialism or mentions the professionals of the movement should not be surprising, since he is a creative writer rather than a philosopher. More significant, however, is the fact noted by students of his thought that Mallea openly rejects the basic existential tenet of "existence preceding essence."[84] He has also attacked existentialism on the grounds that it tends to restrict man, to encircle him and thus limit his possibilities. This view is clearly expressed in a more recent essay, "El análisis y las esencias" (1950), published in the collection *Notas de un novelista* (1954): "The worst thing about existentialism is that it is a matter of a closed philosophy. An ontology that infers no possibility of change is worse than physical death . . . transcendency defines life itself in its biological as well as in its higher aspects. One lives to the degree that one transcends."[85] Mallea's interpretation of existentialism as a "closed philosophy" could, of

83. *Ibid.*
84. Polt, *The Writings of Mallea*, pp. 49-50.
85. Edward Mallea, *Notas de un novelista* (Buenos Aires, 1954), pp. 18-19.

course, be challenged; indeed, the debate revolving about the precise status of human liberty in existential thought continues to the present. Although there may well be some question regarding Mallea's understanding of existentialism's subtleties it is clear that he accepted much of the movement's spirit. It is also true that he rejected those aspects of existentialism which did not fit his own estimate of human potentialities. For our purposes it is significant that the themes which make up the literary periphery of existentialism—solitude, anguish, the pressing need for real communication with others—have figured prominently in Mallea's search for *argentinidad*. Moreover, the fact that this existential flavor in his work is apparent as early as the mid-thirties is noteworthy, since the popular diffusion of this philosophy in most of the Western Hemisphere occurs considerably later. It may be recalled, however, that these existential elements represent only a part of the Mallean *argentinidad*: telluricism—the mystique of the land—as well as Frank's dialectical concept of each individual's "sense of the Whole" also played important roles in its formulation. Lastly, *argentinidad* is for Mallea a spirit, an attitude, a code of disinterested social effort, which has yet to be realized. In short, *argentinidad* does not describe the national essence as it is or was, but rather how it could and should be.

That references to existentialism appear so frequently in the discussion of Erro and Mallea may come as a surprise to those unfamiliar with the Argentine intellectual scene of the late twenties and early thirties. North Americans—unless they had a professional interest in philosophy—were generally unaware of even the terminology of the movement until its diffusion, principally through the French, shortly after World War II. Similarly, among intellectuals in northern Spanish America, existentialism became widely known only after 1946, a fact that is well corroborated by a cursory examination of articles appearing in the leading literary and intellectual reviews of the continent in the thirties and forties. In Argentina, however, familiarity with what was then called "existential philosophy" (the term existentialism being of later coinage) dates from the late twenties. This interest was understandably centered about the Germans who were then developing the new philosophy: Heidegger, and the earlier phenomenologists. The link with European existential thought through Ortega is quite apparent, yet Ortega and his *Revista de Occidente* were read in other parts of Spanish America as well as in Argentina. The presence of several first-rate philosophical minds in the country, particularly Alejandro Korn (1860-1936) and Francisco Romero (1891-1962), must not be discounted. The older of the two, Korn, could hardly be called a precursor of existentialism; yet as a recent student of Argentine philosophy has pointed out,[86] the great emphasis upon the creativity of the individual found throughout Korn's work provides an intellectual climate quite conducive to existential philosophizing. As for Romero, his work in certain fields peripheral to existentialism—philosophical anthropology and the philosophy of values—no doubt helped contribute to this climate.

Two other writers—Miguel Angel Virasoro (1900-65) and Carlos Astrada (1894———)—were more directly involved in existentialism, though they are much less famous than Korn and Romero. Both are first and foremost philosophers and may be considered essayists only if a very broad definition of the genre is accepted: they are not well known outside Argentina, and surprisingly enough they are often overlooked even by their own compatriots.[87] Zum Felde suggests one explanation for this obscurity, at least in the case of Astrada, when he points out that he espoused the cause of Nazism early in the forties.[88] Virasoro, coincidentally, wrote his earliest articles in the ephemeral Rightist review, *Inicial*, whose very *raison d'être*, as its director proclaims, was to fight what he considered to be the good fight against "International communism and the Judaizing press."[89] The magazine was quite clearly anti-Semitic; and Virasoro, albeit in a highly philosophical, highly intellectualized manner, collaborated in this aspect of its program. I do not know if Virasoro held to these political and religious prejudices in his later career; however, in the purely philosophical writings of his maturity, such as his *La libertad, la existencia y el ser* (1942), there are no traces of these views. But it is the Virasoro of the mid-twenties who interests us here. The *Inicial* articles, "El problema de la cultura y la nueva sensibilidad," show the same concern for crystallizing the national essence found in the works of Mallea and Erro. Virasoro's intellectual frame of reference, however, was not yet existential. His guides were the German neo-Kantian philosophers, Spengler and Ortega. As one might expect, he favors vitalism, activism, and

86. Juan Carlos Torchia Estrada, *La filosofía en la Argentina* (Washington, 1961), pp. 250-54.
87. Neither Virasoro nor Astrada are discussed in Torchia Estrada's book, see note 86 above. They are also not treated in Risieri Frondisi's extensive article, "¿Hay una filosofía iberoamericana?" *Realidad*, No. 8 (March-April, 1948), pp. 158-70.
88. Zum Felde, *Indice crítico*, p. 437.
89. See the statement of policy published on the cover of the 2nd issue of *Inicial*, I (Dec., 1923).

the "sportive" or "spontaneous" spirit typical of vigorous, new cultures. Like some of his mentors he enjoys drawing historical parallels: pre-Socratic Greece, a young, flowering, culture, becomes less "spontaneous," less "sportive" upon being "Judaized"; similarly, the incipient culture of the New World must not be "contaminated" (this is not Virasoro's exact terminology, but the implication seems clear) by influences which would limit its sportive vigor. Such was the case, Virasoro claims, when western Europe underwent the transformation of its original early Greek spirit by "Latin-Judaic" influences.[90] How these ideas might be specifically applied to Argentina and America is not made clear; but throughout these early essays Virasoro repeatedly proposes a national "asceticism," defined as a kind of conservation of vital energies—a "training" process which will enable the nation to live by the "sport-concept."[91] Students of Ortega will note here many ideas similar to those expressed in the Spanish essayist's *Origen deportivo del estado*—composed, incidentally, in 1924. Virasoro's articles of 1927-28, published in the important review *Síntesis*, reveal a greater approximation to existential thought. In his conclusion to "Una teoría del yo como cultura" (1927), he states, for example, "The being of the ego is thus its self-realization . . . not the pure abstract being excogitated by Parmenides, but a continual becoming."[92]

Among those most responsible for this surprisingly early cultivation of existentialism in Argentina, Carlos Astrada occupies an important place. Astrada's *El juego existencial* (1933) may well be the first book-length work in Spanish America to employ a clearly existential frame of reference. Although he studied with Heidegger in Freiburg and was well acquainted with the German philosopher's commentators, Astrada states at the outset of the book that he considers the work to be an original interpretation of the master's philosophy.[93] Although the title of Astrada's book—the existential "Game" or "Gamble"—suggests the Orteguian interest in the "sportive" basis of society, this similarity is only superficial. Astrada's objectives, tone, and conceptual framework are entirely different and, moreover, surprisingly modern. Witness his definition of

90. Miguel Angel Virasoro, "El problema de la cultura y la nueva mentalidad argentina," *Inicial*, I (Dec., 1924), 11-25.
91. Miguel Angel Virasoro, "Introducción a la nueva sensibilidad," *Inicial*, II (August, 1925), 115.
92. Miguel Angel Virasoro, "Una teoría del yo como cultura," *Síntesis*, I (Dec., 1927), 36.
93. Carlos Astrada, *El juego existencial* (Buenos Aires, 1933), pp. 9-12.

existence as "the game of risking one's being." Astrada's amplification of this idea bears citation: "Existence is essentially null.
The knowledge of the nothingness which is existence is the game in
which man is placed."[94] Further on, Astrada develops the concept
of "the game" as an *asidero* (handle) or *sostén* (support) by which
man "maintains" his existence: In an essentially meaningless, "null"
world the very notion of man's concept of the world is derived from
this continuous act of "risking" or betting one's being.[95] Again, the
similarity to the vocabulary of more recent existential writers—to
Sartre, for example—is striking. However, Astrada leaves a great
deal unexplained, and the question of how original his treatise is, as
compared with the main lines of Heideggerian philosophy, could not
be answered without an extensive analysis of his thought, a task
which would be beyond the scope of this study. More relevant to
our purposes is the fact that Astrada's influence upon Argentine
intellectual life was not limited to this one rather technical work.
As a writer of philosophical essays in the important review *Sur*
during the thirties, he undoubtedly reached a wide audience. His
articles, in the main explanations of and commentaries upon the
leading early existential writers, have more than just routine interest.
In "De Kierkegaard a Heidegger" (October, 1936), for example,
Astrada employs the noun *existencialismo* at a time when the movement was universally referred to as "existential philosophy" or
"existential thought," making him, in all probability, the first
Spanish American writer to so use this term. Lastly, the role of *Sur*
itself in the germination and fertilization of existentialism in Argentina merits attention. At about the time that Astrada was writing
in the review, articles on the new philosophy by his compatriots
Erro, Mallea, and Bernardo Canal Feijóo began to appear. Notable,
too, was *Sur's* publication, in the summer of 1932, of a portion of the
Spanish translation of Heidegger's *Sein und Zeit*.

To conclude, the early diffusion of existentialism in Argentina
had a marked effect on the content and tone of several of the country's
major writers: the manner in which the *argentinidad* theme is
handled by Erro and Mallea is one of the best examples of this
influence. We shall observe a parallel situation in other countries—
most markedly in the work of an important group of recent Mexican

94. *Ibid.*, p. 26.
95. There is some difficulty in translating the verb "jugar," which can mean either
"to play" (any game, with stakes or not) or "to gamble, to risk." Astrada's context
suggests the latter as the best English rendering of his idea.

essayists. The efficacy of the existential viewpoint in resolving such questions as the meaning of the national essence, the uniqueness of the American destiny, and the nature of the new humanism will be explored later. At this point, however, the work of several other Argentine essayists who have contributed to the discussion of *argentinidad* must be examined briefly.

Bernardo Canal Feijóo, a close contemporary of Mallea, Martínez Estrada, Erro, and Borges, has probed the Argentine essence from several interesting vantage points. In his *El reverso humorístico de la tristeza criolla* (1940), a speech delivered at the Universidad Nacional del Litoral, he attempts to analyze the Argentine spirit on the basis of three traits: 1) "the spirit of evasion" 2) "the self-critical frame of mind" and 3) "the connaturalness of the spiritual creation."[96] He maintains in regard to the first two points that although Argentina is apparently the most autocritical of Spanish American nations, this self-analysis frequently lacks authenticity; that the Argentine intellectual, once having approached the problem of writing about himself and his country, backs off and chooses not to face up to realities. A case in point, he feels, is Martínez Estrada, whose *Radiografía de la Pampa* Canal had attacked earlier in *Sur*.[97] Canal Feijóo's third point, that of the relation of the Argentine spirit to the land, is more fully developed. Like so many other Argentine writers, he feels that the land itself has had a decisive role in shaping the national character—indeed the nation's basic disorder derives from "the feeling of the country's extension, its wilderness; that is, its inability to fill up this vastness, to possess it completely with the infinite power conferred upon organic nations."[98] Paralleling the view of Sarmiento of a century earlier, Canal emphasizes that the vastness of Argentina's territory infects the soul of the inhabitant with a "terror" of nature and with a "sense of the dissolution or disintegration of the inner unity of one's being."[99] The Argentine, under these forces, develops an acute sense of nostalgic sadness; his is the strange fate of "suffering absence while remaining in his place." As one might suppose, this same alienation exists to an even greater degree among the immigrants, the newcomers to Argentina who are faced not only with the painful experience of leaving their own

---

96. Bernardo Canal Feijóo, *El reverso humorístico de la tristeza criolla*, (Publicación No. 43 de la "Extensión Universitaria" de la Universidad Nacional del Litoral [Santa Fe, 1940]), pp. 2-5.
97. See Canal Feijóo, "Radiografías fatídicas," *Sur*, No. 37 (Oct., 1927), 63-67.
98. Canal Feijóo, *Reverso humorístico*, p. 9.
99. *Ibid.*, p. 13.

country, but with the even more painful obligation to make a new homeland for themselves. But despite the apparent sadness of the Argentine *criollo*, Canal feels that the authentic Argentinian really faces life with a "certain smile," which, while not actually expressing a sense of humor, is the "reverse" of his sadness. With this final observation, Canal Feijóo leaves his reader in the air. Although a number of interesting problems are touched upon lightly, the *Reverso humorístico de la tristeza criolla* in effect reaches no conclusions.

Canal's tightly organized, well-documented historical essay *Teoría de la ciudad argentina* (1951), is quite different. In this study he presents the provocative thesis that the interior cities of the nation have never had a legitimate *raison d'être*, and that Buenos Aires' uniqueness lies in the fact that she is "the first Argentine city [that was] by origin necessary and authentic."[100] The provincial cities, he argues, were established not on the basis of economic necessity, nor to suit the needs of transportation or administration. Perhaps the only explanation of their location is that the conquerors, sensing the ethnic and linguistic differences among the region's Indian tribes, attempted to set up cities in conformity with the centers of indigenous population. Obviously, cities established in this manner could enjoy only an artificial existence. Even in the colonial period, Canal notes, the government was forced to adopt policies to maintain a "synthetic balance" between the coast and the hinterland. Often—and this point is well substantiated by pages of documentation—the people of the interior cities had literally nothing to do, the officials nothing to administrate, and the municipal councils nothing to decide. The continued existence of such cities, like their birth, stemmed only from "a formal and abstract decision, which rather resembles a rite, a magic rite."[101] Canal's essay is clearly an important contribution to the traditional Argentine polemic of the city (i.e., Buenos Aires) versus the country: the questions he discusses—the peculiar nature of Argentine demography, the relationships of man and land—have fascinated the nation's writers from Sarmiento to Martínez Estrada. In the light of this polemic, one is immediately tempted to ask if Canal Feijóo "favors" the *porteños*—the people of Buenos Aires—or the *provincianos*; this question, however, cannot be answered readily. He does criticize Sarmiento's polarity of "civilization and barbarism" as inadequate for deciding the problems of city versus country. In Canal's terms, however, the virtual collapse of urban society in

100. Bernardo Canal Feijóo, *Teoría de la ciudad argentina* (Buenos Aires, 1951), p. 45.
101. *Ibid.*, p. 16.

the interior during the Rosas regime could be explained as the expected reversion from an artificially maintained situation to one
which would be more "natural." This point leads to another crucial
idea in Canal Feijóo's thesis: that there is in fact a natural, "organic"
pattern of growth for societies and nations. For example, he views
the rise of Buenos Aires and its assumption of the functions of the
political and economic capital of the nation as a "biological" phenomenon.[102] Granted this naturally ordained hegemony of Buenos Aires,
the notion of a loose Argentine confederation is unthinkable. The
suggestion that the nation would fare better if a new, centrally
located capital were established is likewise untenable, since Canal
Feijóo holds that the organic structure of a nation may not be
arbitrarily altered: "The being of a nation is not a theorem, or a
robot-like mechanism; it is a biological entity. . . ."[103] Canal Feijóo's
essay abounds in analogies drawn from the natural sciences and
particularly from biology. For example, in discussing the problem
of the recent overexpansion of Buenos Aires, he presents a striking
physiological metaphor of the city as a living organism which exists by
means of the dual functions of assimilation and elimination. The
"urban metabolism" of Buenos Aires, however, cannot cope with
the tremendous mass of country people who have flocked to the city
in recent years. Since this movement into the city has not been
justified by any substantial increase in industrialization or other
economic opportunities (as has been the case recently in western
Europe and the U.S.A.), this human influx gives rise to frustration,
aimlessness, crime, and delinquency. Stated in terms of his organic
metaphor, Buenos Aires has become incapable of assimilating and
eliminating the "toxins" and "impure residues" brought into its
body by this "unnatural" population pressure.[104] The victim of
this condition, the individual whose hopes for a better life in the
metropolis, have been crushed by the city's inability to absorb him
and "has lost or cannot find his land."[105] The interesting implication
here is that the city—at least a city which has grown to a size inconsistent with its ability to function properly and "organically"—
alienates man from his soil, from the natural, life-sustaining contact
with the land. What Canal Feijóo does not indicate clearly is
whether he believes, as some of his compatriots do, that *any* modern

102. *Ibid.*, p. 148.
103. *Ibid.*, pp. 185-86.
104. *Ibid.*, pp. 222-24.
105. *Ibid.*, p. 225.

city, by definition, has an alienating effect upon man. This may in fact be his position, for later in his essay he argues that the modern city destroys traditional family life, and that despite the attempt to rationalize human existence "man continues to be the inhabitant of a geographic, climatological, scenic, and geological world. . . ."[106] In short, authentic man remains a child of nature. A paradox is thus suggested by Canal's view of urban growth: on the one hand the city is a "natural" development of the nation or society; and on the other, it tends to destroy man's very essence by cutting him off from the soil, from the natural realm which affords him his authenticity.

A possible resolution of this paradox is suggested when Canal Feijóo calls for what he terms an "extraordinary metaphor"; "the urbanization of the countryside."[107] He argues that such a program —he refrains from outlining it in any detail—would bring about "a wonderful resolution of the old Sarmientan antinomy."[108] He urges, moreover, that like cities, rural areas must be thought of as "human biological and organic unities" and not "mere material objects." He maintains that although his plan for "urbanization" of the rural areas may appear strange, it is justified since it is a reaction against the "mechanical fact of the city."[109] Here again disdain for the modern city is in evidence; a further indication of this position is seen in the final pages of the essay where Canal rebukes certain Argentine sociologists and historians for their denigration of the well-developed culture of the *estancia* (large ranch or plantation). As with his earlier work, the weakest part of Canal Feijóo's essay is the hazy conclusion. The plan for urbanization of the rural areas is not sketched out, and the author's ambivalent view of the city is not clarified. The fact that there is a vague lack of coherence in Argentine character ("a certain difficulty in his being") resulting from the absence of marked climatic and geographic problems, is presented with little support and in a superficial manner. In a final ambivalent note Canal observes that the Argentine possesses both a basic optimism and a basic fear or terror.[110] In short, the most impressive part of this work, dedicated incidentally "to the search for authenticity in Argentine essence and history,"[111] is the well-

106. *Ibid.*, p. 235.
107. *Ibid.*, p. 227.
108. *Ibid.*
109. *Ibid.*, p. 230.
110. *Ibid.*, p. 262.
111. *Ibid.*, p. 251.

substantiated study of urban development during the colonial period; the broader objectives of the author are unfortunately not attained.

We have already discussed the main lines of Ezequiel Martínez Estrada's thought in connection with Spanish American radicialism and the new humanism. Martínez Estrada has written a great deal specifically about his own country, however, and his contributions to the *argentinidad* polemic are substantial. Most of what he has said on the subject flows from his basic philosophical premise that natural man is good until corrupted by modern civilization. Thus his massive, well-documented study of the Gauchesque theme in Argentine culture, the *Muerte y transfiguración de Martín Fierro* (1948), is built around the propositions that the Gaucho was by nature good; that the "civilizing" regime of Sarmiento corrupted and then destroyed him; and that at the turn of the century a complicated national mythology arose aimed at falsifying the character of the authentic Gaucho while obscuring the crime of his eradication. Given Martínez Estrada's general attitudes, one concludes that he considered the Gaucho's way of life representative of a genuine agrarian society and that he viewed its disappearance as a great loss. The point is substantiated by his consistent and bitter critique of the city, as in his essay *Cabeza de Goliat* (1940). We have seen that Martínez Estrada, like Rilke, considered the modern city to be "a thing against nature"; in the specific case of Buenos Aires he has metaphorically described the metropolis as a gigantic octopus whose tentacles (i.e., its rail lines) reach out to carry its corruption deep into the country.[112] The city dweller is in a sense kept prisoner by the city; he is alienated or "dispossessed" from the natural realm, the source of all his genuine being. Only at night, when Buenos Aires sleeps and the "rational" world of daily activity ceases, do the city dwellers come into contact with the life-giving forces of nature.[113] Some parallelism with Canal Feijóo's study of Argentine urban development is evident here. Both writers stress the abnormal growth of Buenos Aires—the unnaturalness of this encephalitic giant's head on the body of a dwarf.[114] Where Canal will say that the organism of the city is incapable of eliminating the toxins it consumes, Martínez Estrada will say of Buenos Aires: "It brutally and blindly absorbs the riches of the interior . . . the giant eats up every-

112. See above, Chapter V, p. 137.
113. Ezequiel Martínez Estrada, *Cabeza de Goliat* (Buenos Aires, 1940), p. 37.
114. These views are substantiated by demographic fact: Of Argentina's 21.5 millions (1964 estimate), approximately one fourth live in Buenos Aires or in the city's metropolitan area.

thing. . . . It nourishes itself on poverty and backwardness, on ignorance and on solitude."[115] The part of the "jail-city" that pleases Martínez Estrada most is the great public park of Palermo, precisely because it is "the opposite of the city."[116] Yet the reader of *Cabeza de Goliat* becomes strangely aware of the author's great fascination, if not affection, for Buenos Aires. Just as Sarmiento, who feared the political and social implications of Gaucho culture, was at heart a fervent admirer of the colorful individualist of the Pampas, Martínez Estrada hates the city in the abstract, but loves many of its inhabitants and many of its picturesque corners. This affection is seen in his lovely descriptions of certain streets, in his impressively poetic prose describing night in the metropolis, and in a series of fine vignettes dealing with its stores, kiosks, and pawnshops.

In what way do Martínez Estrada's views of the city and the country define his *argentinidad*? The answer to this question has often been suggested in his work. In a more recent essay, *Exhortaciones* (1957), he notes that although he has made his message clear repeatedly, people fail to listen: "Must I spend the rest of my days repeating myself like a broken record? We have no roots in the land (nor in the heavens); we feel no love, sympathy or affection for our unknown neighbor. . . . We do not know how to make gifts, to donate, to make offerings . . . we do not feel that we are a people, a mission, a task, a destiny. . . ."[117] The destiny of Argentina, he indicates, though he does not state it outright, is to return to a simple, anarchic, communal life in contact with nature—the implication being that kindness, altruism, and mutual cooperation will come forth "naturally" under such circumstances. Does Estrada literally mean that all the material advantages of modern life must be sacrificed in order to return to this state of primitive bliss? Is life in a world of highly developed social structures, of factories, of mass communications and modern cities an impossibility for the altruistic, sympathetic innocent of Estrada's dream? The answers to these questions, though never given directly, are apparently affirmative. Our earlier observation of what Martínez Estrada thinks of constitutions, formalistic social organizations, cities, and political structures certainly bears this view out.[118]

Although Argentina does not appear to be following this path, other nations do. A few years before his death Martínez Estrada

115. Martínez Estrada, *Cabeza de Goliat*, p. 86.
116. *Ibid.*, p. 94.
117. Ezequiel Martínez Estrada, *Exhortaciones* (Buenos Aires, 1957), p. 28.
118. See above, Chapter V, pp. 138-39.

seemed to have found his utopian dream close to realization in present-day Cuba. In a provocative essay, "El nuevo mundo, la isla de Utopia y la isla de Cuba" (March, 1963), he maintains that the island of Utopia, described by Thomas More in the sixteenth century, may no longer by thought of as truly "imaginary": it exists today in the Antilles; it is the Cuba of Fidel Castro.[119] Estrada argues that More's book must be thought of as a brilliant intuitive prognosis, rather than as a mere speculative work. That Castro himself—a classic underdog—and his regime would appeal to Martínez Estrada comes as no surprise. Keeping in mind Estrada's aversion to formalized government, constitutions, and complex legal apparatus, the attraction of the present Cuban regime with its day-to-day operations may be appreciated. The repeated efforts of the *Castristas* to establish the idea that Cuba's revolution has been primarily agrarian is another facet of this appeal; and certainly the photographs of thousands of city workers abandoning their shops and offices to toil in the cane fields could not fail to impress a person of Estrada's bent. Overtly, this essay reveals nothing of Martínez Estrada's present concept of *argentinidad*. He may well have believed, however, that a Castro-like movement in his own country would have provided the conditions for the eventual establishment of an Argentine Utopia.

Martínez Estrada's ideas are extreme, his basic outlook decidedly radical, and his view of reality highly subjective. As such, they have given rise to bitter criticism as well as to ardent admiration. Of contemporary students of *argentinidad* there is hardly one who has not reacted in one way or another to Estrada's work. We have noted Canal Feijóo's critique of his *Radiografía de la Pampa*[120] and Sebreli's characterization of his career as "a useless rebellion."[121] Of a more personal nature was the sharp clash between Estrada and Jorge Luis Borges over the latter's praise of the Aramburu government, a regime which Martínez Estrada disliked as much as he did that of Perón.[122] Perhaps his most devoted admirer is the poet, novelist, and essayist H. A. Murena, whose evaluation of Estrada has already been noted.

119. Ezequiel Martínez Estrada, "El nuevo mundo, la isla de Utopía y la isla de Cuba," *Cuadernos Americanos*, XXII (March-April, 1963), 117. See also Martínez Estrada's *Mi experiencia cubana* (Montevideo, 1965).
120. See note 97 above.
121. See above, Chapter V, p. 134.
122. See Jorge Luis Borges, "Una efusión de Ezéquiel Martínez Estrada," *Sur*, No. 242 (Sept.-Oct., 1956), pp. 52-53.

Murena, consistent with his interest in the work of his mentor, is himself deeply concerned with the question of *argentinidad*. He has crystallized this concern in a series of essays published as the collection, *El pecado original de América* (1958). At the root of Murena's concept of the Argentine and American essence (the distinction between the two seems nonexistent in his writing) is the idea that as inhabitants of the New World "we left everything when we came over from Europe or from Asia."[123] The American finding himself "outside of history," is not precisely alone or abandoned, but rather "alienated" or "dispossessed." This term is crucial, for Murena argues that "dispossession is the essence of the human predicament."[124] Here again, the parallel with existential terminology is clear: the notion of man's existence as a search for *un lieu*, a residence in an alien world, has become a commonplace in the last few decades. Implied in this idea too, is the hint that Americans, by dint of their unique, "ahistorical" existence are in some way closer to the bedrock of the human essence. But the crux of Murena's essay is that the terror of "dispossession"—of living without the paternal guidance of a clear historical tradition—leads to an almost pathological escapism. The American—and certainly the Argentine of this century is in mind here—attempts to hide the disturbing fact of his alienation by elaborate subterfuges: the pursuit of material comfort, the superficial cultivation of erudition, and many others. He may even feign psychic or physical maladies rather than recognize that he is a pariah, "one of the dregs of the earth—the most wretched of the wretched."[125]

In the brilliant chapter, "El acoso de la soledad," Murena states: "The awareness that we do not exist and the desire to exist, make us exist falsely."[126] To clarify his point he analyzes the cult of falseness in Argentine letters: he condemns a number of important authors for producing what is termed "nationalistic art" rather than genuine "national art." The chief targets for this attack are the "folkloric" writers of the "Martín Fierro" group and their leaders of the twenties, Jorge Luis Borges and Ricardo Güiraldes. These men, Murena feels, were not genuinely sensitive to the national materials that they rather crudely utilized. They are writers of the superficially picturesque, who escape "by the easy route of national-

123. H. A. Murena, *El pecado original de América* (Buenos Aires, 1958), p. 115.
124. *Ibid.*
125. *Ibid.*
126. *Ibid.*, p. 45.

ism, of the past. . . ." They have failed to get to the core of the
nation's essence because they have not recognized the fact of "dispossession" and, equally important, they have been insensitive to
the fact of solitude, inherent in Argentine geography: "Our world,
our present and our obstacle is solitude; therefore it is imperative
that we confront it. Only by coming face to face (with solitude) will
we achieve our liberty, that is, will we exist, will we create art and
not artifice."[127] Each individual's confrontation with solitude will
bring about a spirit of "communion"; and from this individual act of
communion, a sense of community will arise. The exact character
of this relationship or communion with nature is the theme of the
final essay in the *Pecado original de América*. Acutely aware of its
significance as a literary motif throughout Spanish America, Murena
discards the simplistic subject-object relationship suggested by the
phrase "man versus nature." Works such as Güiraldes' *Don Segundo
Sombra* and Rivera's novel of the Amazon jungle, *La Vorágine*, fail to
reveal the genuine American essence because the natural realm
always seems to be "in front of" man as a distinct object. In the
writings of those authors who are successful in their presentation of
this relationship—Mallea, the Chilean poet Pablo Neruda, and
presumably Martínez Estrada—nature is omnipresent, but it is
"behind" rather than "in front of" man. In a sense nature has been
absorbed, assimilated, transcended; or, to use the term suggested by
Murena, it has been "trans-objectivized." Here, as in his penetrating
essay on the current political situation, "El estridor del conformismo,"[128] Murena has not provided final answers, but instead has
offered thought-provoking alternatives to traditional dilemmas.

127. *Ibid.*, pp. 64-65.
128. See above, Chapter V, pp. 143-45.

VII / THE SEARCH FOR ESSENCE

IN MEXICO AND ELSEWHERE

ARGENTINA HAS NOT BEEN UNIQUE AMONG SPANISH American nations in her concern for self-knowledge. Although the discussion in this chapter will be centered on Mexico—unquestionably the northern focus of Spanish American intellectual activity, just as Argentina is the southern focus—a brief examination of the search for essence in Chile, Peru, and Cuba will underscore the fact that this quest is indeed continental in scope.

Considering the country's unique physical features it is not surprising that Chilean essayists should be concerned with geography. Indeed, Benjamin Subercaseaux has written an entire essay, *Chile, o una geografía loca* (1943), precisely on this subject; and Luis Durand, in his *Presencia de Chile* (1942), introduces his study of *chilenidad* by a fine essay on Chilean landscape. Durand's book does more than describe the nation's physical aspects; as such it has greater relevance to our study. In an effort to probe the national character, Durand concentrates on analyzing the rural *criollo*, and particularly the distinctively Chilean *roto*.[1] The *roto*, he feels, combines much of the "two proud and strong races which formed him";[2] and, although the term *rotada* (trick, gambit, scheme) is of recent coinage, Durand finds this manifestation of the *roto* spirit to have been deeply in-

1. The term *"roto"* literally means "a broken man." It apparently became common in the period following World War I when the Chilean economy was dealt a severe blow by the development of the synthetic nitrate industry in the United States. When this happened thousands of destitute workers ("*rotos*") spread south from the abandoned nitrate fields in the North, creating a class somewhat like the "Okies" and migrant workers of the North American depression years. Gradually, however, the term became generalized in meaning so that it included virtually any one of the poor—usually Mestizo—classes.
2. Luis Durand, *Presencia de Chile* (Santiago, 1942), p. 111.

grained in national life for centuries. The essay includes chapters on Chilean folklore, music, dance, and the native love of horses. Though unquestionably interesting, the *Presencia de Chile* falls short because of the lack of any unifying insight on the part of the author. There is no attempt to interpret Chilean experience in terms of universal experience; there is no conviction that some mission, some *raison d'être* should be sought for the nation. In short, Durand limits himself almost exclusively to the picturesque. Though Chile's intellectual and literary activity is very substantial, she apparently lacks the passionate commitment to the quest for essence found elsewhere. This situation prevails despite the fact that she has had typical "nativist versus cosmopolite" polemics (the subject is discussed by Ricardo A. Latcham, in a recent article),[3] fine universities, important literary reviews, and creative writers of great merit.

The Andean countries have already been discussed in connection with our analysis of indigenism and radicalism. In Peru, essayists such as Antenor Orrego and José Carlos Mariátegui were especially interested in studying the Indian and his role in modern society. Though they approached Peruvian reality armed with a very specific set of socio-political tenets, their work nonetheless led to a deeper understanding of the national essence in its totality. The radicals were not alone in this undertaking. Among more conservative writers, Victor Andrés Belaunde—historian, scholar, and editor of the influential review *Mercurio Peruano*—published his *Meditaciones peruanas* in the early twenties and, some two decades later, *Peruanidad elementos esenciales* (1942). The *Mercurio* itself was an important vehicle of *peruanidad*: the statement of policy published in the journal's first number announced that the *Mercurio Peruano* was to serve as "the organ of genuine *peruanidad*" and that it was "to dig deep into the native soil, to penetrate the secrets of . . . past life and to sketch out (Peru's) problems." Although the *Mercurio* was at times capable of maintaining considerable tolerance in its views, more often its pages reflected the markedly conservative position of its editor. Nevertheless Belaunde is no mere propagandist; as the author of substantial studies in Peruvian history he is well equipped to provide an interesting contrast to the Leftist writers we have already discussed.

Belaunde begins his earlier essay, the *Meditaciones peruanas*, by acknowledging the fact that "Peru is sick."[4] Like many writers of

3. Ricardo A. Latcham, "La querella de criollismo," *Bolivar*, No. 34 (Oct., 1954), 563-93.
4. Víctor Andrés Belaúnde, *Meditaciones peruanas* (Lima, 1923), p. 9.

the period, he accuses his countrymen of "side-tracking national ideals"; he speaks of a lack of will, a lack of originality and a lack of enthusiasm among the intellectuals of the day. He credits González Prada with having pointed out these same national ills, but he repeatedly attacks him for his negativism, for his simplistic interpretations of Peruvian reality and particularly for his "antireligious dogmatism."[5] Belaunde argues (the fact that these ideas were conceived at about the period of World War I must be borne in mind) that while the radicals denigrate all forms of religion, they have themselves merely substituted a rigid "scientific" dogmatism for religious dogmatism.[6] Perhaps some Marxists did "worship" science, as Belaunde claims; but certainly this view reveals his insensitivity toward those radicals—Mariátegui, for example—who exalted the passionate, spiritual, and mystical aspect of the Revolution. Moreover, the fact that "scientific dogmatism" may just as easily be employed to justify a regime of markedly Rightist tendencies, such as that of Díaz' Mexico, casts further doubt on Belaunde's facile equation of scientism and radicalism.

When Belaunde states that the radicals' preoccupation with antireligious propaganda has led them away from an objective study of the Indian, his position is even less tenable. However, his statement that the Leftists' preoccupation with the lower economic classes has produced only a partial view of national problems is more justified. Belaunde's thinking on the Indian, the landholders, and related problems does not follow a typically conservative pattern. He is quite capable of criticizing Peru's "coastal plutocracy" with its absentee landlords, its corruption, and its love of bureaucracy. And, in an essay composed as early as 1915 calling for official governmental action to study and defend the Indian, he appears to be a devoted *indigenista*.[7] Although his attitude is tinged with a bit of paternal disdain, he notes the great contributions of the Indians to Peruvian nationhood. In passing he advises his countrymen to accept the ethnic composition of the nation as it is rather than cherish illusions about a massive European immigration which, he feels, will never take place. Very probably Belaunde's advice came as a response to the then popular view, promulgated by his compatriot Francisco García Calderón, that the "inferiority" of Indian or mestizo nations

5. *Ibid.*, p. 54.
6. *Ibid.*, pp. 59-60.
7. The essay in question, "La cuestión social en Arequipa," is dated 1915 and is included in Belaunde's *Meditaciones peruanas*, pp. 130-45.

could be ameliorated by attracting huge numbers of white immigrants.[8] To conclude, the *Meditaciones peruanas* is, as its title
suggests, a random collection of thoughts on various national problems; it has little unity, and there is no intensity in the author's search
for the Peruvian essence. However, Belaunde seems to recognize
this shortcoming: in an epilogue to a later edition (1932) he notes
with concern "the absence of a movement of collective introspection
aimed at discovering our profound reality."[9] This lack is attributed
to two causes: the narrow partisanship of both the Right and the
Left, and the constant reliance of Peruvian intellectuals on "the
ever-changing ideological structures of the European world."[10]

Despite the promise of its title, Belaunde's essay of 1942, *Peruanidad*, is essentially a defense of the Spanish legacy to the New
World. The keynote of the book is found in the opening pages when
Belaunde declares "we can conceive of no conflict between Hispanism
and indigenism." As in his earlier essay he takes the Leftists to task
for not concerning themselves with the Indian's spirituality; for not
dealing with him as a human being, but rather as a scientific problem.
By contrast, he lauds the pro-Indian campaign of Las Casas and
other liberal Catholics of the colonial period. He argues that the
Leftists' complete rejection of colonial culture has led them to
formulate a very incomplete concept of *peruanidad*: the ethical and
juridical ideals of Spain are not only part of the historical past but
they also deserve to be recognized and incorporated in a modern
democratic Peru. Belaunde of course does not emphasize the fact
that the indigenism of Las Casas and the "liberal" theologians of
Salamanca represent only a minority opinion of sixteenth-century
Spanish thought on the subject.

The quest for *peruanidad*, like the quest for *chilenidad*, has not
produced works which penetrate the inner core of the national
essence. The sharp division between writers of the Left and Right
may lie at the root of this situation. In a nation of radical indigenists
on one side and conservative Hispanophiles on the other, there is
little or no common ground upon which writers may meet. Yet Peru
has not suffered any lack of intellectual activity—even by comparison
with Argentina or Mexico. Her philosophical essayists include such
outstanding figures as Alejandro Deústua, a leader in the revolt
against positivism; Mariano Ibérico and Honorio Delgado, both of

8. See above, Chapter II, pp. 26-29.
9. Belaunde, *Meditaciones peruanas*, p. 46.
10. *Ibid.*, p. 47.

whom were conversant with phenomenology and existentialism at an early date; and several very capable neothomists, such as Alberto Wagner de Reina.[11] Peruvian intellectual life has also been enriched by journals of high quality: the Leftist *Amauta* of the late twenties, the conservative *Mercurio Peruano*, and short-lived but very substantial magazine of literary and philosophical essays, *Mar del Sur* (1948-53).[12]

Any discussion of Cuban intellectual or literary life must begin in the very recent past. Although the island produced great writers in the nineteenth century—the magnificent figure of José Martí comes immediately to mind—it is difficult to speak of a distinctively Cuban literature until the advent of nationhood. The work of Fernando Ortiz (1881——), one of the first major writers to emerge after independence, was noted earlier in connection with our discussion of race and racism. Aside from his interests in anthropology and ethnology, Ortiz has played an important role in the island's general intellectual life as the founder of several literary reviews and especially as the editor of one of the continent's oldest, most respected journals, the *Revista Bimestre Cubana*. Félix Lizaso, in his study of Cuban essayists, notes that as early as 1914, Ortiz was intensely concerned with creating an active sense of *cubanidad* among his compatriots.[13] His speech to the "Sociedad Económica de Amigos del País" is a strong exhortation to the intellectuals that they direct their activities toward this end. Ortiz' essays of 1914 and 1924, *Entre cubanos* and *La decadencia cubana: Conferencia de renovación patriótica*, were also composed with a similar objective in mind.[14]

By the 1920's what may legitimately be called a true generation of writers appears on the island. The founding, in 1927, of the provocative Leftist review *Avance* marked an important step in the solidification of this generation's ideals. Among these writers—the *Avance* group—are the essayists Juan Marinello and the late Jorge Mañach (1898-1961). Marinello is the author of several books related to the search for national essence: among these *Sobre la inquietud cubana* (1930) and *Americanismo y cubanismo literario* (1932) are noteworthy. Our attention, however, will be centered

11. For a good resumé of twentieth-century philosophic trends in Peru see Augusto Salazar Bondy, "Panorama de la filosofía en el Perú en los últimos 50 años," *Mar del Sur*, V (Dec., 1950), 42-50.
12. A new review bearing the provocative title *Peruanidad* appeared in the Summer of 1963.
13. Félix Lizaso, *Ensayistas contemporáneos* (Habana, 1936), pp. 34-41.
14. See also Fernando Ortiz, "Los factores humanos de la cubanidad," *Revista Bimestre Cubana*, XLV (1940), pp. 165-69.

upon Mañach and particularly upon his essay, *Indagación del choteo* (1928), a work which despite its qualities has enjoyed less fame than Mañach's celebrated biography of José Martí.

Spanish Americanists frequently note that the literature of recent decades is characterized by a narrowing focus, by a concentration upon the very specific, the very circumstantial, the very personal. We have witnessed in our own study a gradual shift from the broader Americanism of the turn of the century to a more restricted interest in the nation, and in the individual. This narrowing of the essayists' focus does not necessarily lead to a sterile parochialism; often it may be the very process by which fruitful universal insights are gained. Mañach's introductory remarks to the *Indagación del choteo* bear this point out: "The very period in which we live ... demands the re-evaluation of things formerly considered trivial or ridiculous and prides itself in discovering the significance of the insignificant."[15] Citing the sociologist Simmel on the need and value of a "microscopic" study of society, he argues, "There is a vital interest in this. ... The minute and immediate is what consititutes our surroundings, our 'neighborhood,' that with which our existence is in constant contact. ..."[16]

The particular detail of Cuban character which Mañach investigates as the possible key to the national essence is the *choteo*. In its common definition the term refers to a general attitude of not taking anything seriously;[17] but upon close scrutiny, Mañach finds that the *choteo* is essentially an act or habit of disrespect, stemming from a deep-lying repugnance for all authority. Probing further, he finds that in the *choteo* there is an element of "subterfuge in the face of power"; that the *choteador* expresses, by his seemingly gross and pointless ridicule, a state of impotence or of annoyance when confronted by authority.[18] Mañach links this analysis of the *choteo* with a European thinker whom we have already met in a different context: Max Scheler. In this case, it is the German philosopher's study of resentment to which Mañach refers: "Isn't it possible that the *choteo*, in its role as a destroyer of values, may be a product of resentment?" he asks.[19] In Scheler's work "resentment" is generated when the attempt to realize a value is frustrated; while the resentment itself leads to the eventual "transvaluation" of the original

15. Jorge Manach *Indagacion del choteo* (Havana, 1928), p. 6.
16. *Ibid.*, p. 7.
17. *Ibid.*, p. 13.
18. *Ibid.*, p. 29.
19. *Ibid.*, p. 35.

value. Although Mañach feels that the Schelerian analysis is helpful, he points out that the *choteador* may be successful in destroying the value which he attacks by his *choteo*. The final definition of the term, then, is based on an irrational "affirmation" of the ego: "The *choteo* is a strong urge for independence which becomes externalized in a joke which is completely destructive of authority."[20]

Mañach views the *choteo* as a product of a definite historical situation rather than as a constant in the Cuban personality. The liberation of the island from Spanish authority in 1898, he argues, demanded that an "escape valve" for pent-up feelings be found: hence the *choteo*. Though the historical circumstances which first produced this phenomenon have changed, many traits of Cuban character may still be explained by it. The man who laughs or wise-cracks during the most touching scene in a movie is a *choteador* because he prefers to cover up this vulnerable spot in his nature rather than compromise his "jealously guarded independence" in a show of emotion. Many other examples could be given. Our study of *mexicanidad* will reveal some remarkably similar works by essayists who, like Mañach, are capable of unearthing great riches in a linguistic quirk, a proverb, or a common interjection.

As in the case of Argentina's essayists, the search for national essence often leads to prescription as well as to description. Thus, the *Indagación* ends on a plea for the development of a new Cuban culture, characterized by respect, but not coercive respect, and by authentic enthusiasm rather than by the *choteo*: "The *choteo* as mental libertinism is on the defensive. The time to be critically light-hearted, correctly audacious, and conscientiously disrespectful has arrived."[21] One wonders whether Mañach might not have thought of these words when he, along with virtually all of Cuba's intellectuals, cast his lot with the Castro regime. That Mañach felt that Castro had not brought about his desired reorientation is evidenced by his criticism of the regime and his subsequent exile from the island.

* * *

"It is not a question of interpreting that which is Mexican, that which gives us our identity as human, but rather the reverse—of interpreting that which is human as Mexican."[22] In this statement, the young Mexican essayist Emilio Uranga has provided a succinct

20. *Ibid.*, p. 41.
21. *Ibid.*, p. 88.
22. Emilio Uranga, *Análisis del ser del mexicano* (Mexico, 1952), p. 23.

summation of the course that the search for *mexicanidad* has taken in the last few decades. These developments, however, are best appreciated in historical perspective. The men of the Generation of the *Ateneo*, it will be recalled, were imbued with a fervent Americanism, with a compelling desire to refute the values of scientism, and often with a marked sensitivity to the indigenous peculiarities of the New World. The early careers of these writers—Vasconcelos, Caso, Reyes, and the Dominican, Henríquez Ureña—coincided with the decade of the Mexican Revolution; however the immediacy of the conflict and the chaos of the times prevented them from formulating their views on the Mexican essence before the twenties and thirties.

Essays on the Mexican character had been written well before this period: one investigator of the nation's cultural history cites Ezequiel Chávez' study of 1901, "Ensayo sobre los rasgos distintivos de la sensibilidad como factor del carácter mexicano," as perhaps the first effort of this kind in the century.[23] Nevertheless, the Chávez work and others like it are either very short or very limited in scope. Since they were written before the traumatic experience of the Revolution they can hardly be expected to reveal the depth which characterizes later essays of this type. The years immediately following the end of hostilities saw Mexicans gradually become aware of a genuine rebirth of the nation. The new Mexico was an enigma and a challenge; understandably the search for essence acquired a new urgency and greater intensity. The superb poet Ramón López Velarde reflects this search beautifully in his poems and in his less known prose pieces. Shortly before his death (1921) he wrote: "Drinking in the atmosphere of her own enigma, the new *Patria* ceaselessly entreats us with her deep throaty voice. . . ."[24] At roughly the same time Antonio Caso was also receptive to the voice of the new nation: he published his *Discursos a la nación mexicana* (1922), a work which at least by the similarity of title is reminiscent of Fichte's nineteenth-century essays on German nationalism. Though Caso does not investigate the national character, his book does reflect the groping, the search for a Mexican mission. His interest, as in his earlier essays, is to develop a strong sense of moral responsibility in the Mexican—a sense of heroic, active existence based upon a spirit of disinterest.

23. See Juan Hernández Luna, "Primeros estudios sobre el mexicano en nuestro siglo," *Filosofía y Letras*, XX (Oct.-Dec., 1950), 327.
24. Ramón López Velarde, "Novedad de la patria," *El Maestro*, I (April, 1921), 61.

It is a commonplace that the early history of a group of people exerts much influence on their future development. But with the diffusion of psychoanalytic theory—particularly with the spread of Adler's concepts of the complexes and Rank's analysis of the birth trauma—the well-worn phrase "birth of a nation" took on added significance. The work of Samuel Ramos, which was discussed earlier in connection with the neohumanist movement, must be approached against this background. His essay of 1934, the *Perfil del hombre y la cultura en México,* is placed squarely within the psycho-analytic frame of reference: "Modern psychological doctrines teach us that it is not possible to define the personality of an individual if we do not know about certain childhood experiences. . . . Thus we must go back to the beginnings of our history. . . ."[25] The basic fact of Mexico's birth, and here Ramos reiterates the ideas of both Alfonso Reyes and Waldo Frank, is that Mexicans were "invited to civili-zation's banquet when the table had already been served." Ramos feels that this situation, together with the overwhelming effect of nature in the New World, produced in the early Mexican a sense of being "lost," of being swallowed up in an alien world. These feelings led, in turn, to a sense of inferiority. The other participant in the national birth trauma, the Indian, also receives much attention. Ramos does not accept the notion that the Indian's passivity—or what he interprets as "rigidity"—is simply the result of the treatment given him by the conqueror. Rather, he argues that this char-acteristic was apparent in the pre-Columbian Indian. Ramos denies any inferiority in the Indian but he does hold to a notion of fixed native "differentness," which, "as if by magic," has spread to all Mexicans.[26] This "rigidity," working in conjunction with the in-feriority complex, makes the modern Mexican fundamentally in-flexible and highly resistant to any demand that he alter his nature. However, and this point has provided much leavening for later studies of *mexicanidad,* the Mexican will adopt "masks" which produce a superficial change in his character while preserving his unalterable "spiritual bedrock."[27] This bedrock, the Mexican's sense of inferiority, is the ultimate term in Ramos' analysis, although it is never accepted as anything more real than a psychological complex. Ramos concludes the opening chapter of the *Perfil* by noting a number

25. Samuel Ramos, *El perfil del hombre y la cultura en México* (Mexico, 1934), p. 30.
26. *Ibid.,* pp. 40-41.
27. *Ibid.,* p. 39.

of the specific masks which the Mexican has adopted: vanity, bragadoccio, exaggerated individualism, and the like.

After a short discussion of "French Influence in the 19th Century" —a theme related to his thesis only in that the slavish imitation of European culture may be thought of as another typical mask—Ramos further develops the main lines of his argument. Following the psychoanalytic method, he observes that only by facing the truth, by airing the trauma which has produced the given complex, can it be understood and thus removed. Again he makes clear his debt to Adler, claiming that "what is proposed for the first time in this essay is the methodical utilization of this old observation, but rigorously applying the psychological theories of Adler to the Mexican case."[28] Ramos' study of the Mexican is centered upon the *pelado*— the poor, lower-class, uneducated Mexican male. He calls the *pelado* "an explosive being" whose "explosions" are usually verbal. The *pelado* will typically resort to strong language and especially to a rich vocabulary of phallic terms to express his violent nature. He is touchy, defensive, and exhibits a marked lack of confidence in his dealings with others. All of this, as one might expect, is viewed as a mask for his deep-seated sense of inferiority. In his attempt to play the *valiente* (the "tough guy"), the Mexican will indulge in blatant patriotism and in the cultivation of a national mythology based on power and *hombría* (manliness). Moreover, he will deceive himself into accepting the reality of the false image which he has created.[29] The poor *pelados* are not the only victims of this self-deception; Ramos argues that even the more sophisticated bourgeoisie has been contaminated. They too have accepted "archetypes as stimulants to overcome the problems and difficulties of life."[30] Ramos' approach to the Mexican essence provides a striking parallel with the work of several non-Mexican essayists already discussed: his study of the inferiority complex, for example, is quite reminiscent of Martínez Estrada's treatment of the same theme; and the following passage cannot fail to recall Mallea's discussion of the *argentino visible*, Mañach's dissection of the Cuban *choteador*, or Estrada's critique of the Argentinian who is incapable of "giving himself": "Each individual lives shut up within himself, like an oyster in his shell, in

28. *Ibid.*, p. 67.
29. *Ibid.*, p. 85.
30. *Ibid.*, p. 89.

an attitude of mistrust toward others, exuding evil, so that no one will come too close."[31]

In his chapter on "La cultura criolla" Ramos comes to grips with familiar questions of nativism versus Europeanism. Taking positivism as an example of a European doctrine poorly applied to Mexican conditions, he notes that this movement exaggerated the obvious falseness of the national character by suppressing, without replacing, the essential religiosity of the people. Once forced into the subconscious, this element in the Mexican's make-up asserted itself as the adoration of science, as an acceptance of "scientific superstition."[32] His countrymen, Ramos feels, should be willing to use European intellectual tools, but "in harmony" with Mexican culture. Ramos, like Alfonso Reyes—whom he cites approvingly in the *Perfil*—argues that this cultural heritage is essentially Spanish; that it must nevertheless be adapted to the realities of Mexican life; and that the exalted indigenism of the postrevolutionary period could, if not properly understood, prove as false as was the imitation of Europe during the nineteenth century.[33] In a tone reminiscent of Reyes and perhaps of Rodó (whom he also singles out as one of the few writers to have understood the relationship of the Old World to the New), he points out the sterility of the polemic between "nationalists" and "Europeanizers." He observes: "the Europeanizers are in error, because they do not see European culture from Mexico, but rather they see Mexico from Europe."[34]

The final chapters of Ramos' essay are concerned directly with the Mexican as an individual. Echoing one of his favorite mentors, Max Scheler, he states that "the ultimate objective of human activity [or "spiritual activity," to use the Schelerian term] is not the products of culture, but rather the development of personality."[35] Above all, he calls for an attitude of individual sincerity, of honesty: Mexicans must "have the courage to be themselves." Ramos repeatedly makes the point that the national culture be understood as "universal culture made ours," and that the only way to achieve this synthesis is to recognize that which is essentially Mexican. For example the artist who wishes to achieve universality in his work must search his being for his "most individual notes." When these

31. *Ibid..* p. 91.
32. *Ibid.,* p. 109.
33. *Ibid.,* p. 96.
34. *Ibid.,* p. 133.
35. *Ibid.,* p. 155.

are finally discovered, "in that very instant his work will acquire universal transcendence."[36]

The fact that Ramos set forth these thoughts on *mexicanidad* as early as 1934 is as significant as the ideas themselves. In fact, one important section of the *Perfil* appeared in the review *Contemporáneos* some two years before the complete essay was published. To my knowledge no studies of *mexicanidad* comparable in scope or penetration to the *Perfil* appeared until the late forties and early fifties, when an important group of writers picked up the threads of Ramos' work. The professional philosopher will easily find weak points in Ramos' intellectual armor; indeed, in a recent analysis of contemporary Mexican thought Abelardo Villegas has pointed out serious flaws in Ramos' understanding of the concept of values. Yet the same critic readily admits the historical significance of Ramos' work: ". . . the great merit of Ramos consists in his having removed the discussion of our problems from the realm of the very physical and very concrete . . . to a higher, psychological plane. . . . Ramos holds that the crisis of our problems and its solution resides in a certain way of thinking. . . . Therefore a philosophy such as his . . . acquires major dimensions; the solution of the problems of our situation must grow out of serious reflection, out of the clash of ideas."[37]

Ramos published the *Perfil* in 1934, and despite the provocative ideas presented in the work, the theme of *mexicanidad*—or *lo mexicano* as its cultivators choose to call it—apparently lapsed into oblivion for over a decade. It is easier to explain its reappearance in the late forties then it is to account for its absence. A possible explanation for the resurgence of the theme lies in the indirect experience of World War II. Though it may be an overstatement to speak of "the collapse of European culture," as Villegas does,[38] clearly the horrors of war, coupled with the ominous confrontation of East and West in the postwar period, made Latin Americans—and particularly Mexicans—question Europe's ability to maintain its position as the torchbearer of Western civilization. It is understandable that such doubts should lead to a turning inward and to a marked increase in the study and cultivation of everything American.

It would be inaccurate, however, to say that the theme of *lo mexicano* had completely disappeared during the decade or so following the publication of Ramos' essay: Vasconcelos and Caso, for

36. *Ibid.*, pp. 157-58.
37. Abelardo Villegas, *La filosofía de lo mexicano* (Mexico, 1960), pp. 135-36.
38. *Ibid.*, p. 137.

example, continued to probe at least the periphery of the subject; and in 1938 Ramos himself published a second edition of the *Perfil* containing additional material. But by the thirties Vasconcelos seems to draw away from the mainstream of Mexican intellectual life to devote himself to a rather sectarian defense of his religious beliefs; and Caso, while continuing to produce works of merit, apparently made his major contributions in the decade following the Revolution. The case of Alfonso Reyes is, however, different. Reyes has shown a constant interest in discovering what he would call distinctly Mexican "alternatives and specialities," although he seldom attacked the question of *mexicanidad* as a formal problem. His most important essays centered on *lo mexicano* were *Visión de Anáhuac* (1917) and "Discurso por Virgilio" (1933), both composed well before the period under consideration. During the thirties he was almost constantly away from Mexico, yet he maintained a lively interest in *mexicanidad*, as the pages of his own little journal, *Monterrey*, witness.[39] For a writer of Reyes' classical bent, however, the problem of isolating *mexicanidad* and finding its relationship to "universal man" cannot be considered crucial. His essay of the early forties, "Posición de América," illustrates his thinking on the matter. Borrowing a scheme from the American anthropologist Ralph Linton, Reyes describes any culture as having four distinct "factors" or "levels": universals, specialities, alternatives, and peculiarities. To show the relationship between these he suggests a figure of concentric circles, with universals and specialities occupying the inner areas, as a nucleus. The outer edges of the figure are the alternatives and peculiarities, which are envisioned as whirling about the nucleus. Most important, "we can say that the essence of culture is nourished in a centripetal manner and that its energy is brought from the periphery to the nucleus."[40] Although Reyes is not particularly concerned with Mexico in this essay, it would be easy to apply the scheme he outlines to the question of *lo mexicano*. The outer rim of the circle would be composed of varying degrees of Mexican "alternatives and peculiarities." At the center of the cultural diagram would be the universals, in some mysterious way nourished by the centripetal force of the outer rings, and yet essentially the same at all times and in all places: "some things . . . have not changed

39. For a discussion of this journal see Manuel Olguín, *Alfonso Reyes, ensayista* (Mexico, 1956), pp. 76-78.
40. Alfonso Reyes, "Posición de America" in *Obras Completas de Alfonso Reyes* (Mexico, 1956), XI, 257.

since man has been man and will not change as long as the species exists."[41] Reyes' impressive prose and good intentions notwithstanding, this scheme is merely an analogy and as such it cannot be considered a description of reality. Yet its implications are clear: the discovery and cultivation of that which is distinctively Mexican is the *sine qua non* for the establishment of a genuinely universal Mexican culture.

The increasing tempo of Mexican intellectual activity from the end of the thirties and through the late forties resulted in part from the arrival of the Spanish Republican refugees and their gradual incorporation into the nation's literary, scientific, and artistic life. Certainly such powerful philosophical minds as those of José Gaos and David García Bacca helped spark the activity which was soon to appear. Of the generation of intellectuals who reached maturity in the forties, one of the first to reflect the resurgence of interest in *mexicanidad* was Leopoldo Zea (1912———). Zea, a student of Gaos, is best known for his essays dealing with the intellectual history of Mexico and of Spanish America. Such works as *El positivismo en México* (1943), *Apogeo y decadencia del positivismo* (1944), and *Dos etapas del pensamiento en Hispanoamérica* (1949) have become classics of their genre. Zea's interests in historicism and in philosophical method have led him more toward the consideration of *lo mexicano* as a methodological problem than as a field for characterological analysis. His examination of the possibility of a genuine New World culture and his studies on the relationship of Europe and America are similarly directed. Throughout his work, but more noticeably in his earlier essays, the perspectivism of Ortega—perhaps as interpreted by Gaos—figures prominently. Thus in a piece composed in 1942 and incorporated into his *Ensayos sobre filosofía en la historia* (1948), he states: "In attempting to resolve the problems of man whatever be his place in space or in time, we shall have to take ourselves as we are as our point of departure; we must begin with our own circumstance ... conscious of our abilities as members of this cultural community called humanity, and of our limitations as children of one circumstance. ..."[42]

The crisis of Western culture has come to occupy a very central position in Zea's thought of recent years. Inextricably linked with his Mexicanist concern is the idea that Spanish America in general, and Mexico in particular, may well be called upon to salvage the

41. *Ibid.*, p. 258.
42. Leopoldo Zea, *Ensayos sobre filosofía en la historia* (Mexico, 1948), p. 177.

remains of occidental humanism. In such essays as *La filosofía como compromiso* (1952) and in *América en la conciencia de Europa* (1955) he has explored the possibilities of a future ecumenical role for Latin America: citing Northrop's *The Meeting of East and West*, Zea suggests that the ethnic and cultural miscegenation of Latin America equips the continent to serve as a bridge between the Western nations and the renascent cultures of the Orient.[43] Zea fears that the leading Western power, the United States, by virtue of its Puritan tradition ("a Christianity for individuals who strive to be outstanding by dint of their abilities and at the expense of those whom they consider less able"[44] may well be incapable of carrying on the humanist tradition and thus may fail in the great task of "realizing the only worthwhile kind of history; the history of mankind. A history from which no people nor no man must be excluded."[45] If Latin America is to achieve this goal, and if Mexico is to participate in it, then the basic questions of the *circunstancia* must be answered. Zea feels, moreover, that to achieve universality a group must be able to comprehend other groups; that to do this a people must recognize its own particular gift or "contribution" to mankind: "all peoples always have something to say, something to contribute to the world's experience; and the universality of this contribution is found in the capacity of these peoples to make themselves understood and to understand others. The failure to realize this is what has incapacitated men . . . with regard to that which is universal; they shut themselves up behind locked doors where they become steadily narrower until they die in complete solitude."[46] Carrying Zea's point somewhat further it follows that not only Mexicans must seek to discover themselves and their possible contributions to the human synthesis, but that we must generalize the idea and say that all peoples must pursue a similar course if they wish to achieve genuine universality. As Villegas observes: "This is the supreme paradox of the philosophy of *lo mexicano*; when we Mexicans become aware of our limited, circumstantial existence, it signifies that we are aware of ourselves as universally human."[47]

Zea's stature as a mentor of contemporary thought in his country cannot be overemphasized. As one of the leading professors at the National University he has been training a generation of superb

43. Leopoldo Zea, *América en la conciencia de Europa* (Mexico, 1955), p. 173.
44. *Ibid.*, p. 176.
45. *Ibid.*
46. Cited by Villegas, *Filosofía de lo mexicano* p. 139.
47. Villegas, *Filosofía de lo mexicano*, p. 147.

scholars. One of these, Abelardo Villegas, pays him eloquent tribute throughout the pages of his *Filosofía de lo mexicano* (1960) simply by demonstrating, politely and brilliantly, the intellectual independence of the student from the teacher. Lastly, Zea has played an important role as the "godfather" of the *Hiperión* literary and philosophical circle. As we shall see, some of the most interesting studies of *mexicanidad* to date have appeared in the collection *México y lo mexicano*, written by various members of the group and under Zea's editorship. But before exploring the thought of the *Hiperión* writers and of Octavio Paz, who was closely associated with the group, the hazards inherent in attempting to discover the "ontology of the Mexican"—his distinct essence—must be considered. José Gaos has very astutely pointed out the fundamental logical pitfall: "It is a question of defining or discovering the essence of the Mexican. To do this one must be viewing this essence. It cannot be seen except in Mexicans themselves.... In order to observe it in these people it is necessary to know that they are Mexican, in contrast to other people in general. And to know this, implies (knowing) what a Mexican is.... A vicious circle."[48]

Octavio Paz (1914——) is unique among present-day Mexican writers in that, although primarily a poet, he has made substantial contributions to contemporary letters as an essayist. As might be expected, his essays often deal with problems of poetics and aesthetics;[49] however, Paz has also written several studies dealing with *lo mexicano*, the most important of which are gathered together in his widely read volume, *El laberinto de la soledad* (1950). In his essays Paz brings to bear upon the question of *mexicanidad* a fine poetic sensibility, a rich literary experience, and a dazzling talent for blending elements of prose and poetry together on the same page. The *Laberinto de la soledad* has already gone through several printings, a surprising achievement for a work of its type and one which attests Paz' importance. The fact that many Mexican writers of the most recent generation—essayists such as Emilio Uranga—have dedicated their studies on *mexicanidad* to him gives further evidence of Paz' dominant position in the nation's intellectual life.[50] Perhaps more

48. José Gaos, *En torno a la filosofía mexicana* (Mexico, 1952), p. 21, as quoted by Villegas, *Filosofía de lo mexicano*, p. 183.
49. Paz' two major works in this field are *El arco y la lira* (Mexico, 1956), and *Las peras del olmo* (Mexico, 1957).
50. For further discussion of Paz' influence on his compatriots see George Gordon Wing, "Octavio Paz, Poetry, Politics and the Myth of the Mexican" (Ph.D. dissertation, University of California, 1960), pp. 10-14.

than any other Mexican, Paz is recognized abroad. In France he is well known among the Surrealists; in the United States portions of his *Laberinto* were first featured in the *Evergreen Review's Eye of Mexico*, and recently the complete work has appeared in English translation. Paz himself has traveled widely in Europe and the Orient; at present, he is Mexico's ambassador to India.

Paz' earliest essayistic work appeared in 1929 and 1930 in the review *Crisol*. These articles—dealing with problems of Mexican land tenure—are interesting chiefly in that they demonstrate that despite his "cosmopolitanism" Paz' concern for things Mexican is deeply rooted. During the thirties, when he was gaining recognition as a poet, he produced a number of curious prose pieces which were published in the ephemeral reviews *Barandal*, *Taller*, *Ruta*, and later in *El Hijo Pródigo*. These writings—and they defy precise literary classification—provide an insight into the genesis of many of the fundamental attitudes which were later expanded in his major essays. Titled "Vigilias: Fragmentos del diario de un soñador," they explore several themes: man's existence in a fundamentally alien world, the redemptive function of Eros, and the rationalistic view of the world versus the irrational. A host of questions related to these philosophic themes, but dealing specifically with aesthetics, are also considered: poetry as a method for the discovery of truth, the ambivalent position of the novel, the relationship of prose to poetry, etc. Specific concern for *lo mexicano* is absent in his work of this period. Yet Paz did not escape to the ivory tower: his political position was often expressed in writing as well as in deed. What must be stressed is that this aspect of Paz' thought as well as his recent quest for *mexicanidad* are derived from his world-view, and particularly from the role accorded therein to poetry.[51] Some pertinent examples of this relationship may be observed in the "vigilias." A basic idea is that poetic activity is an act of "pure disinterest"—an unconditioned, unteleological expression of the human essence. The realm of poetic activity, *lo poético* as Paz calls it, is in sharp contrast to the world as it is—the world of purposeful activity, the world rationally conceived, which is viewed as an alien place, "mute, indifferent, irreparably strange."[52] Whether the "world as it is" is a corrupted paradise, or whether man's alienation in it is an unavoid-

51. My view of the relationship between Paz' poetry and politics parallels Wing's thinking on the subject: see note 50 above.
52. Octavio Paz, "Vigilias: Fragmentos del diario de un soñador," *Taller*, I (Dec., 1938), 3.

able concomitant of his very existence is never clearly indicated. However, an interesting parallelism between the existential theme of alienation and the psychoanalytic theories of the birth trauma, popularized by Otto Rank in the twenties, is evident here. Much of Paz' poetry as well as his prose suggests either a literal belief in the birth trauma, or at least an acceptance of it as a very meaningful symbol. Returning to Paz' derivation of politics from poetics, there is an implicit equation between "the poetic realm" (*lo poético*) and that which is essentially and rightfully human. The poetic state, like the prenatal state and certain other states, is not only "disinterested" but passive; man's authentic being "flows" outward during those moments when he is not doing something directed toward an external end. It is as if Paz were saying that the individual must *stop*, must cease to exercise his will (will not to will?) in order that he may truly exist. The mainstream of occidental philosophy of course runs counter to these notions. Similarly, the values of modern technological society are opposed to them. Paz' critique of "bourgeois-capitalist" culture, while it has the ring of a typically Leftist attack of the thirties, is based upon these views of the human essence. Paz' radicalism was in effect an attack upon the values of activity, of work for work's sake, of progress, and of acquisition;[53] all of these destroy man's essence by denying him the realm of the poetic.

The erotic mystique and its corollary idea of communion occupy a very crucial place in Paz' thinking. Like poetry, intense erotic experience makes man one with his genuine essence; such experience, moreover, resolves the individual's solitude into communion. In support of these ideas Paz cities Novalis' views of the sexual urge as a "disguised desire for human flesh," and of woman as "the highest form of bodily sustenance."[54] For Paz the physical fusion of the sex act leads to—or is itself—a communion, a partaking of the flesh of all living things, a way back to the primordial, undifferentiated, atemporal ground of Being: "In love the couple endeavors to participate once again in that state in which life and death, need and satisfaction, sleep and action, words and images, time and space, the fruit and the lip, are all fused into one reality."[55] Paz' essays frequently place the reader on a narrow frontier between rational

53. Paz, "Vigilias," *Taller*, I (Dec., 1939), 16ff.
54. Octavio Paz, "Poesía de soledad y poesía de comunión," *El Hijo Pródigo*, I (August, 1945), 273.
55. *Ibid.*, p. 272.

prose analysis and an only partially comprehensible zone of sur-realistic chaos. His technique of mixing prose and poetry is often extremely effective, although considerable demands are made upon the reader for rapid accommodation to his shifting styles. On one page of the "Vigilias," in a straightforward prose discussion of D. H. Lawrence's contribution to the understanding of the erotic, he states: "its objective is communion: therefore it [Lawrence's eroticism] does not attempt to create a moral code, but a religion." He then goes on to note that "the profound hope of communism is not dissimilar, for it seeks fraternity, the active communion of those who are des-perate, as well as the disinherited."[56] A few lines beyond these, however, his poetic muse takes command and the reader finds him-self involved in an intensely personal prose poem: "Your eyes open, as if to devour me. I sink into them. And, suddenly, they no longer exist, nor do I, a shipwreck like you, you who disappear attached to me, melted. . . . We lose our names, our form, our feelings, every-thing that illusorily gives us individuality, and we are naked, divested of everything . . . in this absolute nudity . . . of our hidden, impalp-able condition."[57]

Paz feels that the genuinely erotic, like the the genuinely poetic, are disinterested, "non-productive," irrational activities and could never be accommodated to the values of bourgeois-capitalist society. The conviction that either this society must reject them, or that they must be distorted to suit the demands of the "establishment," is implicit in much of Paz' work. And since the cultivation of *lo poético* and *lo erótico* are indispensable for the realization of that which is essentially human, it follows that the achievement of this ultimate objective is profoundly frustrated in the contemporary Western world.

Given this rejection of things as they are, what positive positions are open to a thinker such as Paz? Clearly he must be a revolutionary, and, at least during much of the thirties, Paz did embrace the Third International. But after certain historical events—the Moscow trials and his own participation in the Spanish Civil War, he abandoned orthodox communism for the less rigid, but more radical camp of the Surrealists.[58] Since Paz' critique of existing conditions is directed specifically at the bourgeois, highly advanced societies of the West, it

56. Paz, "Vigilias," *Tierra Nueva*, II (Jan.-April, 1941), 38.
57. *Ibid.*, pp. 39-40.
58. See Wing, *Octavio Paz*, pp. 24-58. Wing observes that Paz soon realized that the success of the Revolution—even the kind of revolution for which the Surrealists' yearned—was becoming "increasingly more improbable."

is not surprising that cultures far removed in time, space, and basic philosophy should attract him. He has consistently shown an appreciation for oriental philosophy, for the Dionysian religions of the ancient world and for primitive myth and ritual. To clarify how Paz incorporates these varied elements into an integrated view of reality would be a challenging task, but one which we shall leave undone in order to pursue the matter of *mexicanidad* in his essays.

Paz confesses at the outset of the *Laberinto de la soledad* that for many years the concern for defining the uniqueness of *lo mexicano* appeared to him to be "superfluous and dangerous."[59] It was his opinion that a creative work, be it literary or graphic, could do more to define the Mexican essence than any direct attempt to describe it. This attitude explains, at least in part, why overt treatment of the theme of *mexicanidad* is virtually nonexistent in his prose before 1950. Another probable explanation may be found in his adherence to the internationalism of the Left. By the mid-forties a change in attitude is in evidence. Paz could, if the conditions demanded it, not only be interested in the national essence, but also play the role of the staunch defender of *mexicanidad*. His break with the great radical poet of Chile, Pablo Neruda—clearly one of his most important poetic mentors—illustrates this point dramatically.[60]

Paz conceived of the *Laberinto* while on a trip to the United States. Although it would be unfair to maintain that the essay is merely a justification of Mexicanism produced under the pressure of the antithetical Yankee ethos, it is well to remember that relations between the Mexican-Americans in the Southwest and the non-Latin population of the area were quite strained in the late forties. Indeed, Paz' interest in discovering what it was about the *pachuco* which made him an immiscible element in the North American melting pot, provides the point of departure for the entire book.[61] It was this curious experience of noting the vaguely defined *mexicanidad* which seemed to "float in the air" of Los Angeles which led Paz to ask "the same questions that Samuel Ramos asked himself in the *Perfil.* . . ."[62] It must be made clear, however, that Paz had not proposed to write a formal study of Mexican character. Some years after having

59. Octavio Paz, *El laberinto de la soledad* (2ª edición; Mexico, 1959), p. 10.

60. See Wing, *Octavio Paz*, pp. 94-97 for a good description of this affair.

61. Paz, *Laberinto*, pp. 12-16. The term *pachuco* refers to the youth of Mexican origin living in the southwestern part of the United States, particularly California. The term is clearly deprecatory: it became common during World War II as the name for Spanish-speaking juvenile delinquents—the "zoot-suiters"—of the Los Angeles area.

62. Paz, *Laberinto*, p. 12.

published the *Laberinto* he said of the book: "It does not deal with the psychology of the Mexican; rather it is a description of a vital historical rhythm (that of the dialectic of solitude and communion) at one time and in one people."[63] He asserts, moreover, that his study is to be thought of as tentative, as "circumstantial," to use an Orteguian term.

The first chapter of the *Laberinto* deals specifically with the character of the *pachuco*; although Paz sympathizes with him, he states that he is not interested in the *pachuco* per se. The reason for studying him, Paz claims, is that he represents one possible extreme of Mexicanism: an extreme which is very revealing since the *pachuco* when persecuted (presumably by the police or by belligerent North American street gangs) "achieves his authenticity, his true being, the supreme nakedness of a pariah, of a man who belongs nowhere."[64] Paz views the *pachuco's* pose in Yankee society as that of a "challenge": he wishes to stand out so that his persecutors may better see their prey, for only by being attacked and harassed does he enter into any sort of intimate contact with the world about him: "Persecution redeems him and breaks his solitude: his salvation depends upon gaining access to the very society he seems to deny. Solitude and sin, communion and health become equivalent terms."[65] Two propositions underlie this analysis. In the first place, although the *pachuco's* radical isolation—his solitude—is to a degree explicable in terms of his environment, Paz always considers solitude as a basic condition of man or, better stated, as one term in a dialectical view of human existence. Secondly, he posits this dialectic of "solitude-communion" as a universal process by which the individual does not simply become aware of his genuine essence, but actually creates this essence. In Paz' essay, solitude (perhaps the English word "aloneness" translates *soledad* better) occupies a position somewhat analogous to "inferiority" in Ramos' earlier work. Man in general, and the Mexican in particular, is not necessarily aware of his solitude. He is even less aware of his need for communion, for resolving the imperfection of his aloneness into the state of wholeness or health characteristic of communion. Not only does the *pachuco* fail to appreciate this process, but more important, he intentionally tries to "cover up" his solitude by methods that ironically may be subconscious attempts to resolve the solitude-communion dialectic.

63. Cited by Wing, *Octavio Paz*, p. 77.
64. Paz, *Laberinto*, p. 16.
65. *Ibid.*

Hence the case of the *pachuco* who must attract his persecutors.

When Paz shifts his attention from the *pachuco* to the ordinary Mexican, as he does early in the *Laberinto*, he analyzes first the deliberate techniques employed by the Mexican to obscure his sense of "solitude-sin." Paz then studies the inadvertent indications of genuine *mexicanidad* which crop up in language, customs, and folklore. A listing of the subterfuges which the Mexican uses to hide his radical aloneness (and his concomitant feelings of insufficiency, vulnerability, etc.) provide a rich description of the national character. The Mexican tries to defend his intimacy by being *ensimismado* or self-contained; or he cultivates a code of not "opening himself up," of not allowing the exterior world to penetrate his intimate being. He who permits this penetration is looked upon as something less than a man. The Mexican's attitudes toward women and his sexual mores are consistent with this fear of being vulnerable, of being "open to attack." Hence the "openness" of the female must be viewed as a defect, as an imperfection if not an evil. The Mexican further protects himself by a complex system of formalities and "courtesies"; and his tendency to lie is more a self-deception than a deception of others.[66] Perhaps most important, he is a "dissimulator," one whose mimetic talents are of such an order that he loses his own identity completely in his desire to blend into his surroundings.[67] He becomes, to use Paz' ingenious figure, Mr. Nobody (*Ninguno*), a being so unidentifiable that he even treats himself "as a nobody." So general is this Mexican trait of self-negation that there is a strange pall of nothingness over the land: "stronger than our pyramids and sacrifices, than our churches, our popular songs and uprisings, a silence older than history again reigns in our land."[68]

Paz' discussion of the inadvertent indicators of Mexican character is equally interesting. In the third chapter of the *Laberinto* the national love for the fiesta is discussed as a ritual during which "the Mexican does not amuse himself: he wishes to transcend himself, to scale the wall of solitude which isolates him during the rest of the year."[69] The term "ritual" as applied to the fiesta is not to be taken lightly. Paz is well acquainted with contemporary theories regarding the nature of myth and the function of ritual. This is seen in his knowledgeable citation of writers such as Malinowski, Frazer, and

66. *Ibid.*, pp. 26-38.
67. *Ibid.*, p. 38.
68. *Ibid.*, p. 41.
69. *Ibid.*, p. 44.

Hume (all in the *Arco y la Lira*), as well as in his approach to the specific nature of the Mexican fiesta: "Everything takes place in a magic world: time is *other time* (situated in a mythic past or in pure present-ness); the space in which it takes place changes in nature, it becomes detached from the rest of the Earth, it is bedecked and converted into a 'festival place'. . . ."[70] The analysis of the fiesta as ritual helps illumine Paz' conception of being and existence. The individual Mexican who "scales the wall" of his aloneness and enters into the fiesta's communion is, as Paz puts it, returning "to a remote and undifferentiated, prenatal or presocial state, so to speak."[71] There is a fascinating vagueness about the phrase "so to speak" (*por decirlo así*) in this contest. Is Paz speaking metaphorically, or does he hold to the view that there is—or was—another world existing parallel to "the real world"? Certainly this is the same realm to which poetry leads us—the atemporal state of wholeness, of primordial being where such terms as "the one" and "the all" seem to lose all meaning. Perhaps Paz should not be pressed into answering such questions; for even when he is writing prose he is a poet at heart, and his work is grounded upon a fundamentally poetic vision of the world.

The specific fiesta upon which Paz focuses his attention is the *Día de Difuntos* (all Saint's Day), a holiday particularly interesting since it combines a spirit of unrestrained merrymaking with the remembrance of the deceased. The common people's attitude toward death provides another fascinating passage through his labyrinth, for here again the Mexican's essence is revealed. Paz points out that in most advanced Western societies death no longer has any significance beyond that of a rationally understood terminus of biological existence. And in present day Mexico even the educated and sophisticated share this view. For the pre-Columbian Indian and for the orthodox Catholic (Paz treats both as extinct species), death was quite another matter. Although the cosmology of these two groups was profoundly different, "in both systems life and death have no autonomy; they are the two faces of the same coin of reality. All their meaning is derived from other values which control them. They are references to invisible realities."[72] Despite the fact that the contemporary Mexican (excluding of course the sophisticate) does not consciously hold to this notion of a "life-death unity,"

70. *Ibid.*, p. 45.
71. *Ibid.*, p. 46.
72. *Ibid.*, p. 51.

neither does he accept completely the modern scientific view. Though he may, like the typical North American or European, fear death, he nonetheless prefers to meet it quickly "face to face, with disdain or irony." This attitude is partially a result of his denigration of life—his sense of being "nobody." The apparently offhand mocking of death (the custom of eating candy skulls during the fiesta, the burning of firecracker skeletons, etc.) becomes an expression of the worthlessness of life. As Paz puts it, the Mexican shrugs his shoulders asking, "why should I care about death if I don't care about life?"[73] The Mexican, unlike the Aztec or the contemporary primitive who may have a similar cosmology, cannot "give himself over" (*entregarse*) to death because this entails a sacrifice, an "opening himself up" to someone or something exterior. Furthermore, the contemporary Mexican—despite his heritage from the Aztec—is not a primitive, and hence cannot really look upon death as a "ritual passage." There is, however, one way in which the Mexican may make death a vehicle for communion: he may, in a moment of passion, commit murder. Murder is of course a crime, but in contrast to the impersonal slaughter of modern warfare or the mass extermination practiced in police states, it is a "humanized" act. Paz concludes the discussion on a very unorthodox note: "For us crime is still a relationship—and in this sense it has the same liberating significance of the Fiesta or of confession—Hence its drama, its poetry, and—why not say it outright—its grandeur."[74]

Paz' ability to probe the smallest details of Mexican life and to extract from these insights into the national character is very well demonstrated in his analysis of the *mala palabra*—the strong language of insult, curse, and invective. It will be recalled that others have found this kind of linguistic psychology rewarding: in Mexico, Paz' direct predecessor was Samuel Ramos, who in his *Perfil del hombre* analyzed the inferiority complex of the *pelado* on the basis of his compensatory use of phallic terms. For Paz, however, obscene words are more than simple psychological mechanisms. They comprise the "only living language in a world of anemic words—poetry within the reach of everybody."[75] And most important, these words "confusedly reflect our interior nature. . . ." Paz frequently refers to the obscene as a "social language," as a set of terms imbued with ritualistic magic.

73. *Ibid.*, p. 53.
74. *Ibid.*, p. 55.
75. *Ibid.*, p. 67.

The specific word which he analyzes, in all its Mexican shadings and variants, is the verb *chingar* (to rape, to violate). Why should this particular term be so valuable a key to *lo mexicano*? The answer is found in the fact that, aside from its literal meaning, the basic relationship denoted by the word is one of violence, of "forcible penetration into another...."[76] Although the verb is always "tinged with sexuality" its significance goes beyond the merely erotic—"it stands for the triumph of closed-ness of the male, of him who is strong, contrasted with that which is open (and vulnerable)." Paz argues that the relationship implied by the verb defines much of the Mexican's social environment—a world of "the strong and the weak," of *chingones* and *chingados*.

Paz then shifts his attention to history in an attempt to anaylze the traditional Mexican battle cry, *Viva México, hijos de la Chingada*! ("Long live Mexico, sons of the violated woman!"—to put it delicately). Inquiring into the identity of the *Chingada*, Paz notes that she is, above all else, a Mother—or, more precisely, an archetypal figure of the mother. Moreover, as the "violated mother" she represents the Indian woman of the Conquest, the Doña Malinche, the mistress of Cortes. It follows that the Mexican, like the Argentine Gaucho analyzed by Martínez Estrada, is the product of an illegitimate union, and as such is fatherless and disinherited. In this sense *La Chingada* is "the mother of orphans."[77] To sum up, the "aloneness" of the Mexican has an historical dimension: as the product of the casual union of the Conquistadores and the violated Indian woman he is in a sense an orphan; his "accidental" birth has placed him in a fundamentally hostile world wherein he has been forced to live defensively, circumscribed by a complex armour of mask and dissimulation.

Paz is too sophisticated to believe that the Mexican is unique in his anguished condition: "Actually all women, even those who submit voluntarily, are torn open, are violated by the male. In a sense we are all children of the *Chingada*, children of Eve, simply by virtue of being born of woman."[78] This point is further developed in a brief comparison of the Biblical account of the Fall, the Greek myths revolving about Zeus, "the violator of women," and similar motifs in the cosmology of primitive man. But rather than repeat the work of others who have pointed out the similarities of mythic

76. *Ibid.*, p. 69.
77. *Ibid.*, p. 71.
78. *Ibid.*, p. 77.

patterns among all men, Paz chooses to concentrate his efforts on the specifically Mexican version of this one very basic myth. By stating clearly that he is attempting to isolate "a few traits and emotions which illuminate the universal condition of man by means of a particular light,"[79] he is free to devote himself to a thoroughly Mexican study, while recognizing an essential human universality. In the survey which follows, Paz analyzes a number of important features of the national essence in terms of their mythic nature: the cult of the Virgin of Guadalupe, the hero worship accorded the legendary Cuauhtémoc, etc. Paz concludes his analysis by observing that the essence of the nation is best described as a "breaking away" (*una ruptura*) from the Mother. Not only a breaking away, but also a negation and a search for a way back, for a return from the state of exile and aloneness.[80] Always the poet, Paz uses terms here which have multiple symbolic values: "The Mother," for example, means the *Chingada*, the violated Indian woman ("the long-suffering Mexican mother," to use a popular phrase); on another level "the Mother" is associated with the *madre patria*, Spain, so in this sense the "rupture" is a break with the security and established order of Old World civilization. Finally, in view of the universal character of mythic patterns, separation from "the Mother" is a generalized experience—a bond which links the Mexican to all men.

Paz' presentation of Mexican history, which occupies several chapters in the *Laberinto*, is organized in terms of this same myth. For example, the Reform Movement of 1857 is viewed as the definitive "rupture" with the mother, similar to the manner in which the adolescent breaks away from home and family. Perhaps the best example of Paz' dialectical application of myth is seen in his discussion of the Revolution of 1910-17.

> The Revolution is a search for ourselves and a return to the mother. And thus it is also a fiesta . . . an excess and a waste . . . an orphan's lament and a cry of jubilation, of suicide and of life, all intermixed . . . it is the other Face of Mexico . . . the brutal and resplendent face of the fiesta and death. . . . It is a burst of reality: a revolt and a communion. . . . And with whom does Mexico join in communion in this bloody fiesta? With herself, with her own being. Mexico dares to be. The revolutionary explosion is a portentious festival in which the Mexican, drunk with himself, meets at long last in mortal embrace, the other Mexican.[81]

79. *Ibid.*, p. 72.
80. *Ibid.*
81. *Ibid.*, pp. 79-80.

The closing chapters of the *Laberinto* deal with problems that recur frequently in any discussion of national essence: how may the specific expression of a country's experience—whether literary, political, artistic, or philosophical—be universal and yet genuinely "native"? Is there any meaning in such terms as "Mexican" art, "Mexican" essence, and "Mexican" philsosophy? Paz answers these questions in several ways. He argues that to look for distinctive philosophy in Mexico would be fruitless, for the modes of thought employed by Mexicans have clearly been eclectic and copied from Europe.[82] But he qualifies this view when he notes that the contemporary world is one in which the ideological fount of the Western world has become exhausted. This puts Mexico—and many countries like her—in an unprecedented position: "For the first time Mexico does not have available a set of universal ideas to explain our circumstances. Europe, that storehouse of ready-made ideas now lives as we do: in the present. Strictly speaking, the modern world no longer has any ideas. For this reason the Mexican, like all men, finds himself facing reality alone."[83] Thus, the Mexican must and will discover a genuine universality rather than merely copy European viewpoints. There may, of course, be a certain local flavor or style in Mexican philosophy, but this, like so many other external trappings, will eventually disappear: "*Mexicanidad* will be a mask which when it falls off will at last reveal (only) man.... Mexican philosophy ... will simply and plainly be philosophy."[84] Paz sums up this point very neatly when he adds, shortly afterwards, "our labyrinth is that of all men."

In the closing pages of the chapter titled "Our Times," Paz offers some of the richest fruits of his experience as a poet, as a diplomat, as a Mexican, and as a man. He reminds his countrymen that there are no longer any set formulas to solve the problems of their past history, present essence, or future goals. Yet it is Mexico's responsibility that they be resolved.[85] In doing so the nation will perform a service not only to herself but to all other nations, for at the heart of things, the human condition is everywhere the same. Mexico must also realize that she is one of the "nations of the periphery"—the emerging nations who, though they have stood by for centuries as mere spectators or "objects" of history, are fast becoming

82. *Ibid.*, pp. 133-34.
83. *Ibid.*, p. 151.
84. *Ibid.*, p. 153.
85. *Ibid.*, p. 172.

"agents of historical change." Unlike the older nations of Europe, these countries have no well established guidelines for the future. They have realized—or will soon realize—the uselessness of copying European solutions to traditionally European problems. The anguish which this realization produces can only be overcome by working out their own new and, in this sense, radical solutions.[86]

In words of eloquent sincerity Paz expresses the wish that the Mexican's quest for essence will resolve itself positively in the creation of "a world in which neither deceit, bad faith, pretense, greed, violence, nor subterfuge hold sway. A society which will not make of man an instrument. . . . A human society."[87] Finally the Mexican—and certainly all men—must have faith: faith that when all masks are shed, when all subterfuges are abandoned, when he is alone and naked he will find that "Out there, in the open solitude, the hands of others who are alone are awaiting us."[88] The words of Octavio Paz, the poet, leave little that we may add.

It is always difficult to determine the impact of a given work upon the intellectual milieu in which it was produced. An abundance of evidence, however, points to the fact that in the case of Paz' *Laberinto de la soledad*, this impact was very substantial. Mexican journals of the early fifties, for example, blossom forth with scores of articles dealing with the general theme of *lo mexicano* and especially with articles organized along the lines suggested by Paz. The highly regarded review *Filosofía y Letras*, published by the National University, is particularly rich in essays of this type: Jorge Carrión's "De la raíz a la flor del mexicano," Alfonso García Ruiz "Sociogénesis del mexicano," and Angelina C. de Morelón's "Algunas formas del valor y de la cobardía en el mexicano."[89] The publication, in 1952, of the series *México y lo mexicano* (under Zea's direction) is a further indication of the *Laberinto's* catalytic effect. Our discussion of the quest for *mexicanidad* will be concluded by examining two items from this series, *Mito y magia del mexicano* by Jorge Carrión (1925———), and *Análisis del ser del mexicano* by Emilio Uranga (1921———).

Carrión gives a hint of the methodology to be employed in the *Mito y magia* in his shorter essay "De la raíz a la flor del mexicano"

86. *Ibid.*, p. 174.
87. *Ibid.*, p. 173.
88. *Ibid.*, p. 174.
89. These articles, and others on related themes, appear in Volumes XX (Oct., 1950) through XXIII (June, 1952) of this review. For more on Paz' impact see Wing's dissertation, especially the first two chapters. The reaction of Mexico's intellectuals to Paz has not been unanimously positive: for an interesting and penetrating dissection of his *mexicanidad*, see Villegas, *Filosofía de lo mexicano*, p. 211-12, note 1.

(1951). He states here that his technique will be to seek the thread of "*lo mexicano* . . . throughout the course of its traumatic, painful birth—the Conquest; and follow it through the infantile stammerings of the colonial period."[90] Carrión's method is thus clearly psychoanalytic. Paz—whom Carrión cites in his essay—relied heavily on this technique in the *Laberinto*, but the psychoanalytic was only one of several approaches he employed. Of equal importance were ideas stemming from his poetics, from existentialism, and from oriental thought. Carrión is considerably more one-sided: he apparently accepts the proposition that the psychoanalysis of the individual may be applied to the group, and it is with the conceptual tools of the analyst that he probes *lo mexicano*. Thus, he finds in the Mexican character a basic polarity of femininity (associated with the Indian background) versus masculinity (associated with the Spanish conqueror).[91] The Mexican of the Conquest, like a libidinous adolescent, has on one hand an Oedipal attraction to the feminine image (*La Chingada* of Paz?) and, on the other, a yearning for a powerful, godlike father-image. Much of this same polarity, Carrión argues, continues to the present day, where it shows up in the Mexican's religious symbolism, popular beliefs, and penchant for myth-making.[92]

Carrión's book-length essay, the *Mito y magia del mexicano* (1952), is cast within the same psychoanalytic frame of reference. He states at the outset that traditional tales, legends, and myth—regardless of their historical truth—have great value in determining the psychological nature of a people. In accord with his admitted mentors, Jung and Adler, he feels they illuminate childhood experience and hence are essential to the understanding of the mature individual or nation.[93] In this manner Carrión analyzes the conflicts of the modern Mexican as the clash of "the maternal principle" with "the paternal." These two "principles" have several layers of meaning: the maternal is traced to the Indian background and is characterized by a "pre-logical" or magical view of reality, while the paternal is associated with the Spanish conqueror and with a rationalistic or scientific attitude toward the world.[94] Carrión's discussion of the Wars of Independence provides another illustration

90. Jorge Carrión, "De la raíz a la flor del mexicano," *Filosofía y Letras*, XXI (Jan.-June, 1951), 13.
91. *Ibid.*, pp. 21-22.
92. *Ibid.*, pp. 23-24.
93. Jorge Carrión, *Mito y magia del mexicano* (Mexico, 1952), pp. 16-17.
94. *Ibid.*, p. 10.

of his method. This conflict is seen as a protest against the father-image—the hated authoritarian *paterfamilias*, identified with the Spaniard. Throughout this discussion Carrión borrows frequently from his predecessors, Ramos and Paz; his debt to these writers is particularly evident in his treatment of the fiesta and of Mexican attitudes toward women.[95]

In his attempt to analyze Mexican hero-worship Carrión has deliberately questioned Ortega's injunction not to "psychologize history."[96] He argues that while the purely historical study of a Zapata, a Cuauhtémoc, or a Villa has undeniable value, the analysis of such heroes as mythic figures has even greater significance since it reveals the desires, aspirations, and needs of the people. The real Emiliano Zapata, for example, is "only the grain of sand about which the popular mollusk manufactures the pearl, the legend."[97] Similar examples abound in the essay. After the "trauma" of the Conquest, the father figure in the indigeneous mythology (Quetzal-cóatl) is necessarily forgotten—or, better stated, is pushed into the collective subconscious. Meanwhile in response to the psychic needs of the people, the maternally compassionate figure of the Virgin of Guadalupe takes his place.[98] Somewhat different is Carrión's interpretation of the myth of the *héroes cadetes*—the young cadets who died martyrs' deaths in the defense of Chapultepec Castle during the North American invasion of 1848. Historical research has established the age of the youthful defenders as about 18, yet popular belief always pictures them as boys of perhaps 14 or 15. Carrión argues that the significance of this modification of their true age lies in the fact that there was, and perhaps still is, an essentially adolescent spirit about the Mexican which leads him to identify with this age group.[99]

Much of Carrión's essay is sprinkled with bits of political and social criticism in the guise of psychoanalysis. For example, when he attacks Mexico's Fascists, aristocrats, *sinarquistas*, and other "authoritarian types," Carrión claims to do so not for their political or economic philosophy, but because they have rejected the profound indigenous sensibility toward death—"so alive, so moving, so full of

95. *Ibid.*, p. 11.
96. *Ibid.*, p. 22.
97. *Ibid.*, p. 13.
98. *Ibid.*, p. 46.
99. *Ibid.*, pp. 30-31.

laughter."[100] North America too comes in for some sharp criticism, particularly for its racistic tendencies. Here again explanations are sought in psychoanalytic rather than purely economic or social factors: "In all racistic ideas the motif of sexual repugnance lies latent and hidden."[101] And among his own countrymen he finds that the enmity toward the Yankee frequently takes the form of the desire to violate at least "two or three *gringas*" during one's lifetime.[102] There is much in the *Mito y magia del mexicano* that is open to criticism. Carrión's frequent attempts to force political phenomena into the psychoanalytic mold seem especially questionable, as are his psychological explanations of certain features of Mexican speech. Yet Carrión presents many brilliant insights, for he is a provocative writer and one who is capable of rising to impressive stylistic heights.

Emilio Uranga begins his *Análisis del ser del mexicano* (1952) by acknowledging first his debt to Octavio Paz and secondly his allegiance to a specific generation of intellectuals: the *Hiperión* group. Uranga's characterization of this circle of writers reveals a good deal about his own intellectual development. He underscores the group's "discovery" of existentialism some three or four years earlier (about 1948), its fundamentally historicist orientation, and, most important, its devotion to "the imperative of clarifying the morphology and dynamics of the Mexican being."[103] He further states that while the group recognizes that Mexico has always been interested in self-knowledge, it now proposes a philosophically oriented, profound probe of the national essence: in short, an "ontology" of the Mexican. Uranga and his generation are not content merely to examine the national essence. As activists they feel that the very process of ontological investigation will "bring about moral, social and religious transformations of this essence."[104]

Uranga's intellectual equipment, as seen in the *Análisis del ser del mexicano* and in earlier shorter essays,[105] is decidedly existential. Uranga is not, however, an orthodox follower of any one trend within the movement. He draws upon Sartre, Heidegger, and Ortega; most important, he has frequent recourse to what might be called

100. *Ibid.*, p. 101. The treatment of death in the Mexican essayists (Paz, Carrión, and Uranga) is remarkably similar to the approach of Norman O. Brown as set forth in his recent book, *Life Against Death* (Middletown, Conn., 1959).
101. Carr ión, *Mito*, p. 32.
102. *Ibid* ., p. 34.
103. Emilio Uranga, *Análisis del ser del mexican o* (Mexico, 1952), p. 10.
104. *Ibid.*, p. 11.
105. See Uranga's "Dos teorías de la muerte: Sartre y Heidegger," *Filosofía y Letras*, XVII (Jan.-March, 1949), 55-71.

the poetic periphery of existentialism. The best way to attack the core of Uranga's position is to analyze exactly what he means by "historicism" and by "ontology." Early in his essay he points out that historicism has created a climate of interests in Mexico, a "broad movement of awareness," as he puts it. This movement itself is directed not toward an "historical" search for Mexican essence but rather toward a deeper "ontological" quest: "history must say, if not the last word, at least the next to the last word regarding the essence of the Mexican."[106] The term "historicism," as defined by Uranga, suggests a philosophy of history and an accompanying method of evaluating the validity of historical investigation. The historicist position, he holds, calls for the clear recognition of the limitations inherent in any analysis of the past; every historian writes from a given point in time and from a given situation, a *circunstancia*, to use Ortega's word. Historicism thus points out "the circumstantial connections of every thought, regardless of how universal it may strive to be."[107] If I interpret Uranga correctly, he feels that the historicist method clarifies the various changing conceptual structures which encompass and describe reality. This reality itself, he indicates, has a structure of its own, one which must be called "ontological." Later in the essay he argues that "ontological structures" are not valid *only* in a given historical moment; they have a universal and atemporal quality.[108] Uranga then qualifies his description of the ontological structure. He states that while it may be completed, it may never be modified. Any such "completion" must come, he adds, "from ontology itself."[109] Although his meaning is far from clear, one gathers that the "ontological structure," as used in reference to the Mexican nation, is not very different from the familiar concept of the "national soul"—wine of rather old vintage despite the newness of the historicist-existential bottle.

Although it is clear that Uranga is concerned with the ontological structure of human beings, rather than with ontology as a philosophical problem involving being in the widest sense, a number of questions still remain regarding his use of this concept. Does he view being, the ontological structure, as an undifferentiated, amorphous "ground of being"? Or are there an infinite number of "onto-

106. Uranga, *Análisis del ser*, pp. 13-14.
107. *Ibid.*, p. 10.
108. *Ibid.*, p. 75.
109. *Ibid.*

logical structures" corresponding to all groups and all individuals?
An answer may be found in the fact that Uranga consistently doubts
the notions of the universality of man and of a general human nature:
early in his essay he states " . . . we are not very certain of the
existence of man in general."[110] Yet when Uranga cites Heidegger
on matters of basic definitions, as he does quite frequently, he is
unconcerned that his mentor does not speak of the "German ontological structure" but simply of "man" and of his essence. Uranga
accepts, with some reservations, the fundamental Heideggerian
concepts of man as "accidental" and of human existence as a "pro-
posal," or "program" (from the German *aufgegeben*).[111] What
Uranga does not state—perhaps because it is obvious—is that when
he reads the word "man" in Heidegger's works, he does not imagine
a group of blond beer drinkers in a Freiburg tavern: in his mind's
eye he sees the swarthy *pelado*, white cotton trousers, the *maguey*
cactus, the eagle, and the serpent. Uranga's essay is based on the
conviction that the entire problem of universal man versus specific
man—the Mexican, in this case—is, in fact, meaningless. He deplores
the fact that Mexicans—and other non-Europeans—have confused
the philosophic notion of universality with a simplistic idea of
European cosmopolitanism. His own position is one which " . . .
refuses to recognize as 'human' all those constructs of the Europeans. . . ."[112]

There remain some unresolved problems surrounding Uranga's
use of the term "ontological structure." We saw that the ontological
structure was viewed as something which may never be changed or
modified, but which may nonetheless be "completed." Thus it has a
growth, though perhaps "development" would be too strong a word
to use in its description. Traditionally "ontology" suggests a static
concept—"being" rather than "becoming"—yet as used by Uranga
the word seems to denote a degree of dynamism and change. But if the
ontological structure of the Mexican is in fact conceived of as an
unchangeable essence which can only be "completed" or "added to"
by "ontology itself," can Uranga and his generation do anything to
accomplish their stated goals of bringing about a moral, social, and
religious transformation of the Mexican's being? Though he avoids
the question, the answer seems clear—their role is one of description,
of revelation, perhaps. To the extent that revelation can bring about

110. *Ibid.*, p. 20.
111. *Ibid.*, p. 19.
112. *Ibid.*, p. 23.

change—as in psychoanalysis—the efforts of writers like Uranga can produce real effects.

Leaving aside the question of whether the ontological structure of a people may be altered, specifically what has Uranga revealed about the Mexican? The point of departure for his description is the existential concept of man's "accidental" status: man has no *raison d'être*, he is a chance "addition" to the world, or in Uranga's echoing of the Sartrean concept, he is "in excess" (*está de más, está fuera*).[113] The Mexican, Uranga notes, is particularly sensitive to this situation in that he possesses a certain "proximity to accident" and a "desire to saturate life with chance. . . ." His love of the lottery and his attitude of distrust toward his fellow men stem from an attempt to cope with "accidentalness" by living a life in which rational prognosis and faith in a foreseeable pattern of events hardly exist.[114] Uranga realizes, of course, that the "accidental" nature of human existence is the same everywhere, but he feels that it would be ridiculous for him to study Frenchmen or Germans when he is so thoroughly familiar with Mexicans. He finds, moreover, that the Mexican sensitivity to "accidentalness" is particularly acute. Aside from its expression in the love of the lottery and other games of chance, it is expressed by a basic feeling of *zozobra* ("worry," "anxiety" related to the verb *zozobrar*, "to sink," "to founder," or "to capsize"). In short, the Mexican goes through life ever cognizant of his chance existence and always more or less in fear that he may founder on some unseen rock or reef.[115] Uranga points out that few Mexican writers have ever isolated this fundamentally *zozobrante* character of the Mexican; the oversight is especially evident among the essayists. He criticizes writers like Caso, Ramos, Zea, and Luis Villoro for having dealt merely with the *autognosis* of the Mexican rather than with his *ontology*.[116] He feels that the value of his own contribution to the study of *mexicanidad* lies in the fact that he has worked the rich mine of "intuitive insights" which the poets have provided: " . . . the only originality we claim is that of having listened to the poets."[117]

113. *Ibid.*, p. 31.
114. *Ibid.*, pp. 24-25.
115. *Ibid.*, pp. 41ff.
116. *Ibid.*, pp. 62-65. Uranga is particularly critical of Luis Villoro's essay, "Soledad y comunión," *Filosofía y Letras*, XVII (Jan.-March, 1949), 115-19. Villoro's article was delivered as a speech on Oct. 29, 1948, at the Faculty of Philosophy and Letters. The speech is a rather early example of Mexican existential interest. Villoro speaks of Gabriel Marcel and other Existentialists; he also employs much "solitude-communion" antithesis.
117. Uranga, *Análisis del ser*, p. 100.

Uranga dedicates the last portion of his essay to one such poet—Ramón López Velarde. López Velarde's unique sensitivity to the Mexican *zozobra*, coupled with an intuitive appreciation of the "dialectic of solitude"—to use Paz' term—provide the elements of Uranga's final synthesis of the Mexican essence. As he uses the term *zozobra*, and as he finds it used in Velarde's poetry, the word acquires a meaning that is somewhat different from its dictionary definition. Rather than standing for a "capsizing" or "foundering," it suggests a kind of "oscillation between two possibilities, between two inclinations, without knowing which it would be better to grasp and which it would be better to reject mercilessly."[118] The *zozobrante* nature of the Mexican places him in a decidedly uncomfortable position: he suffers as he "zigzags" or "flutters" between vital choices. The point of *zozobra* is not a placid dead center, but a constant slipping off the razor's edge first to one side then to another. In the tightly packed prose of his concluding chapter Uranga notes " . . . our character provides a permanent crisis with no hope of normalcy."[119] By fusing a fertile insight of existentialism—the accidentalness of human existence—with a penetrating analysis of the Mexican *zozobra*, Uranga has reached this provocative conclusion. Provocative not only for Mexicans, but for others as well, for Uranga maintains that "personality viewed as *zozobra* is not a closed receptacle, rather it is an irrigation duct." That Mexico can learn to live in a state of perpetual crisis may in fact be of great value to others: "We have a lesson to teach, we owe the world the lesson of a vitalized crisis. . . ."[120]

To conclude, Emilio Uranga is a relatively young man from a relatively young continent. As such, and as a man of the twentieth century, he does not claim to speak with absolute certainty. It will be recalled that when he discusses the crucial problem of the concept of universal man he says "we are not very certain of the existence of man in general. . . ."[121] It is in this light that we must appreciate his contribution to the search for essence. And although Uranga may doubt the philosophic validity of "man in general," he can not be relegated to the ranks of the narrow nationalists. He is, as are a host of his contemporaries throughout Spanish America, deeply committed to the old truth that a profound knowledge of oneself not

118. *Ibid.*, p. 95.
119. *Ibid.*, p. 99.
120. *Ibid.*
121. *Ibid.*, p. 97.

only clears the path to real understanding of others, but leads also to genuine human fraternity. At heart he must agree with López Velarde when the poet writes

> My brethren of all ages
> See in me their own moment's pause,
> Their own lament, their own mad striving. . . .[122]

122. The original verse—which I have translated rather freely—is cited by Uranga on p. 99 of the *Análisis del ser*:

> Mis hermanos de todas las centurias
> reconocen en mi su pausa igual
> sus mismas quejas y sus propias furias.

VIII / CONCLUSION

THE REVOLUTIONARY SPIRIT WHICH UNDERLIES SO MUCH of contemporary Spanish American life and culture continues unabated. The dynamism, the restlessness—the *zozobrante* mood of the continent—make any conclusions which we may draw only tentative.

One of the most important of these tentative conclusions concerns a traditional problem in Spanish American studies: the question of viewing the area in terms of national versus hemispheric developmental patterns. As viewpoints, these two positions are more complementary than mutually exclusive. Yet Spanish Americans— as well as outsiders—frequently ask themselves if there exists in fact a genuine *Hispanic American* culture, or merely a conglomerate of very different nations each following her own historical trajectory and only vaguely related to the others by the single bond of language. The evidence presented here clearly argues for the continental or hemispheric position. The scientism of the late nineteenth century had established itself as firmly in Mexico as in Argentina; racistic explanations of the continent's problems may be found in the writings of Alcides Arguedas—whose native Bolivia is one of the most "Indian" nations of Latin America—as well as in the essays of José Ingenieros who came from white, cosmopolitan Buenos Aires. In the first decade of the present century, when the bastions of Positivism came under fire, Uruguay's Rodó, Mexico's Vasconcelos, and the Dominican Republic's Henríquez Ureña all joined in the attack. Our exploration of the theme of the American destiny showed how Venezuela's Picón Salas, Mexico's Alfonso Reyes, Argentina's Ricardo Rojas, and even North America's Waldo Frank all contributed to the "rediscovery" of the continent. Although our analysis of radicalism centered about the Peruvian essayists, the writings of Argentina's Martínez Estrada and H. A. Murena provide evidence that passionate defenders of the radical tradition exist elsewhere. Similarly, the search for the national essence has followed a remarkably parallel course throughout the continent. Argentina's Eduardo Mallea and Mexico's Octavio Paz both pointed out that the route toward authenticity was to be found by following essentially the same path: the dialectic of solitude—communion and the tearing away of the merely circumstantial mask. Although there are always some differences in national flavor and slight variations in timing, we have here a clearly discernible pattern and one which certainly supports the concept of an integral Spanish American culture.

An historical survey of this pattern leads to another important conclusion. The seventy years covered by our study witness a steadily increasing growth of confidence among Spanish American intellectuals. The defensiveness of the positivist period soon gave way to a mood of enthusiastic affirmation during the early decades of the present century. The rediscovery of America rekindled the spark of messianism and the dream of Utopia which have always been associated with the New World. With each new decade Spanish Americans have asserted the values of their culture with increasing conviction. They have even suggested that the continent is destined to play an ecumenical role in a dangerously divided world. Stated in the simplest terms, Spanish Americans are losing their inferiority complex. They feel that they have important things to say and they wish to be heard. This new attitude may surprise Europeans and North Americans: they may question how an "underdeveloped" area and one which has had a peripheral relationship to the mainstream of Western life can solve problems which older and wiser nations have failed to solve. Spanish American writers have defended their position well, however. Paz and Reyes make a good case for considering Spanish America as a bridge between the worlds of East and West; Mallea and others suggest that modern man must seek a new sense of genuineness in the land itself; and scores of antiracists have pointed out that Hispanic America's process of ethnic blending may provide a model for a world in which skin color continues to be a major divisive force.

That contemporary Spanish American essayists are deeply concerned with questions of universal scope does not imply that they are no longer interested in their own national or regional culture. Rather, there is a growing appreciation of the old truth that self-knowledge necessarily precedes any real knowledge of others. Thus another conclusion to be drawn from our study is that the dilemma of "nativism or universalism" which traditionally has plagued Spanish American lettters is at last beginning to be resolved. The rich essayistic production of recent decades centered on themes of "authenticity" and "autognosis" bears this point out, for seldom is the search for national essence an end in itself.

The best of contemporary Spanish American essayists, their philosophic and literary sophistication notwithstanding, are rarely bookish or pedantic. One has the distinct feeling when reading their works that he is dealing with real men, with "hombres de carne y hueso." To conclude, what stands out most sharply in their essays are certain qualities of spirit: the commitment of the writer to his vocation; the difficult to describe, but omnipresent search for a new humanism; and among many, an almost mystical yearning for communion with all men.

BIBLIOGRAPHY

THE MAJORITY OF THE ITEMS LISTED BELOW ARE CITED OR referred to in either the text or footnotes. The few additional uncited entries are books or articles which I have found valuable for general background.

Alberini, Coriolano. "Waldo Frank en la Facultad de Filosofía y Letras," *Síntesis*, No. 29 (Oct., 1929), 117-25.

Alexander, Robert J. *Communism in Latin America.* New Brunswick: Rutgers University Press, 1957.

Anderson Imbert, Enrique. "La Argentina, Erro y la filosofía," *Sur*, No. 45 (June, 1938), 32-43.

————. *Historia de la literatura hispanoamericana.* 2 vols. México: Fondo de Cultura Económica, 1961.

Andrade Coello, A. *Rodó.* Quito: Imp. de la Universidad Central, 1913.

Arciniegas, Germán. "La academia, la taberna, y la universidad," *Revista de las Indias*, No. 58 (Oct., 1943), 5-15.

————. *Este pueblo de América.* México: Fondo de Cultura Económica, 1945.

Arguedas, Alcides. *La danza de las sombras.* 2 vols. Barcelona: Sobs. de López Robert, 1934.

————. *Pueblo enfermo: Contribución a la psicología de los pueblos hispano-americanos.* Carta-prólogo de Ramiro de Maeztu. Barcelona: Viuda de L. Tasso, 1909.

————. *Pueblo enfermo.* 3ᵉʳᵃ ed. Santiago de Chile: Ercilla, 1937.

Astrada, Carlos. *El juego existencial.* Buenos Aires: Babel, 1933.

Barbagelata, Hugo D. *Rodó y sus críticos.* Paris: Agencia Gen. de Librería, 1920.

Barzun, Jacques. *Race: A Study in Modern Superstition.* New York: Harcourt, Brace, 1937.

Beck, Vera. "La revista *Martín Fierro*," *Revista Hispánica Moderna*, XVI (Jan.-Dec., 1950), 133-41.

Belaúnde, Víctor Andrés. *Meditaciones peruanas.* Lima: Cía. de Impresiones y Publicidad, 1923.

————. "En torno al último libro de Mariátegui," *Mercurio Peruano*, XX (Mar.-April, 1930), 132-36.

Bernardete, M. J. (ed.). *Waldo Frank in America Hispana.* New York: Inst. de las Españas, 1930.

Borges, Jorge Luis. "Una efusión de Ezequiel Martínez Estrada," *Sur*, No. 242 (Sept.-Oct., 1956), 52-53.

———. *Inquisiciones.* Buenos Aires: Proa, 1925.

Boyd, William C. *Genetics and the Races of Man.* Boston: Little, Brown, 1950.

Bulnes, Francisco. *El porvenir de las naciones latino-americanas.* México: Pensamiento Vivo de América, [1922].

Bunge, Carlos Octavio. *Nuestra América: Ensayo de psicología social.* 6ª edición, texto definitivo, muy corregido. Intro. de José Ingenieros. Buenos Aires: Vaccaro, 1918.

Canal Feijóo, Bernardo. *Medida del criollismo.* Buenos Aires: Porter Hnos., 1929.

———. "Radiografías fatídicas," *Sur*, No. 37 (Oct., 1937), 63-67.

———. *El reverso humorístico de la tristeza criolla.* (Publicación No. 43 de la "Extensión Universitaria.") Sante Fe: Universidad Nacional del Litoral, 1940.

———. "Sobre el americanismo de Ricardo Rojas," *Revista Iberoamericana*, XXIII (July-Dec., 1958), 221-26.

———. *Teoría de la ciudad argentina: idealismo y realismo en el proceso constitucional.* Buenos Aires: Sudamericana, 1951.

Carrión, Benjamín. *Los creadores de la nueva América.* Madrid: Soc. General Española de Librería, 1928.

Carrión, Jorge. "De la raíz a la flor del mexicano," *Filosofía y Letras*, XXI (Jan.-June, 1951), 9-24.

———. *Mito y magia del mexicano.* (Colección "México y lo mexicano," No. 3.) México: Porrúa y Obregón, 1952.

Caso, Antonio. "El enemigo de la tierra," *Repertorio Americano*, IV (1922), 171-73.

———. *La existencia como economía, como desinterés y como caridad.* México: Secretaría de Educación Pública, 1943.

———. *La filosofía de la intuición.* Mexico: Ed. de "Nosotros," 1914.

———. "Max Stirner," *Revista Moderna*, X (March, 1908), 80-84.

———. "Nietzsche, su espíritu y su obra," *Revista Moderna*, VIII (Aug., 1907), 348-58.

———. "Perenidad del pensamiento religioso y especulativo," *Revista Moderna*, XIII (Oct., 1909), 68-72.

Chang-Rodríguez, Eugenio. *La literatura política de González Prada, Mariátegui y Haya de la Torre.* México: Studium, 1957.

Crawford, William Rex. *A Century of Latin American Thought.* Rev. ed. Cambridge, Mass.; Harvard University Press, 1961.

Díaz Rodríguez, Manuel. *Camino de perfección.* Caracas: Ed. Cecilio Acosta, [1942].

Díez de Medina, Fernando. *Sariri: Una réplica al Ariel de Rodó.* La Paz: Tejerina-Librero, 1954.

Dujovne, León. *La obra filosófica de José Ingenieros.* Buenos Aires: A. López, 1930.

———. "Waldo Frank y Spengler," *La Vida Literaria*, No. 15 (Oct., 1929), 7-14.

Durand, Luis. *Presencia de Chile.* Santiago de Chile: Nascimiento, 1942.

Endara, Julio. *José Ingenieros y el porvenir de la filosofía.* 2ª ed. Buenos Aires: Agencia Gen. de Librería, 1922.

Erro, Carlos Alberto. *Diálogo existencial.* Buenos Aires: Sur, 1936.

———. *Posibilidad y realidad de la vida argentina.* Conferencia del Instituto Cultural Joaquín B. González. Buenos Aires: Instituto J. B. González, 1937.

———. *Tiempo lacerado.* Buenos Aires: Sur, 1936.

Ferrater Mora, José. *Ortega y Gasset: An Outline of his Philosophy.* New Haven: Yale University Press, 1957.

Francovich, Guillermo. *Pachamama: Diálogo sobre el porvenir de la cultura en Bolivia.* Asunción: La Colmena, [1942].

Frank, Waldo. *America Hispana: A Portrait and a Prospect.* New York and London: Scribner's, 1931.

———. "El español," *Revista de Occidente*, X (1925), 36-43.

———. "Mensaje a los escritores mexicanos," *Repertorio Americano*, VIII (1924), 305-6.

———. "Necesitamos crear un mundo nuevo," *Cuadernos Americanos*, IX (July-Aug., 1950), 40-47.

———. *The Re-discovery of America.* New York and London: Scribner's, 1929.

Frankl, Víctor E. *Espíritu y camino de Hispanoamérica. La cultura hispanoamericana y la filosofía europea.* Bogotá: Ministro de Educ. Nacional, 1953.

Frondizi, Risieri. "¿Hay una filosofía iberoamericana?" *Realidad*, No. 8 (March-April, 1948), 158-70.

Gáos, José. *Antología del pensamiento de lengua española de la edad contemporánea.* México: Séneca, 1945.

———. "Aportaciones a la historia del pensamiento iberoamericano," *Cuadernos Americanos*, VI (Nov.-Dec., 1947), 142-43.

———. *En torno a la filosofía mexicana.* 2 vols. México: Porrúa y Obregón, 1952.

Garagorri, Paulino. *Ortega, una reforma de la filosofía.* Madrid: Revista de Occidente, 1958.

García Calderón, Francisco. "Las corrientes filosóficas en la América Latina," *Revista Moderna*, XI (Nov., 1908), 150-56.

———. *La creación de un continente.* Paris: P. Ollendorf, 1913.

———. *Les démocraties latines de l'Amérique.* Paris: Flammarion, 1912.

———. "Ortega y Gasset y nuestro tiempo," *Repertorio Americano*, XX (1930), 147-48.

———. *Le Pérou contemporain, étude sociale.* Paris: Diyarric, 1907.

Ghiano, Juan Carlos. "De ensayistas," *Ficción*, No. 27 (Sept.-Oct., 1961), 86-90.

González, Manuel Pedro. *José Martí, Epic Chronicler of the United States in the Eighties.* Chapel Hill: University of North Carolina Press, 1953.

González Prada, Manuel. *Horas de lucha.* Buenos Aires: Ed. Americalee, 1946.

————. *Pájinas libres.* Edición definitiva... Prólogo y notas de Luis Alberto Sánchez. Lima: Editorial P.T.C.M., 1946.

Groussac, Paul. "La paradoja de las ciencias sociales," *La Biblioteca,* II (Oct., 1896), 309-13.

Haya de la Torre, Víctor Raúl. *Espacio-tiempo histórico.* Lima: Ed. La Tribuna, 1948.

Henríquez Ureña, Max. *Rodó y Rubén Darío.* Habana: Soc. Ed. Cuba Contemporánea, 1918.

Henríquez Ureña, Pedro. "Conferencias sobre el positivismo," *Revista Moderna,* XII (July, 1909), 301-10.

————. "Marginalia: José Enrique Rodó," *Revista Moderna,* IX (Dec. 1907), 240-42.

————. *Obra crítica.* ed. Emma Susana Speratti Piñero. Prólogo de Jorge Luis Borges. México: Fondo de Cultura Económica, 1960.

————. "Profesores de idealismo," *Revista Moderna,* XIV (June, 1910), 213-16.

Hernández Luna, Juan. "Primeros estudios sobre el mexicano en nuestro siglo," *Filosofía y Letras,* XX (Oct.-Dec., 1950), 327-36.

Ingenieros, José. *Crónicas de viaje.* 6ª ed. Buenos Aires: L. T. Rosso, 1919.

————. *Hacia una moral sin dogmas: Lecciones sobre Emerson y el eticismo.* Buenos Aires: L. T. Rosso, 1917.

————. "Nacionalismo e indianismo: Carta a Ricardo Rojas," *Revista de América,* II (May-Aug., 1913), 185-94.

————. *Obras completas.* Revisadas y anotadas por Aníbal Ponce. 16 vols. Buenos Aires: L. T. Rosso, 1939.

Jiménez Rueda, Julio. "La visita de Waldo Frank," *Contemporáneos,* IV (1929), 357-58.

Junco, Alfonso. "El hispanismo auténtico es el mejor indigenismo," *Mercurio Peruano,* No. 196 (July, 1943), 279-82.

Kantor, Harry. *The Ideology and Program of the Peruvian Aprista Movement* ("University of California Publications in Political Science," Vol. IV, No. 1). Berkeley and Los Angeles: University of California Press, 1953.

Kaufman, Walter. *The Owl and the Nightingale.* London: Faber and Faber, 1959.

Korn, Alejandro. "Filosofía argentina," *Nosotros,* LVII (1927), 52-65.

Latcham, Ricardo A. "La querella de criollismo," *Bolívar,* No. 34 (Oct., 1954), 563-93.

Le Bon, Gustave. *Lois psychologiques de l'évolution des peuples.* Neuviéme édition. Paris: Félix Alcan, 1909.

Lizaso, Félix. *Ensayistas contemporáneos.* Habana: Trópico, 1938.
López Velarde, Ramón. "Novedad de la patria," *El Maestro,* I (April, 1921), 61-63.
Maeztu, Ramiro de. "El mito de la raza," *Repertorio Americano,* (1927), 214-15.
Mafud, Julio. *El desarraigo argentino.* Buenos Aires: Americalee, 1959.
Mallea, Eduardo. *La ciudad junto al río inmóvil.* Buenos Aires: Anaconda, 1935.
————. *Conocimiento y expresión de la Argentina.* Conferencia pronunciada el 12 de sept. de 1934 en el Palacio Giustiniani, Roma. Buenos Aires: Sur, 1935.
————. *Historia de una pasión argentina.* Con un prólogo de Francisco Romero. Buenos Aires and Mexico: Espasa-Calpe, 1939.
————. *Notas de un novelista.* Buenos Aires: Emecé, 1954.
————. *El sayal y la púrpura.* Buenos Aires: Losada, 1947.
Mañach, Jorge. *Indagación del choteo.* Rev. ed. Habana: Avance, 1928.
Marías, Julián. *El existencialismo en España.* Bogotá: Ed. "Universidad Nacional de Colombia," 1953.
Mariátegui, José Carlos. *El alma matinal.* Lima: Amauta, 1959.
————. *Defensa del marxismo.* Lima: Amauta, 1959.
————. *Siete ensayos de interpretación de la realidad peruana.* Lima: Amauta, 1959.
Martí, José. "El partido liberal," in *Obras completas,* Vol. II. La Habana: Trópico, 1946.
————. "La verdad sobre los Estados Unidos," in *Obras completas,* Vol. I. La Habana: Trópico, 1946.
Martínez, José Luis (ed.). *El ensayo mexicano moderno.* 2 vols. Mexico: Fondo de Cultura Económica, 1958.
Martínez Estrada, Ezequiel. "Análisis funcional de la cultura," *Lunes de Revolución,* No. 47 (Feb. 15, 1960), 3-5.
————. *Cabeza de Goliat: microscopía de Buenos Aires.* Buenos Aires: Club del libro A.L.A., 1940.
————. "El complejo Chandala," *Cuadernos Americanos,* IX (Jan.-Feb., 1950), 116-29.
————. "El estímulo de vivir," *Nosotros,* XI (Dec., 1917), 457-66.
————. *Exhortaciones.* Buenos Aires: Burnichon, 1957.
————. "Lo real y el realismo," *Cuadernos Americanos,* XVII (July-Oct., 1958), 258-64.
————. *Muerte y transfiguración de Martín Fierro.* 2 vols. Mexico: Fondo de Cultura Económica, 1948.
————. "Norteamérica la hacendosa," *Sur,* No. 193 (Nov.-Dec., 1950), 146-55.
————. "El nuevo mundo, la isla de Utopía, y la isla de Cuba," *Cuadernos Americanos,* XXII (March-April, 1963), 89-122.
————. *Radiografía de la Pampa.* Buenos Aires: Babel, 1933.
————. "Tesoros velados," *Nosotros,* XI (Oct., 1917), 193-99.

Maurín, Joaquín. "Arciniegas o la conciencia de América," *Cuadernos* No. 1 (July-Aug., 1953), 101-4.

Mead, Robert G., Jr. *Breve historia del ensayo hispanoamericano.* México: Studium, 1956.

Mistral, Gabriela (pseud., Lucila Godoy Alcayaga). "El grito," *Repertorio Americano*, IV (1922), 45.

——. "México y los Estados Unidos," *Repertorio Americano*, IV (1922), 365.

Molina, Enrique. "Concepción filosófica," *Atenea*, XVIII (Dec., 1941), 281-317.

——. "La filosofía en Chile en la primera mitad del siglo XX," *Atenea*, XXVIII (Sept.-Oct., 1951), 213-77.

——. *Filosofía americana.* Paris: Garnier, 1914.

——. "José Ingenieros," *Atenea*, II (Nov., 1925), 411-18.

Monterde, Francisco. "Nueva salida de Ariel," *Cuadernos Americanos*, I (May-June, 1942), 101-6.

Murena, Héctor A. *El pecado original de América.* Buenos Aires: Sur, 1958.

——. "El estridor del conformismo," *Cuadernos*, No. 60 (May, 1962), 10-24.

Nin Frías, Alberto. *Ensayos de crítica e historia.* Valencia: Sempere, 1907.

Ocampo, Victoria. "Carta a Waldo Frank," *Sur*, No. 75 (Dec., 1940), 11-15.

Olguín, Manuel. *Alfonso Reyes, ensayista.* Mexico: Studium, 1956.

Orrego, Antenor. "Apuntes para una filosofía o interpretación del pensamiento," *Amauta*, I (Dec., 1926), 17-21.

——. "¿Cuál es la cultura que creará América?" *Amauta*, II (April, 1928), 3-4. Serial article continued in Sept. issue, pp. 14-16 and Oct. issue, pp. 8-9.

——. *El pueblo continente: Ensayos para una interpretación de la América Latina.* Santiago de Chile: Ercilla, 1939.

——. "¿Qué es una filosofía?" *Amauta*, III (Nov.-Dec., 1929), 1-3.

Ortega y Gasset, José. *El espectador*, Vol. II of *Obras completas.* 4ª ed. Madrid: Revista de Occidente, 1957.

——. "La voluntad del barroco," *Revista de América*, IV (June-July, 1914), 87-96.

Ortiz, Fernando. "Los factores humanos de la cubanidad," *Revista Bimestre Cubana*, XLV (1940), 165-69.

Paz, Octavio. *El arco y la lira.* México: Fondo de Cultura Económica, 1956.

——. *El laberinto de la soledad.* 2ª edición revisada y aumentada. México: Fondo de Cultura Económica, 1959.

——. *Las peras del olmo.* México: Imp. Universitaria, 1957.

——. "Poesía de soledad y poesía de comunión," *El Hijo Pródigo*, I (Aug., 1945), 271-78.

——. "Vigilias: Fragmentos del diario de un soñador," *Taller*, I (Dec., 1938), 3-6.

——. "Vigilias: Fragmentos del diario de un soñador," *Taller* II, (Dec., 1939), 11-22.

——. "Vigilias: Fragmentos del diario de un soñador," *Tierra Nueva*, II (Jan.-April, 1941), 32-43.

Picón Salas, Mariano. *Buscando el camino*. Caracas: Cultura Venezolana, 1920.

——. *Europa-América: Preguntas a la esfinge de la cultura*. México: Ed. Cuadernos Americanos, 1947.

——. *Hispano-América, Posición crítica*. Santiago de Chile: Imprenta Universitaria, 1931.

——. *Regreso de tres mundos: Un hombre en su generación*. México: Fondo de Cultura Económica, 1959.

Polt, John H. R. *The Writings of Eduardo Mallea*. ("University of California Publications in Modern Philology," Vol. 54.) Berkeley and Los Angeles: University of California Press, 1959.

Ramos, Samuel. "Antonio Caso," *Ulises*, I (June, 1927), 12-20.

——. "Antonio Caso, filósofo romántico," *Filosofía y Letras*, XI (April-June, 1946), 179-96.

——. "La crisis del humanismo," *Universidad de México*, 2ª época, IV (Aug., 1937), 1-10.

——. *Hacia un nuevo humanismo: Programa de una antropología filosófica*. México: La Casa de España, 1940.

——. *El perfil del hombre y la cultura en México*. México: Imp. Mundial, 1934.

——. "Sociología de la obligación moral," *Universidad de México*, 2ª época, I (May, 1936), 26-30.

Repertorio Americano. "Del homenaje argentino a J. C. Mariátegui," XX (1930), 344-47.

——. "Del homenaje peruano a J. C. Mariátegui," XX (1930), 308-10.

——. "Del tributo cubano a José Carlos Mariátegui," XXI (1930), 121-23, 142-44.

Reyes, Alfonso. "José Ortega y Gasset," *Cuba contemporánea*, XVI (Jan., 1918), 53-54.

——. *Obras completas de Alfonso Reyes*. México: Fondo de Cultura Económica, 1955.

——. "Treno para Ortega y Gasset," *Cuadernos Americanos*, XV (Jan.-Feb., 1956), 65-67.

Rodó, José Enrique. "América," *El Cojo Ilustrado*, IX (Aug. 15, 1900), 526.

——. *Ariel*. Prólogo de Leopoldo Alas. Buenos Aires: Sopena Argentina, 1948.

——. *Obras Completas*. Compilación y prólogo de A. J. Vaccaro. Buenos Aires: Ed. Antonio Zamora, 1948.

Rodríguez Alcalá, Hugo. *Ensayos de Norte a Sur*. México: Studium, 1960.

Rodríguez Monegal, Emir. *El juicio de los parricidas*. Buenos Aires: Deucalión, 1956.

Rojas, Ricardo. *La argentinidad.* 2ª ed. Buenos Aires: Roldán, 1922.
————. *Obras completas.* 16 vols. Buenos Aires: J. Roldán, 1924.
Romanell, Patrick. *The Making of the Mexican Mind.* Lincoln, Nebraska: University of Nebraska Press, 1952.
Romero, Francisco. *Ortega y Gasset y el problema de la jefatura espiritual y otros ensayos.* Buenos Aires: Losada, 1960.
Salazar Bondy, Augusto. "Panorama de la filosofía en el Perú en los últimos 50 años," *Mar del Sur,* V (Dec., 1950), 42-50.
Sánchez, Luis Alberto. *Balance y liquidación del novecientos.* Santiago: Ercilla, 1941.
————. *¿Existe América Latina?* México: Fondo de Cultura Económica, 1945.
Sánchez Reulet, Aníbal (ed.). *La filosofía latinoamericana contemporánea.* Washington: Unión Panamericana, 1949.
Sánchez Villaseñor, José. *Ortega y Gasset, Existentialist.* Translated by Joseph Small. Chicago: H. Regenery, 1944.
Sanín Cano, Baldomero. *El humanismo y el progreso del hombre.* Buenos Aires: Losada, 1955.
Sartre, Jean Paul. *Sartre on Cuba.* New York: Ballantine, 1961.
Scheler, Max. *Man's Place in Nature.* Translated, with an introduction by Hans Meyerhoff. New York: Noonday, 1961.
Scobie, James R. *Argentina, A City and a Nation.* New York: Oxford University Press, 1964.
Sebreli, J. J. *Martínez Estrada, una rebelión inútil.* Buenos Aires: Palestra, 1960.
Soto, Luis E. "Ricardo Rojas y la americanidad," *Revista Iberoamericana,* XXIII (July-Dec., 1958), 317-33.
Snyder, Louis L. *Race, A History of Modern Ethnic Theories.* New York: Longmans, Green, 1934.
Stabb, Martin S. "Indigenism and Racism in Mexican Thought: 1857-1911," *Journal of Inter-American Studies,* I (Oct., 1959), 405-23.
Tablada, J. J. "México en Norteamérica: como se juzga nuestra cultura," *Repertorio Americano,* III (1922), 406-7.
Tamayo, Franz. "Carta de Americanos para Americanos," *Repertorio Americano,* XIII (1926), 177-80.
————. *La creación de la pedagogía nacional.* La Paz: Ed. de "El Diario," 1910.
Torchia Estrada, Juan Carlos. *La filosofía en la argentina.* (Serie "Pensamiento de América.") Washington: Unión Panamericana, 1961.
Torres, Carlos Arturo. *Estudios de crítica moderna.* Madrid: América, 1917.
————. *Idola fori,* (3ᵉʳᵃ ed. No. 9 "Selección Samper Ortega de Literatura Colombiana.") Bogotá: Minerva, 1935.
Ugarte, Manuel. *The Destiny of a Continent.* Edited by J. Fred Rippy and translated by C. A. Phillips. New York: Knopf, 1925.
————. "Noticias Yanquis," in *An Anthology of Spanish American Literature.* Prepared under the auspices of the Instituto Inter-

nacional de Literatura Iberoamericana by a Committee consisting of E. H. Hespelt and others. New York: Appleton-Century, 1946.

Uranga, Emilio. "Dos teorías de la muerte: Sartre y Heidegger," *Filosofía y Letras*, XVII (Jan.-March, 1949), 55-71.

——. *Análisis del ser del mexicano*. (Colección "Méxcio y lo mexicano," No. 4.) México: Porrúa y Obregón, 1952.

Uriel García, José. *El nuevo indio. Ensayos indianistas sobre la sierra superuana*. 2ª ed. corregida. Cuzco: Rozas Suc., 1937.

Valle, Rafael Heliodoro. *Historia de las ideas contemporáneas en Centroamérica*. México: Fondo de Cultura Económica, 1960.

Vasconcelos, José. "La educación en México," *Repertorio Americano*, V (1922), 376-78, 386-89.

——. *Obras completas*. 3 vols. México: Libreros Mexicanos Unidos, 1957.

Villegas, Abelardo. *La filosofía de lo mexicano*. México: Fondo de Cultura Económica, 1960.

Villoro, Luis. "Soledad y comunión," *Filosofía y Letras*, XVII (Jan.-March, 1949), 115-19.

Virasoro, Miguel Angel. "Introducción a la nueva sensibilidad," *Inicial*, II (August, 1925), 102-16.

——. "El problema de la cultura y la nueva mentalidad argentina," *Inicial*, I (Dec., 1924), 11-25.

——. "Una teoría del yo como cultura," *Síntesis*, I (Dec., 1927), 13-36.

Vitier, Medardo. *Del ensayo americano*. México: Fondo de Cultura Económica, 1945.

Wahl, Jean A. *A Short History of Existentialism*. New York: Philosophical Library, 1949.

Wing, George Gordon. *Octavio Paz: Poetry, Politics, and the Myth of the Mexican*. Unpublished dissertation, University of California at Berkeley, 1960.

Zaldumbide, Gonzalo. *José Enrique Rodó*. Madrid: Ed. América, 1919.

Zea, Leopoldo. *América en la conciencia de Europa*. México: Los Presentes, 1955.

——. *Dos etapas del pensamiento en Hispanoamérica: Del romanticismo al positivismo*. México: El colegio de México, 1949.

——. *Ensayos sobre filosofía en la historia*. México: Stylo, 1948.

——. *The Latin American Mind*. Translation of *Dos etapas del pensamiento en Hispanoamérica*. Translated by James H. Abbott and Lowell Dunham. Norman, Okla.; University of Oklahoma Press, 1963.

——. "Ortega el americano," *Cuadernos Americanos*, XV (Jan.-Feb., 1956), 132-45.

Zum Felde, Alberto. *Proceso intelectual del Uruguay*. Montevideo: Claridad, 1941.

——. *Indice crítico de la literatura hispanoamericana: El ensayo y la crítica*. México: Guaranía, 1954.

APPENDIX

SOME JOURNALS DEALING WITH THE CONTEMPORARY
SPANISH AMERICAN ESSAY

THE FOLLOWING ENUMERATION IS NEITHER EXHAUSTIVE nor bibliographically complete. I have merely listed those journals in which I have found valuable material by and about essayists of twentieth-century Spanish America. In the case of some journals I have added a brief descriptive note. For further information on Spanish American periodicals see Boyd G. Carter, *Las revistas literarias de Hispanoamérica* (México: Studium, 1959); and John E. Englekirk, "La literatura y la revista en Hispanoamérica," *Revista Iberoamericana*, XXVI (Jan.-June, 1961), 9-79; *Revista Iberoamericana* XXVII (July-Dec., 1961), 219-79; and *Revista Iberoamericana*, XVIII (Jan.-June, 1962), 9-73.

Abside. Mexico, 1937-56. A journal of ideas. The best of modern Catholic thought. Oswaldo Robles, Sánchez Villaseñor, Alberto G. Méndez Plancarte, Valenzuela, and others.

Amauta. Lima, 1926-30. Invaluable for study of the Leftists, particularly the *Apristas.* Antenor Orrego, Waldo Frank, Mariátegui, Luis Alberto Sánchez, etc.

La Antorcha. Paris, 1931-32. Ephemeral publication of José Vasconcelos while in Europe.

Atenea. Univ. of Concepción, Chile. 1924——. Chile's most important literary and intellectual journal. Directed for many years by Enrique Molina.

Atlántida. Buenos Aires, 1911-14.

Avance. Havana, 1927-30. Important vehicle for Cuban writers and intellectuals of the late 1920's. Interesting for political radicalism as well. Mañach, Carpentier, Marinello, Novás Calvo, and others.

Babel. Buenos Aires, 1939-51. Directed by "Enrique Espinoza," pseud. of Samuel Glusberg. Interesting and sophisticated. Decidedly radical orientation. Contributors include: Martínez Estrada, P. Henríquez Ureña, Sydney Hook, Ed. Wilson, Kafka, Camus, etc.

Bolívar. Bogotá, 1951——. Rather conservative "replacement" for the *Revista de las Indias* which ceased publication in 1951. Features Catholic intellectuals—C. Finlayson, Wagner de Reina, Derisi, Frankl—as well as others.

Casa de Cultura Ecuatoriana. Quito, 1945-54. Directed by Benjamín Carrión. Important for *indigenista* orientation. Features such writers as Pío Jaramillo Alvarado, Jorge Icaza, and Carrera Andrade.

Claridad. Buenos Aires, 1926-41. Decidedly Leftist. Important for study of Argentine and general Spanish American radicalism.

El Cojo Ilustrado. Caracas, 1892-1914. Invaluable for study of writers of the *modernistas* and the *arielistas*: Rodó, C. Zumeta, C. A. Torres, F. García Calderón, Blanco Fombona, *et al.*

Contemporáneos. Mexico, 1928-31. Directed by B. Ortiz de Montellano. The vehicle of the "Generation of Contemporáneos": Abreu Gómez, Villaurrutia, Torres Bodet. Much translation from foreign sources and reprints of other Spanish American journals.

Cuadernos. Paris, 1953-65. One of the very best Spanish language journals published today. Organ of the "Congreso por la libertad de la Cultura." Articles by Arciniegas, H. A. Murena, Antenor Orrego, L. A. Sánchez, Díez de Medina, etc.

Cuadernos Americanos, Mexico, 1942——. Another very major literary journal of contemporary Spanish America. Includes articles from all over the hemisphere, but with special attention to Mexican themes and writers.

Cuba Contemporánea. Havana, 1913-27. An important journal of its day. Includes many non-Cubans among its collaborators.

Cultura Universitaria. Caracas, 1947——.

Ficción. Buenos Aires, 1956-65. Includes many of the best recent Argentine writers: Borges, L. E. Soto, Martínez Estrada, etc.

Filosofía y Letras, Mexico, 1941-54. Published by the Faculty of Philosophy and Letters of the National University. Much Ramos, Caso, Zea, O'Gorman. By mid-forties a number of articles on existentialism appear.

El Hijo Pródigo. Mexico, 1943-46. Edited by Paz, Alí Chumacero, Sánchez Barbudo, O. G. Barreda, and others. Much foreign translation, particularly from contemporary French writers.

Hispania. Amherst, Massachusetts, 1918——. Organ of the American Association of teachers of Spanish and Portuguese. Articles, chiefly by North Americans, on a wide range of Hispanic literary subjects.

Humanismo. Mexico City and Habana, 1952-60. Edited by Cubans and Mexicans; by late fifties became associated with Castro movement. Interesting for development of *castrista* ideology.

Inicial. Buenos Aires, 1923-24. Markedly Rightist and anti-Semitic. Important for study of Virasoro.

Kollaysuyo. La Paz, 1939-42; 1951-52. Earlier series more *indigenista.* Later series is more general.

Les Lettres Françaises. Buenos Aires, 1941-47. Unusual review with collaborators from France and Argentina. Directed by Roger Caillois.

El Maestro. Mexico, 1921. Ephemeral journal published by the Secretaría de Educación, then headed by Vasconcelos. Most outstanding contributor is Ramón López Velarde.

Mar del Sur. Lima, 1948-53. An impressive and sophisticated review. Much interest in foreign literary and intellectual movements: existentialism, Zen, psychoanalysis, etc. Contributors include Mariano Ibérico, A. Salazar Bondy, Octavio Paz.

Martín Fierro. Buenos Aires, 1924-27. Extremely important for poetic movements of the period. Less important for the essay.

Mercurio Peruano. Lima, 1918-31; 1939-53. Gives a good general review of Peruvian intellectual life. Becomes noticeably more conservative after 1939.

Minera. Buenos Aires, 1941-? Often listed as *Cuadernos Minerva.* Primarily a philosophical journal.

Nosotros. Buenos Aires, 1907-34; 1936-43. A major literary journal of its period.

La Nueva Democracia. New York, 1920——. Published by the Committee on Cooperation in Latin America. Articles on a wide range of general Latin American subjects.

Proa. Buenos Aires, 1924-25. Important for the *"Martínfierristas,"* Borges, Güiraldes, some early work of Mallea.

Realidad. Buenos Aires, 1947-49. A "review of ideas." Directed by Francisco Romero. Contributors include Erro, Mallea, Martínez Estrada, R. Frondizi, Ascoli, etc.

Repertorio Americano. San José de Costa Rica, 1919-57. Extremely valuable "review of reviews" type publication. Reprinted items from leading periodicals of the hemisphere. Directed for over twenty-five years by García Monge.

Revista Bimestre Cubana. Havana, 1831-35; 1910-59. One of the oldest publications in Spanish America. Directed by Fernando Ortiz in recent years.

Revista Chilena. Santiago, 1917-30.

Revista Cubana. Havana, 1935-57.

Revista de América. Bogotá, 1945-51. A solid, continentally oriented journal. Directed by Arciniegas and R. García Peña. Contributors include Gabriela Mistral, L. Alberto Sánchez, Díez de Medina, and Sanín Cano.

Revista de América. Paris, 1912-14. Directed by F. García Calderón. Contributors from Spanish America and from Spanish Americans living in prewar Paris: Ingenieros, Pérez Petit, Gerardo Murillo ("Dr. Atl"), etc.

Revista de Filosofía. Buenos Aires, 1915-29. Directed by Ingenieros, and often reflecting his intellectual position.

Revista de las Indias. Bogotá, 1936-51. An excellent review of wide interests. Chief contributors: Arciniegas, Sanín Cano, Díez de Medina, etc.

Revista Hispánica Moderna, New York, 1934——.

Revista Iberoamericana. Mexico, 1939——. Organ of the Instituto Internacional de Literatura Iberoamericana.

Revista Moderna. Mexico, 1898-1911. Helpful for early work of the *Ateneo* writers: Caso, Henríquez Ureña, etc.

Revista Nacional. Montevideo, 1938——.

Revista Nacional de Cultura. Caracas, 1938——. Directed by Picón Salas until 1940, then by Juan B. Plaza.

Ruta. Mexico, 1938-39.

Síntesis. Buenos Aires, 1927-30. An important journal of literary and philosophic orientation. Writers of widely varying viewpoint: Borges, Virasoro, C. Astrada, Gerchúnoff, etc.

Sur. Buenos Aires, 1931———. Founded by Victoria Ocampo, continues to be Argentina's greatest literary and intellectual journal. Virtually all important Argentine writers have published in it. Also features much foreign literature, translations, etc.

Taller. Mexico, 1938-41. Much by Paz, R. Solana, María Zambrano, and others.

Tierra Nueva, Mexico, 1940-42. Articles by Zea, J. L. Martínez, Paz, Alí Chumacero, etc.

Universidad de México. 1946———. Important journal with wide variety of articles. Especially interesting for the *mexicanidad* theme. An earlier journal bearing the same title appeared in 1931-33.

Universidad: Mensual de Cultura Popular. México, 1936-38. Directed by Miguel N. Lira. Leftist leaning. Articles by Ramos, R. Heliodoro Valle, and many foreigners.

Valoraciones. Buenos Aires, 1923-28. Particularly rich in philosophic articles. Korn, Romero, frequent contributors, also some Mexicans: Torres Bodet, Reyes, and Ramos.

La Vida Literaria. Buenos Aires, 1928-31. Includes articles by important Argentine writers—Gerchúnoff, Martínez Estrada—and many foreigners. Leftists predominate.

INDEX